CHEMICAL CRIMES

CHEMICAL CRIMES

Science and Poison in
Victorian Crime Fiction

CHERYL BLAKE PRICE

THE OHIO STATE UNIVERSITY PRESS
COLUMBUS

Copyright © 2019 by The Ohio State University.
All rights reserved.
Library of Congress Cataloging-in-Publication Data

Names: Price, Cheryl Blake, author.
Title: Chemical crimes : science and poison in Victorian crime fiction / Cheryl Blake Price.
Description: Columbus : The Ohio State University Press, [2019] | Includes bibliographical references and index.
Identifiers: LCCN 2018046299 | ISBN 9780814213919 (cloth ; alk. paper) | ISBN 081421391X (cloth ; alk. paper)
Subjects: LCSH: English fiction—19th century—History and criticism. | Crime in literature. | Poisoners in literature. | Poisoning in literature. | Criminals in literature. | Murder in literature.
Classification: LCC PR878.C74 P75 2019 | DDC 823/.087209008—dc23
LC record available at https://lccn.loc.gov/2018046299

Cover design by Andrew Brozyna
Text design by Juliet Williams
Type set in Adobe Palatino

♾ The paper used in this publication meets the minimum requirements of the American National Standard for Information Sciences—Permanence of Paper for Printed Library Materials. ANSI Z39.48-1992.

CONTENTS

Acknowledgments   vii

INTRODUCTION The Victorian Chemical Criminal   1

CHAPTER 1   "The Science of Murder": Educating the Female
              Chemical Criminal in L. E. L.'s *Ethel Churchill* and
              Bulwer's *Lucretia*   28

CHAPTER 2   Medical Bluebeards: Gothic Medicine and the
              Poisoning Doctor in the Fiction of Ellen Wood   68

CHAPTER 3   Chemicalized Bodies and Criminal Intent: Unruly
              Bodies and the Limitations of Forensic Science in
              Early Detective Fiction   103

CHAPTER 4   L. T. Meade's Female Mad Scientists: Science Fiction
              and the Transformation of the Chemical Criminal in
              Fin de Siècle Detective Fiction   139

AFTERWORD   174

Bibliography   179
Index   191

ACKNOWLEDGMENTS

I BEGIN my acknowledgments by thanking Barry Faulk, Meegan Kennedy, and Eric Walker. I could not have written this book without their help. Paul Fyfe was never obligated to help me, but he always did. George Robb has been lovely and supportive at key moments in this book's creation. My colleagues and dean at my current academic home, the University of North Alabama, are truly wonderful and supportive. I especially want to acknowledge my chair and faculty mentor, Cynthia Burkhead, who is always available to share her wisdom. Katie Owens-Murphy, Christa Raney, Matt Duquès, Nancy Atkinson, Kelly Latchaw, and Lisa Minor have all been the best of intellectual friends. Dana Burbank always managed to get me more copy allowances, which were desperately needed during the revision of this book.

I want to express my sincerest gratitude to the three readers who gave their time to review and comment on the manuscript. They were insightful and rigorous, and their suggestions undoubtedly made this book stronger. Two have opted to remain anonymous, but I can gladly thank Caroline Reitz by name. I have also been lucky in my editors, Kristen Elias Rowley and Lindsay Martin, and further thanks go out to the rest of the staff at the Ohio State University Press.

Much of the research for this book was supported by Florida State University's International Program's London Fellowship, and I thank Kathleen Paul and Lisa Bowers-Isaacson for making my stay in London intellectually and personally fulfilling. The University of North Alabama's Laura Harrison Professorship helped support the final stages of preparing this manuscript, and I thank the Harrison family for all that they give to North Alabama. I am grateful to my students, both undergraduate and graduate, for their unfailing willingness to dive into the depths of Victorian crime fiction with me.

The librarians at the British Library, Florida State, the University of Illinois Urbana–Champaign, and University of North Alabama libraries were great aids in finding sources. I thank them all for their help and their generosity in forgiving my late book returns.

Revised and expanded version of "Medical Bluebeards: The Domestic Threat of the Poisoning Doctor in the Popular Fiction of Ellen Wood" by Cheryl Blake Price from *Victorian Medicine and Popular Culture*, edited by Louise Penner and Tabitha Sparks, © 2015. Reprinted by permission of the University of Pittsburgh Press. Louise and Tabitha were great editors; I appreciate their comments as well as the feedback from the anonymous reviewers of this collection.

My family has been unfailingly supportive. My deepest thanks go to my parents and sister as well as David and Diane Price. Elise and Beau were born during the writing of this book and gave me perhaps the best gift a writer can get: a reason to take a break.

Matt Price deserves the most thanks. This book is dedicated to him.

INTRODUCTION

THE VICTORIAN CHEMICAL CRIMINAL

IN THE 1851 article "The Philosophy of Murder," John Paget writes, "the offence of poisoning, [in] spite of its superatrocious character, seems capable of working upon whole cities and communities, as with an individual or personified power; indeed, . . . one might imagine it to be *a circumambient presence.*"[1] This book is deeply interested in the Victorians' belief that they were saturated in poisons to the extent that, as the *Illustrated Times* declared, poison was "the Crime of the Age."[2] Poison was by no means the most frequently committed crime, and yet it captured a disproportionate share of the Victorian imagination. Beatings, stabbings, and shootings were all more common, but an increase in criminal poisonings, peaking around midcentury, seemed enough evidence that England was experiencing a poisoning epidemic. Cryptic reports warned, "cases of undetected poisoning are of much more frequent occurrence than is generally supposed," suggesting to anxious readers that their homes might be infested with secret poisoners.[3] Admitting that "there is nothing *very* alarming [about poison crime statistics], taken in comparison with the numericals of other modes of murder," Paget hyperbolically suggests, "it is highly probable that not more than one

---

1. Paget, "Philosophy of Murder," 174. Emphasis mine.
2. "Crime of the Age," 64.
3. "Undetected Poisonings," 419.

murder of this kind in twenty is discovered."⁴ Alluding to the idea of poison as a secret crime that leaves behind little evidence, this writer prompts his readers to ask just how many guilty men and women were sharing their beds, making their food, or dispensing their medicines. In the Victorian era, pondering how many poison murders went unpunished was a terrifying prospect, but one that proved fascinating nonetheless.

A large part of this fascination, as Paget recognizes, is poison's "personified power" and ability to infiltrate "whole cities and communities." Paget speaks geographically, but poison's circumambient presence seeped into other kinds of communities as well—particularly the communities of crime fiction. Poison might not have really been as frequent a crime as Paget suggests, but it certainly shows up persistently in Victorian writing. This is because there was something new and particularly formidable about the Victorian poisoner. As one commentator put it, "the modern poisoner has discarded the rough agencies of his earlier brethren. He treats you *secundum artem*, and gives you the benefit of the latest discoveries in toxicology. He considers your circumstances—your little peculiarities of constitution—your habits, and then passes his arm under your own, and, with soft expressions of sympathy and commiseration, blandly edges you into your grave."⁵ The "modern poisoner" is dangerous because of his ability to turn the Victorians' cherished ideals—intelligence, civility, and compassion—to criminal ends. He is a refined criminal who uses beguiling "soft expressions of sympathy" to mask his murderous intentions. He knows his victim intimately and thoughtfully takes into consideration their "little peculiarities of constitution" as well as "the latest discoveries in toxicology" to create a personalized poison that will dispatch his victim with the least amount of trouble. This secretive criminal effects his *modus operandi* of slipping death into food, drink, or medicine through his access to domestic spaces. Poisoning has always been a domestic crime, but its fusion with current science in the nineteenth century was a new, troubling development. Victorian poisoners were not like the poisoners of the past; instead, they transformed into a rarified group of criminals who drew from scientific knowledge and methodology to perpetrate domestic crime: The poisoner had become the chemical criminal.

This book has two primary goals. The first is that it explores why fictional poisonings transitioned into chemical crimes during the nineteenth century. The answer, this book argues, is that the chemical criminal allowed authors to interrogate the professionalization of science, which was one of

---

4. Paget, "Philosophy of Murder," 174.
5. "Poison," 277. *Secundum artem* is Latin for "according to the [standard] practice."

the most significant revolutions that occurred in the nineteenth century. Poison offered a venue for discussions about science because, more than any other type of criminal, the poisoner practiced "a scientific art or profession."[6] Andrew Mangham is correct in pointing out the nineteenth-century belief that "every successful poisoner needs to have a high level of chemical and biological knowledge."[7] The Victorians recognized that "the vulgar methods of the knife, the bullet, or the bludgeon" need no special training or preparation, but "the [poison] bowl needs for its effective management a scientific precision of plan and a subtlety of execution."[8] This combination of science and crime transformed the nineteenth-century poisoner into the chemical criminal, which this book defines as a type of poisoner who employs scientific knowledge, practices, or methodology to commit crime. In real life and in fiction, Victorian poisoners are scientifically proficient, either through formal training (as the many instances of poisoning doctors attest) or by educating themselves before committing their crimes. Appearing as professionally trained chemists and doctors and just laypeople who employ scientific methodology in the commission of their crimes, chemical criminals provide an important outlet to discuss the progress and growing power of science in the nineteenth century, particularly in relation to the domestic sphere.

The second goal of this book is to investigate the interesting correlation between chemical crime and innovations in genre development. Tracing chemical crime across Victorian crime fiction reveals its appearance when authors are experimenting with genre; in fact, this occurs so frequently that chemical crime is present at almost every significant moment in the development of Victorian crime fiction. This book also argues that poison's fluid nature and its ability to mix, mingle, and transcend boundaries makes the chemical criminal an ideal figure for generic experimentation.[9] Authors harness this fluidity and apply it structurally, and the chemical criminal appears at the origins of sensation, detective, and science fictions—and when the boundaries of genres like the Newgate novel expand and anticipate later genre developments. This figure's presence at these critical moments in the development of crime fiction, and the examinations of science that inevitably accompany them, indicates that reactions to science played a large role in shaping these developments. By focusing on chemical crime's appearance

6. "Sale of Poisons," 117.
7. Mangham, "'Drink it up Dear,'" 107.
8. "Poisons and Poisoners: Old and New," 171.
9. "Generic" in this context applies to "genre" instead of the more commonly used meaning of "general."

at these generically significant moments, this book traces how reactions to Victorian science inspired change in nineteenth-century crime fiction.

To introduce the chemical criminal and demonstrate how authors use this figure for these dual purposes, this book begins with an examination of a text that is both an appraisal of Victorian science as well as an example of generic innovation: Wilkie Collins's *The Woman in White*. First published in serial form beginning in November of 1859, *The Woman in White* is widely credited as the first sensation novel, a genre of Victorian crime fiction featuring suspenseful criminal plots situated within the home. The novel outlines a criminal conspiracy to fake the death of Laura Fairlie, the wife of Sir Percival Glyde, by changing her identity and incarcerating her in an insane asylum so her husband and aunt can inherit her fortune. The mastermind of this plot is Count Fosco, who is greatly aided in this enterprise by the years he spends "in the ardent study of medical and chemical science."[10] Fosco's treachery is directly indebted to his status as a chemical criminal; without the two times Fosco uses his "half-ounce bottle"—once to drug Laura's maid, Fanny, for access to a letter she is carrying, and a second time to incapacitate Laura so she can be smuggled into the asylum—he would not have been successful in his identity-switching scheme.[11]

Fosco is especially useful for opening this discussion because he represents so many of the characteristics that define the trope of the chemical criminal. To begin with, like many of his fictional brethren, Fosco's characterization is influenced by real-life chemical criminals, whose cases often garnered an immense amount of public attention. Collins's background in journalism made him alert to the shifting interests of his readers, and with Fosco he capitalized on the public obsession with a spate of mid-century poisonings. In particular, the case of the convicted murderer William Palmer had a special resonance with Collins (as it did with other authors, such as Charles Dickens), and it had a significant impact on the writing of *The Woman in White*.[12] Palmer was a surgeon and the second son of an upwardly mobile lumberman in the town of Rugeley and by all accounts seemed to be an ordinary, middle-class professional—except for the string of suspicious deaths that followed him throughout his adult life. Palmer, who preferred betting on racehorses to doctoring, was always in need of money. Conve-

---

10. Collins, *Woman in White*, II: 348.
11. Collins, *Woman in White*, II: 350.
12. Dickens was so disturbed by Palmer's innocent appearance that he published "The Demeanour of Murderers" in *Household Words* in 1856. In the article, he contradicts the majority of other commentators on the case by claiming Palmer's guilt is clearly apparent from his appearance and manners.

niently for him, financially burdensome relatives, like his mother-in-law, had a habit of dying. On two occasions when his debts became especially pressing, death rescued him. First wife and then brother—each insured for £13,000—died and relieved his financial embarrassments. Being close to Palmer certainly seemed to have a fatality to it, but he was not charged with murder until the unexpected death of his business associate, John Cook. Cook had profited from a winning streak, and shortly thereafter sickened and died while being assiduously medicated by his friend Palmer.

Palmer coalesces several assumptions about the chemical criminal that make him an attractive model to the budding sensation novelist. Sir James Fitzjames Stephen summed up the fascination with the Palmer case when he wrote:

> His career supplied one of the proofs of a fact which many kind-hearted people seem to doubt, namely, the fact that such a thing as atrocious wickedness is consistent with good education, perfect sanity, and everything, in a word, which deprives men of all excuse for crime. Palmer was respectably brought up; apart from his extravagance and vice, he might have lived comfortably enough. He was a model of physical health and strength, and was courageous, determined, and energetic.[13]

Palmer's intelligence and training in the medical field, his respectable middle-class upbringing, and his robust appearance reflect a paradox for Victorian conceptions of criminality. Although class assumptions firmly placed crime on the bottom rungs of the class ladder, the most captivating fictional villains were quickly becoming middle- or upper-class, refined, cunning, personally attractive, and blessed with scientific aptitude. To a society heavily invested in visible legibility, the criminal *du jour* did not look or act as expected. There was a damning amount of circumstantial evidence against Palmer, for example, but his personal appearance and deportment, which did not fit expectations of criminal physiognomy, caused many to question his guilt. Drawing from Palmer and other high-profile criminals like him, fictional chemical criminals reflected a break from the usual type and drew similar mixed reactions to their villainy. As Margaret Oliphant writes in her review of *The Woman in White*, instead of a hulking ruffian, Collins has created "a new type of the perennial enemy to goodness" that "is more inter-

---

13. Stephen, *History of the Criminal Law*, 424.

esting, and seizes on our sympathies more warmly than any other character in the book."[14]

Chemical criminals like Count Fosco are able to hold the discordant status of a sympathetic criminal because poisoning is "the crime of civilization," while violence, in his words, is "a method largely adopted by the brutal lower orders of the people, but utterly abhorrent to the refined and educated classes above them."[15] The Victorians cast poison as a nonviolent crime, enabled by modernity, and defined their own criminal preferences against those of a barbaric past:

> The crime of murder has prevailed in all ages since the fall of man. In the first instance this was effected by physical violence and the shedding of blood. The advancement of civilization has led to the discovery of other methods of effecting the object—methods less brutal and more diabolical. Murder is not now confined to cases of sudden impulse or ungovernable passion. The modern assassin adapts his expedients to the refinement of the age, bringing to his aid the appliances of science, and often masking deliberate treachery under an assumed pretence of affectionate attentions.[16]

Despite the fact that poisoning crimes could be horrendously painful and torturous, the perception of poison's civilized qualities made it an ideal weapon for a Palmer—or the villain of a sensation novel—to distinguish themselves from common, lower-class criminals. Martin Weiner identifies the cultural trend that discouraged bloody, physical crimes on the basis that they were barbaric. Especially for upper- and middle-class men, violence became stigmatized and "when a 'respectable' man killed, then as now, it was usually with a weapon—poison, a gun—which required less directly and sustainedly 'violent' action."[17] Sir Percival Glyde's violence and excitability allow readers to quickly identify him with an earlier tradition of the swaggering, violent criminal type. Fosco's forays into the criminal realm are elegant in comparison. He masterminds complex plots, is affable to his victims, and (when intervention is necessary) is aided not with force, but with a drop or two of his poison bottle.

"The wise man's crime is the crime that is *not* found out," Fosco notes. He knows that the best way to circumvent justice is to use something that is material, yet invisible, and does not result in heaps of incriminating evi-

---

14. Oliphant, "Sensation Novels," 566.
15. "Crime of the Age," 64.
16. Scoffern, "Secret Poisoning," 201.
17. Weiner, *Men of Blood*, 170.

dence. Violent crimes are risky, the Victorian commentator Paget writes, because "once unlawfully spilled," blood "will flow to the world's end after the criminal," and the law has "a keen eye for bloody spots and bloody knives."[18] Percival's forceful actions against Laura result in incriminating bruises that Marian notes are "a weapon to strike him with"; but Fosco would never make the mistake of blundering through a murder and leaving behind so much evidence.[19] If applied correctly, chemicals could work relatively imperceptibly, and poisoning offered the murderer, in Paget's words, relative "secrecy and safety."[20] The ideal poison has the rare distinction of being colorless, odorless, and tasteless, but the clever murderer could still use poisons, like the bitter-tasting prussic acid, if they slipped them into strongly flavored food or drink.

Getting poison into the body of your victim unnoticed is the first step, but scientific acumen is necessary to escape detection. Fosco, learned in medicine and described as "one of the first experimental chemists living," would use his familiarity with the diseases of the human body and precise dosing techniques to create a poison that imitates a natural disease.[21] A successful poisoning can be a ticklish business. If given slowly over a period of days, arsenic produces symptoms similar to those of infectious diseases like English cholera and could easily fool overworked or inattentive medical men.[22] Given in one large dose, however, arsenic evokes a violent reaction that clearly indicates foul play. As tests for certain poisons became more reliable, chemical criminals began taking into account the traces chemicals left in the body. The popularity of chemicals such as strychnine (which is the poison that Palmer supposedly used to kill Cook) in the latter half of the century attests to the preference for chemicals that quickly decomposed or were forensically invisible. Fosco himself is frank about his capabilities and explicitly states that had Anne Catherick not suddenly died, he would "have assisted worn-out Nature" with his poisons and "opened the doors of the Prison of Life."[23] After her lengthy illness, he is confident no inquiries would be made about the nature of Catherick's death.

Although Fosco insists he only used his chemical knowledge twice (and both times in relatively harmless ways), his "withering eloquence" on the subject of poisons and drugs perhaps inspires more fear than his actions.

---

18. Paget, "Philosophy of Murder," 172.
19. Collins, *Woman in White*, I: 453.
20. Paget, "Philosophy of Murder," 172.
21. Collins, *Woman in White*, I: 332.
22. Dickinson, "Memoranda," 139.
23. Collins, *Woman in White*, II: 365.

Fosco explains, "Chemistry, especially, has always had irresistible attractions for me, from the enormous, the illimitable power which the knowledge of it confers. Chemists, I assert it emphatically, might sway, if they pleased, the destinies of humanity."[24] Fosco's boasting about the mysterious "illimitable power" offered by criminal chemistry reveals that it is not what he has done, but rather what he *could* have done with the "scientific assistance" of his poison bottle that haunts the narrative.[25] This ambiguity—the scientific specificity yet ghostly presence—of Fosco's poisons is a trademark of Victorian chemical crimes. Andrew Mangham argues that in pre-nineteenth-century works, "poisons were frequently identified simply as 'poison' and descriptions of their effects have more to do with melodrama than actual fact," and in Victorian texts, there is "a new attention to detail" that "identified and discussed a number of deadly poisons."[26] On the other hand, Margaret Hallissy writes that before the twentieth century, "the image of poison is surrounded by magic and mystery, enshrouded in medical ignorance."[27] Both of these critics are correct; in fiction, Victorian poison is discussed scientifically, but it also is still imbued with mystery. Ian Burney might put it best when he writes that the Victorians understand poison as being both "physically distinct (and thus capable of detection and containment) and evanescent (and thus the stuff of mystery and romance)."[28] True to its dual nature, the science of chemical crime is inseparable from its romance. When Laura describes her drugging, she relates that a glass of water given to her by the count "had so strange a taste that it increased her faintness" and a bottle of smelling salts made her "giddy on the instant."[29] Afterward, she loses track of time and hallucinates before awaking in the asylum. Her symptoms are suggestive of an opiate, but which one, and how Fosco's two chemicals work in concert, is not revealed.[30] This book finds that despite the amount of rich detail about the scientific processes and methodologies that chemical criminals employ, fictional chemical crime remains deeply enigmatic.

The Victorians frequently highlight hard domestic realities by placing them against poison's ephemerality. As a quiet, sophisticated crime that necessitates an intimacy with the body of the victim, poison is the domestic

---

24. Collins, *Woman in White*, II: 365.
25. Collins, *Woman in White*, II: 349.
26. Mangham, "'Drink it up Dear,'" 96.
27. Hallissy, *Venomous Woman*, xiii.
28. Burney, *Poison, Detection, and the Victorian Imagination*, 181.
29. Collins, *Woman in White*, II: 75.
30. Collins's novel *Jezebel's Daughter* is another illustration of the enduring link between poison and romance, as the "experimental chemist" Fontaine uses modern science to resurrect lost Renaissance poisons that have almost magical effects on the human body.

murder *par excellence*. Fosco's use of poison—colloquially known as "inheritance powder"—against his niece to secure a rich legacy for his wife reflects poison's reputation as a family affair. The domestic nature of poisoning in part accounts for its association as a woman's crime. Dr. John Scoffern notes that it is "obvious" why "poisoning has ever been the favoured scheme of woman's murder practice": "It needs no strength of hand, no unwavering presence of mind, face to face with your victim; it makes no noise, spills no blood, is quiet, undemonstrative; and as far as murder can be, is elegant."[31] Poison may have a persistent reputation as a woman's crime, but as Fosco demonstrates, that does not mean that chemical criminals are exclusively female or that their male counterparts do not raise similar anxieties about the safety of the domestic sphere. Fosco and his literary brethren take advantage of women's unequal legal and social positions to victimize them within the home, while the female chemical criminal uses her domestic position to promote her murderous plans. The gendering of the chemical criminal, then, as Ian Burney notes, is only "an element of, but not the exclusive referent for, Victorian reflections of the subject of criminal poisoning."[32] This book will take a deep interest in the entanglement of gender and crime since all chemical criminals, regardless of their gender, raise anxieties about science's role in bringing about domestic tragedies.

The domestic nature of chemical crime draws attention to one of poison's most well-known inconsistencies: its association with the foreign. It is unsurprising, even rising to the level of uninspired, that Collins furnishes his chemical criminal with a foreign ancestry. Especially in the first half of the century, Victorian writers often traced poison's history to foreign, not domestic, sources. Accounts of historic poisoners, such as the lengthy 1856 series on "Poisoners and Slow Poisons" in *Reynold's Miscellany* or George Hogarth's 1837 contribution on "The Poisoners of the Seventeenth Century" for *Bentley's Miscellany* overwhelmingly focus on foreign criminals.[33] The persistent association between poisons and the foreign results in the appearance of many foreign poisoners in Victorian fiction, although cases of actual foreign poisoners operating on English soil were nonexistent.[34] Particularly

---

31. Scoffern, "Secret Poisoning," 117.
32. Burney, *Poison, Detection, and the Victorian Imagination*, 23.
33. Hogarth's two papers on "The Poisoners of the Seventeenth Century" were published in 1837 and 1838. The series "Poisoners and Slow Poisons" in *Reynold's Miscellany* was published in 1856. The latter only contained three examples of English poisoners, and featured far many more examples of foreign poisoners.
34. There are a few exceptions, such as Thomas Neill Cream, who was Scottish-born but had immigrated to the Americas. After committing poisonings in Canada and the United States, he continued his crime spree in England.

in regard to the modern Italians, the Victorians believed "vindictiveness, and subtlety must be acknowledged to be strong features in the character of that people," and that they had retained the "superiority" of their ancestors' poisonous arts.[35] Fosco even seems to recognize himself as a cliché. When he insists on Marian being a witness to her sister's signature on a document, he reminds Marian that: "We Italians are all wily and suspicious by nature, in the estimation of the good John Bull. Set me down, if you please, as being no better than the rest of my race. I am a wily Italian and a suspicious Italian."[36] Fosco's evocation of himself as an Italian stereotype, however, is just one his tricks; by drawing attention to his foreignness, he draws suspicion away from his reluctance to have both himself and his wife act as witnesses to the signing away of Laura's fortune. It is a reminder that (to borrow Marian's words) the "strikingly original and perplexingly contradictory" Fosco is not a stereotype at all.[37] "Subtract from him his eccentricities, his Italianisms, and his corpulency," an anonymous reviewer wrote in 1860, and what one finds is "a very undecipherable villain."[38] The *Saturday Review*'s insightful writer identifies that Fosco does not represent a foreign stereotype but rather a paradox.

Fosco demonstrates that one of the paradoxical characteristics of the chemical criminal is that they are paradoxical. He is, to use Maria Constantini's words, one of the "uncanny forces of otherness" in the novel that "eroded the limen between diversity and sameness, and generated hybrid forms which altered the local perception of identity."[39] As Constantini recognizes, Collins uses Fosco's enigmatic nature to explore the instability of identity—and Fosco's poisons become one of the vehicles for identity erosion in the novel. Fosco claims that he can manipulate the identity and personality of others through his use of chemistry:

> Mind, they say, rules the world. But what rules the mind? The body. The body (follow me closely here) lies at the mercy of the most omnipotent of all potentates—the Chemist. Give me—Fosco—chemistry; and when Shakespeare has conceived Hamlet, and sits down to execute the conception—with a few grains of powder dropped into his daily food, I will reduce his

---

35. Hogarth, "Poisoners of the Seventeenth Century" (1837), 230.
36. Collins, *Woman in White*, I: 365.
37. Collins, *Woman in White*, I: 330.
38. "Woman in White," 249.
39. Costantini, "Land of Angels," 28.

Palmer, would seem to be that the transformation had already occurred. *The Woman in White* uses the ambiguity of poison to show that the criminal to fear is the one who fuses its two villains: It is not the foreigner, but rather the Palmers of the world, the Fosco in Glyde's British clothing, who present the greatest threat to the domestic sphere.

With *The Woman in White*, Collins invokes an exploration of science and crime that will recur throughout his later writings, including works like *Armadale, The Law and the Lady, The Legacy of Cain, Heart and Science*, and *Jezebel's Daughter*. This reading of the novel demonstrates that Collins's domestication of crime—the defining innovation that sensation fiction makes—has direct links to his concerns about Victorian science. It is not a coincidence that sensation fiction develops when nineteenth-century science is accumulating prestige and an increased presence in the Victorian home. Sensation fiction is preoccupied with exploring the cause and effect of schisms within the domestic sphere, and Collins recognized that science, along with other factors like restrictive laws and social customs, had a role to play in these ruptures. In this case, Collins applies science to one of sensation fiction's defining concerns, identity, and finds that science contributes to crises of identity and depersonalization in the modern world.

MOVING FROM DETECTIVE-SCIENTIST TO SCIENTIFIC CRIMINAL

The Woman in White demonstrates the need to reexamine how crime fiction reacted to scientific modernity. In the chapters that follow, *Chemical Crimes* traces how authors use the chemical criminal to interrogate Victorian narratives of scientific progress in crime fiction, including the genres of Newgate, sensation, detective, and gothic fiction. Through this approach, *Chemical Crimes* charts how nineteenth-century crime fiction responded to, and was shaped by, cultural perceptions about the progress of Victorian science. A focus on the criminal applications of science offers a corrective to the current way of understanding the development of Victorian crime fiction by moving the critical focus back onto the *criminal* and away from the detective. Focus on the detective has overwhelmingly dominated both genre studies of Victorian crime fiction and analyses of the interrelationship between nineteenth-century science and crime; when charting the big picture of nineteenth-century crime fiction, critics have consistently woven a tale about the emergence and rise of the detective. Heather Worthington rightly points out that the detective is so "central to the accepted developmental narrative of crime fiction" that much nineteenth-century criticism uses the term "crime fiction" synonymously for "detective fiction."[47] This way of viewing nineteenth-century crime fiction has resulted in an emphasis on the detective, who exemplifies "the emergence of the intellectual professions as new repositories of social power."[48] Following D. A. Miller, who argued for "a radical *entanglement* between the nature of the novel and the practice of the police" and explored how the novel "systematically participate[s] in a general economy of policing power," subsequent critics have fleshed out the detective as the representative figure of disciplinary power.[49] The critical importance of the detective in determining the generic characteristics of crime fiction is illustrated by the tendency for critics to divide this literature into three phases: the pre-detection fiction of the early nineteenth century, the emergent detective stories developing at mid-century, and the late century legitimization of detective fiction as a popular literary movement that has its epitome in Arthur Conan Doyle's Sherlock Holmes series.

Science plays a large part in this legitimization of the literary detective, and critics have identified a causal link between the rise of the detective and their increasing reliance on science or scientific methodology. Works like Ronald R. Thomas's *Detective Fiction and the Rise of Forensic Science* and Worthington's argument that detective fiction is highly influenced by the medical case study suggest that the popularity of fictional detectives is a function of their scientific competence. As Charles Rzepka puts it, "the story of the development of the detective genre largely coincides with the history of narrative practice in these reconstructive sciences and with its popular dissemination."[50] This approach presents a progressive account of Victorian crime literature, which charts the trajectory of nineteenth-century crime fiction as aimed teleologically toward a scientized detective form. In other words, critics have connected the development of crime fiction to its willingness to absorb and promote the Victorian sciences, the apex of this project being the scientific detection of Sherlock Holmes.

The argument that Victorian crime writers helped legitimate forensic science is fueled by the narratives of nineteenth-century scientists who actively worked to promote the reliability of new methodologies in the detection of crime. In *Poison, Detection, and the Victorian Imagination*, Ian Burney investigates how forensic scientists tried to establish their cultural authority and legitimize their tests for poison. Using the Foucauldian idea of discipline,

---

47. Worthington, *Rise of the Detective*, 3.
48. Kayman, "Short Story from Poe to Chesterton," 46.
49. D. A. Miller, *Novel and the Police*, 2.
50. Rzepka, *Detective Fiction*, 33.

Burney argues that Victorian forensic toxicologists worked to make poison visible through accurate toxicological tests. Forensic toxicologists did face challenges in their quest to control how the public viewed poison and needed to create narratives "through which poison might be positioned as, first and foremost, an object of scientific intervention."[51] This process required scientists to separate poison from its deeply ingrained cultural context, a process Burney describes as "taming poison's unruly past."[52] By working to demythologize poison in their public appearances and writings, toxicologists sought to expose poison and bring it under the scope of material science. Burney argues that the toxicologists' project involved disciplining poison not only through scientific tests but also through cultural narratives by emphasizing scientifically realistic ways of interpreting poison. The results of these efforts are found in articles, like the one written for the *Edinburgh Evening Courant*, that try to assuage public anxiety by arguing:

> There is a Nemesis on the track of even the most skilled and cunning administrator of these subtle poisons; for science, as it gives the bane, affords the antidote also, *pari passu*; and the skilled scientific expert has tests not less subtle by which he can certainly demonstrate the presence of most poisons in the body even after it has long been in the grave, and even when the quantity to be experimented on is infinitesimally small.[53]

If one only looks at articles like those in the *Edinburgh Evening Courant*, they would expect to find toxicological figures, in the form of doctors or chemists, appearing in a detective role to reveal the presence of poison in Victorian fiction. Significantly, toxicological figures are rarely employed in this manner until very late in the century, and in Victorian crime fiction, it is more common to find characters employing science for chemical crimes rather than accurate toxicological detection. Scientists were never able to fully divest poison from its aura of mystery, and Burney concludes, "poison could not be fully contained within a framework of rational procedures. Poison spoke essentially to imagination, anchored in public and scientific conceptions of history, crime, and the body, and toxicology was inescapably embedded in this network of associations."[54]

I follow Burney's conclusions by showing how authors resisted toxicology's efforts to discipline poison by combining the scientific realities of

---

51. Burney, *Poison, Detection, and the Victorian Imagination*, 45.
52. Burney, *Poison, Detection, and the Victorian Imagination*, 45.
53. *The Edinburgh Evening Courant*, 228.
54. Burney, *Poison, Detection, and the Victorian Imagination*, 173–74.

poison with its imaginative possibilities. This perspective allows this book to question scholarly narratives that tie developments in crime fiction to a scientifically sophisticated detective. A narrow focus on the detective-scientist and his legitimization of science has caused scholars to overlook fictional offenders, many of whom predate forensic investigation, who adapt scientific methodology, technology, and knowledge for the commission of crimes. To once again quote Fosco, "the hiding of a crime, or the detection of a crime" is "a trial of skill between the police on one side, and the individual on the other. When the criminal is a brutal, ignorant fool, the police, in nine cases out of ten, win. When the criminal is a resolute, educated, highly-intelligent man, the police, in nine cases out of ten, lose."[55] Fosco suggests that the police are ill-equipped to deal with any but the most simplistic crimes, and that scientific criminals (like himself) are safe from their methods of detection. In other words, Fosco argues that the true innovators are the criminals, and that forensic detection is merely playing catch-up. Yet literary critics have consistently overlooked the fact that Victorian authors usually present the detective's use of science as *reactionary* instead of *proactive*. By analyzing the chemical criminal, this book corrects this oversight by showing that the literary detective's increasing reliance on science is mirrored, and in many cases anticipated, by chemical criminals. Just as early authors of crime fiction, Dennis Porter notes, "invented the fine art of detection as a counterpart to the fine art of murder," fictional detectives often employ science in response to scientifically sophisticated poisoners.[56] Literary detectives were adapting science, like toxicology, to deter and solve crime, but this was in response to antagonists who had already turned to cutting-edge science to avoid detection. Not only did authors present chemical criminals who were at the forefront of scientific innovation, but these villains are also shown subverting forensic science altogether. *Chemical Crimes*, therefore, both illustrates how the chemical criminal challenges the rise of Victorian science and offers an alternative way of examining the development of crime fiction that is not dominated by the disciplining detective (or systems of detection) that D. A. Miller identifies in *The Novel and the Police*. This book's focus on the chemical criminal across Victorian crime fiction reveals just how much authors were willing to challenge the supposed disciplinary force of forensic detection and suggests that generic developments were inspired as much by the scientific innovations of the criminal as they were by the detective.

---

55. Collins, *Woman in White*, I: 352
56. Porter, *Pursuit of Crime*, 22–23.

A THEORY OF POISON

In its examination of how Newgate, sensation, detective, gothic, and science fictions portray science and how these portrayals affect the changes occurring within these genres, *Chemical Crimes* is deeply indebted to previous work done in the fields of genre studies, crime fiction, and literature and science. The latter two areas especially have relied heavily on New Historicist work influenced by the writing of Michel Foucault. This book's goal of moving away from the disciplining detective signals that its New Historicist methodology will somewhat differ from previous studies, in that it draws inspiration from Jacques Derrida rather than Foucault. The subject matter inspires this shift, since the Victorians' perception of poison as slippery, indeterminate, and invisible is evocative of Derrida's work on the *pharmakon*. The trouble nineteenth-century writers had defining a chemical composition as a "poison" begins to suggest the complex and unfixed nature of Victorian poison, particularly since the division between a beneficial medicine and a destructive poison was shifting and indistinct. The eminent Victorian toxicologist Alfred Swaine Taylor wrote "that it is difficult, if not impossible, to comprise in a few words an accurate description of what, in medical language, should be understood by the term 'poison.'"[57] Not only was poison difficult to define, but in many cases a potentially deleterious chemical substance could have beneficial medical applications. Opiates, for example, were one of the most effective Victorian medicines for reducing pain and inducing sleep as well as one of the most criminally abused drugs. The dual nature of Victorian poison is similar to the *pharmakon*, which Derrida points out is a Greek word that simultaneously means "remedy" and "poison." In *Plato's Pharmacy*, Derrida teases out the overlapping semiotic meanings of the *pharmakon*, refusing to let its meaning rest in the binary construction of "antidote" or "toxin." For Derrida, the *pharmakon* has a slippery hybridity that collapses binary distinctions, or in his words, "this *pharmakon*, this 'medicine,' this philter, which acts as both remedy and poison, already introduces itself into the body of discourse with all its ambivalence."[58]

Derrida's notion of the *pharmakon* is useful for theorizing how the Victorians employed poison in their literary and cultural discourses because, like the *pharmakon*, poison was "apprehended as a blend and impurity," which "acts like an aggressor or a housebreaker, threatening some internal purity and security."[59] Victorian poison, then, is best defined not by its chemical

---

57. Taylor, *On Poisons*, 10.
58. Derrida, *Dissemination*, 70.
59. Derrida, *Dissemination*, 128.

composition, but by its power to invade, react with, and transform the body. Derrida reminds us that poison not only illustrates how bodies can be corrupted but also reveals that these bodies were never discrete or stable to begin with: "If the *pharmakon* is 'ambivalent,' it is because it constitutes the medium in which opposites are opposed, the movement and the play that link them among themselves, reverses them or makes one side cross over into the other (soul/body, good/evil, inside/outside, memory/forgetfulness, speech/writing, etc.)."[60] This book argues that authors use poison as a symbol of Derridean ambivalence, using it to assault some of the Victorians' most cherished binary oppositions—male/female, private/public, innocence/guilt—revealing the internal contradictions of these terms. Sylvia Pamboukian notes that in one of the Victorian definitions of poison, it "signifies not only physical disturbance to an individual but also moral or social harm to the social body, perpetrated by the hated or the ostracized."[61] Representative of dangerous hybridity, poison not only threatens the purity of the individual body but also breaks into various facets of the social "body," disrupting seemingly stable cultural constructions.

The Victorian poisoner shares the disruptive characteristics of their chemicals. Again, Derrida's work in *Plato's Pharmacy* becomes useful for interpreting this Victorian symbol for, as he notes, the term *pharmakeus*, like the *pharmakon*, has a multiplicity of meanings, including "a magician? a sorcerer? even a poisoner?"[62] For the Victorians, the poisoner (like poison itself) was not a stable referent, but rather an ever-shifting figure that absorbed and reflected pressing social anxieties. The fictional poisoner appears in a number of guises—such as the middle-class wife or the socially mobile professional man—that were of particular Victorian concern and which authors used to analyze sites of cultural contestation. In the words of Piya Pal-Lapinski, the poisoner and their chemicals "signified various kinds of border-crossings."[63] The indeterminacy and fluidity of the poisoner meant that this figure was highly adaptable to a variety of contexts; when authors desired to tackle the problematic confluence of science and crime, the chemical criminal arose as a venue for these explorations.

Additionally, *Chemical Crimes* employs Derrida's ideas to interrogate the idea of crime fiction as a disciplinary form. As well as exploring the *pharmakeus*, Derrida writes on its synonym, *pharmakos*, which, while meaning "poisoner," also applied to a particular form of "scapegoat." Societal evils

---

60. Derrida, *Dissemination*, 127.
61. Pamboukian, *Doctoring the Novel*, 99.
62. Derrida, *Dissemination*, 117.
63. Pal-Lapinski, Exotic Woman, 36.

would be projected onto these scapegoats (who were drawn from traditionally othered social categories, like the indigent), and during annual festivals they would be ritually expelled from the city in order to purge social ills from the body politic. In taking on these evils, the *pharmakos* would be symbolically transformed into a foreign entity that must be cleansed from the body politic. It is tempting to stop here and read crime narratives as following this formula. For example, the eventual isolation of the criminal, whether through incarceration or death, can be read through a disciplinary lens as a symbolic antidote for society's ills. Critics have previously used D. A. Miller's argument in *The Novel and the Police* that the novel "systematically participate[s] in a general economy of policing power" to support these readings.[64] In her dissertation on sensational poison narratives, Randa Helfield follows this line of thinking when she argues that these texts moved to diffuse the threat of the domestic poisoner by associating them with foreignness. Helfield posits that sensation fiction "help[ed] to formulate a unified culture and a strong national identity" by producing "fictions which displaced internal poisons onto foreign figures," thus "creat[ing] a healthier and more harmonious body politic."[65]

Taking into consideration Derrida's full discussion of the *pharmakos*, however, reveals that Helfield's reading does not probe the hybridity of the poisoner far enough. Derrida also writes that the "ceremony of the *pharmakos* is thus played out on the boundary line between inside and outside, which it has as its function ceaselessly to trace and retrace. The origin of difference and division, the *pharmakos* represents evil both introjected and projected."[66] The poisoner is always already a part of the community; as something that is foreign yet still "in the very heart of the inside," the *pharmakos* complicates the idea of foreignness and demonstrates that its expulsion is only illusionary. This becomes apparent in poison narratives through the way that they ultimately treat the fate of their villains, as these fictions are more willing to show their chemical criminals getting away with murder. The majority of texts examined in this book, including Collins's novel *The Moonstone*, Edward Bulwer's *Lucretia*, Ellen Wood's "Mr. Castonel," Charles Warren Adams's *The Notting Hill Mystery*, and several of L. T. Meade's short stories, all have notoriously destabilized endings that do not satisfyingly discipline the criminal. Moreover, texts featuring chemical criminals (such as *The Moonstone* and *The Notting Hill Mystery*) often experiment with narrative structures that largely occlude a clear, meaningful understanding of

---

64. D. A. Miller, *Novel and the Police*, 2.
65. Helfield, *"Poison Pen,"* 45.
66. Derrida, *Dissemination*, 133.

the crime. These narrative structures take on the characteristics of poison by becoming slippery and acting as an additional destabilizing force within the text—a move that further complicates the idea of the crime novel as a disciplinary structure.

I have invoked Derrida's work on the *pharmakon*, but this book does not offer a deconstructive reading of Victorian literature and science. It is not the work of this monograph to argue that texts are endlessly undecidable, nor does it tap into "what many have understood as the anarchic essence of deconstruction, the sense of untrammeled freedom or 'play' where 'anything goes.'"[67] Instead, it applies Derrida's writing on the *pharmakon* to better contextualize and interpret chemical crime. If, as Pamboukian argues, "poison is created, not as a self-evident entity defined by scientists, but through cultural processes in the public sphere," then the Victorians constructed an idea of poison that greatly resembles the *pharmakon*.[68] In Derridean fashion, Victorian poison is fluid, slippery, and metamorphosing. I am not suggesting that the Victorians were proto-deconstructionists, but I am contending that they employed chemical crime as a site of ambiguity (Derrida's work on the *pharmakon*, after all, was only pointing out a linguistic tension that already existed in Western thought) that could blur the boundaries of cultural dichotomies.[69] Informed by Derrida's *pharmakon*, my analysis explores how authors harness the ambiguity of poison to interrogate cultural oppositions (such as male/female, victim/criminal, innocence/guilt) and reveal the fundamental instability of these binaries. Authors do not employ poison in exactly the same way, but they all do productively harness the turbulence of poison for their critique of science and crime. They celebrate poison's undecidability and use it to create meaning instead of trying to discipline or contain it.

The methodology of *Chemical Crimes* reflects my point that poison fundamentally changes whatever it touches. Poison has also transformed the theoretical principle of this book, and, like the most efficient of chemical criminals, this critic blends many ingredients into her interpretative methodology. My theoretical framework borrows from several areas—New Historicism, deconstruction, genre theory, feminism, and gender studies—for

---

67. Kirby, "Deconstruction," 293.
68. Pamboukian, *Doctoring the Novel*, 100.
69. One could almost say that I am suggesting the Victorians anticipated deconstruction, but to use Éamonn Dunne's words, "Deconstruction never began in the first place. It was always already there, from the beginning—from the beginning of the beginning" (J. Hillis Miller, x).

its readings.[70] Drawing from its roots in studies of crime fiction and the field of literature and science, it offers a historically informed framework to demonstrate how authors use poison to scrutinize the logic-driven discipline of science (particularly in relation to gender) and how these engagements with criminal science shape the contours of Victorian crime fiction. In the chapters that follow, readers can expect to find historical context, such as cases of real-life chemical criminals, placed alongside literary texts. What emerges is a contextualized reading that draws inspiration from Derridean thought to provide a highly sensitive account of the ways the Victorians conceptualized chemical crime as a tool for social critique. In doing so, this book shows how a focus on the disciplinary model of reading crime fiction has resulted in a critical misreading of some of the forces shaping this literature.

"ARSENICAL LITERATURE" AND LITERARY INNOVATION

Derrida's work has been useful for theorizing poison as a destabilizing force, but it is also advantageous to examine the way he uses the *pharmakon* to discuss the nature of writing in Western culture. Derrida notes that philosophy has long privileged speech over writing; this philosophical bias derives from the belief that speech offers immediacy and truth, while writing results in confusion, loss of meaning, and an erosion of the memory. Derrida, however, reveals the ideological instability inherent in this mind-set when he illustrates that philosophy is just as reliant on writing as it is on speech. As a society built on the tenets of Western philosophy, the Victorians inherited this fraught perspective on writing. While the advances in literacy and printing technologies heralded the progress of society, the Victorians also believed that writing could be "poisonous." The persistent debates over the supposed dangers of reading crime fiction readily illustrate Victorian anxieties about writing. Throughout the century, public interest in so-called Arsenical literature—comprising Newgate, sensation, gothic, and detective fictions—was a source of acute concern.[71]

The source of this concern was the notion that the boundaries of literature and other writing, like the *pharmakon*, were fluid. For example, Vic-

---

70. A mistranslation of Derrida's statement *il n'y a pas de hors-texte* as "there is nothing outside of the text" may be responsible for the divide between his work and historicism because it suggests that he does not give any critical weight to context. Derrida argues that there is no absolute context, but context can still be useful for reading texts—if one remembers that context cannot alone determine meaning (Limited Inc., 60).

71. "Prospectus of a New Journal," 193.

torian fiction (and crime literature in particular) often turned to real-life events, such as court cases, for inspiration—a move that blurred the distinctions between fiction and reality. *The Woman in White* is a prime example of this blending, as Fosco's characterization and the novel's structure, as John Sutherland has noted, are inspired by the William Palmer poisoning case. The case against Palmer was entirely circumstantial since he was exceptionally good at avoiding detection. Since there was no scientific evidence to convict him, the prosecutors had to build a case on witness testimony. Sutherland writes that Collins more than likely attended Palmer's trial, and was struck by how each witness "contribute[d] a personal fragment to the chain of evidence."[72] This method of layering individual elements to create a single narrative is the basis for the novel's multivocal narration style. The strong influence of the Palmer case on the creation of *The Woman in White*'s structure and themes demonstrates an uncomfortable blending and suggested that literature not only absorbed influences but could also disseminate (sometimes dangerous) ideas.

In the critical outcry against sensation novels like *The Woman in White*, we can see the conception of literature as both causing and remedying criminal violence playing out in Victorian culture. Echoing earlier critics of genres like Newgate fiction, commentators on the sensational literature often labeled this fiction "noxious"—especially since sensation fiction was thought (like poison) to facilitate somatic transformation.[73] Sensation fiction, after all, derives its name from the bodily "sensations" experienced by its readers, and critics worried about what else these powerful texts could transmit. In a review that outlined the dangers of sensation fiction, Henry Mansel declared the genre to be a "poison" that provoked a dangerous "morbid excitement" in its readers.[74] This morbidity was particularly connected to sensation's domestication of crime: "We feel but a feeble interest in an authentic record of the crimes of a Borgia or Brinvilliers [two historical poisoners]; but we are thrilled to horror, even in fiction, by the thought that such things may be going on around us and among us."[75] In a defense of the sensation novel, however, George Augustus Sala declares that the genre is important precisely because it does not obscure the reality of domestic problems. Noting that readers find the same sensational material in newspapers, he writes, "We men and women who live in the world, and have, many of us, lived pretty hard lives too, want novels about That which Is, and not about That

---

72. Sutherland, "Introduction," xvi.
73. Oliphant, "Novels," 257.
74. Mansel, "Sensation Novels," 486, 482.
75. Mansel, "Sensation Novels," 489.

which Was and never Will be."[76] As Sala suggests, sensation novels played an important role in helping the Victorians to reassess some of their assumptions about the home. Indeed, sensation novels often prompted political and social change—a fact that Victorian authors used to validate the genre's production and consumption by the nineteenth-century public.

As the debate about sensation novels attests, concerns about the poisonous potential of literature often erupted at times of literary innovation. Since the use of "poison" as a metaphor for dangerous texts was so prevalent in Victorian culture, *Chemical Crimes* also uses poisonous works to reexamine the nature of Victorian writing, particularly in relation to generic change. Again, Derrida's work is useful for understanding why chemical crime would be an attractive topic for authors wanting to experiment with genre. In "The Law of Genre" he writes, "the law of the law of genre . . . is precisely a principle of contamination, a law of impurity, a parasitical economy."[77] Demarcating generic boundaries creates a system of "belongs" or "does not belong"—in other words, a binary structure that, to borrow from Gérard Genette, presents itself as a "'natural' system."[78] The problem with such a system is that it is not, in fact, natural but "a factitious symmetry heavily reinforced by fake windows."[79] As Hayden White sums up Derrida's deconstructive reading, "genre summons into being a kind of impurity against which it seeks to guard."[80] Generic boundaries are not natural and stable. As a "seduction" that "makes one stray from one's general, natural, habitual paths and laws," the *pharmakon* can be used to reveal the impurity of genre by breaking down its naturalized boundaries.[81]

In the works that *Chemical Crimes* studies, chemical crime signals a straying from generic traditions. Ian Burney has documented the confluence of poison and generic impurity in Victorian toxicological writings, illustrating how sensational discourses bled into scientific treatises on the nature of poisons.[82] In the realm of fiction, chemical criminals are often found at sites of literary innovation or generic exploration. Since the poisoned text is notoriously hybrid, this book charts the development of the chemical criminal through the various genres of crime fiction. It finds that chemical crime appears at moments when new genres develop or when signifi-

---

76. Sala, "Cant of Modern Criticism," 54.
77. Derrida, "Law of Genre," 59.
78. Derrida, "Law of Genre," 60.
79. Derrida, "Law of Genre," 60.
80. White, "Good of Their Kind," 375.
81. Derrida, *Dissemination*, 70.
82. Burney, *Poison, Detection, and the Victorian Imagination*, 59–92.

cant moments of development happen within genres. For example, chemical crime is present in two early detective novels (*The Notting Hill Mystery* and *The Moonstone*) as well as in the first locked-door detective novel (Sheridan LeFanu's 1864 *Uncle Silas*) and the first instance of the detective figure being the criminal (Marie Connor Leighton and Robert Leighton's 1899 *Michael Dred, Detective*). The readings that follow will examine texts considered originators within their genres, such as *The Moonstone*, or works that refigure the boundaries of their genres, like Bulwer's *Lucretia* and its re-visioning of silver fork and Newgate fiction. While acknowledging that it is useful, even necessary, to demarcate generic boundaries when studying the development of forms, this project focuses on points of generic instability and, crucially, how authors implicate science in this instability.

Thus, the chapters that follow are organized not only around the themes of science and crime but also by genre. Chapter 1 argues that the educated female chemical criminal in Letitia Elizabeth Landon's silver fork novel *Ethel Churchill* inspires both the characterization of Bulwer's villain and the generic innovations he makes in his Newgate novel *Lucretia; Or, The Children of Night*. Landon's incorporation of a criminal plot in her silver fork novel and Bulwer's revisioning of *Ethel Churchill* suggest that we reassess silver fork fiction's contribution to the development of Victorian crime fiction, particularly in relation to women and domesticity. Opening with an examination of narratives about Landon's own death by poison, this chapter focuses on how women's scientific education is framed as potentially poisonous in the early nineteenth century. By featuring intelligent women who eventually employ their scientific knowledge and training to commit chemical crimes, both Landon and Bulwer seem to critique programs of education that encourage women to participate in the masculine realm of scientific knowledge. At the same time, these authors also challenge biological essentialist ideas about women's intellectual inferiority and highlight early nineteenth-century society's refusal to accommodate ambitious, highly educated women.

By focusing on the poisoning doctor, chapter 2, "Medical Bluebeards: Gothic Medicine and the Poisoning Doctor in the Fiction of Ellen Wood," reveals the fraught relationship between sensation fiction and Victorian medicine. It argues that in two of Ellen Wood's works, her novel *Lord Oakburn's Daughters* and short story "Mr. Castonel," she uses the uxoricidal poisoning doctor to situate the medical gothic into the domestic sphere. Noting the cultural opposition between medicine/domestic, Wood uses the medical Bluebeard to illustrate how medicine was eroding women's power in the home. Wood, however, is not content to point out the problems of the medical field's relationship to women. Particularly in her later work, *Lord Oakburn's Daughters,* Wood deviates from the medical gothic by featuring female characters who challenge dangerous or immoral medical practitioners in order to assert their management of the home. Wood shares her deep concern with medical issues and proactive stance with many other sensational authors, and this chapter argues perhaps it is time scholars designate a subfield of "medical sensation" to better analyze sensation fiction's engagement with medicine and the home.

Chapter 3, "Chemicalized Bodies and Criminal Intent: Unruly Bodies and the Limitations of Forensic Science in Early Detective Fiction," examines the prevalence of poison in early detective fiction to show how the formation of the genre was influenced by anxiety about science, rather than faith in forensic methodologies. Beginning with an examination of *The Notting Hill Mystery*—a novel by Charles Warren Adams that has claims to being the first detective novel in the English language—this chapter illuminates how poison in early detective fiction reveals the unruliness of bodies. In *The Notting Hill Mystery,* the detective figure Henderson's theory about the deaths of Gertrude Anderton and Rosalie relies on their unruly bodies having unusual reactions to both poison and mesmerism. Similarly, Franklin Blake's body in *The Moonstone* becomes unruly when he unconsciously steals the titular diamond in a chemically induced trance. These two books play with modern forensics' dependence on the standardized body—the assumption that all bodies function essentially the same way—to illustrate how the unruly body can subvert forensic categorization. Both *The Notting Hill Mystery* and *The Moonstone* demonstrate how much early detection fiction questioned the ability of science to deal with the strange and unusual instead of legitimizing forensics as a reliable tool of detection.

Chapter 4 engages questions of gender and genre through a reading of two late-Victorian detective short story series by L. T. Meade: *The Brotherhood of the Seven Kings* and *The Sorceress of the Strand.* The primary criminal figures in both series—Madame Koluchy in *The Brotherhood of the Seven Kings* and Madame Sara in *The Sorceress of the Strand*—are adept female scientists who use their scientific knowledge in the commission of their daring criminal endeavors. Marked as foreign, ageless, and preternaturally beautiful, these women yoke the exotic seductiveness of earlier female chemical criminals with the scientific prowess of a Moreau or Jekyll—indicating Meade's fusion of the detective story with science fiction. These early female mad scientists practice a science that incorporates female concerns and is able to subvert the work of male detectives. Their strange, visionary science also indicates the extent to which science was becoming alienated from the layperson. By the end of the century, even the educated could no longer keep up with cutting-edge developments in science. To redemocritize science, Meade suggests the inclusion of new groups of people, such as women, into the practice of science. This chapter brings this book full circle by demonstrating that at the end of the century as in the beginning, the Victorians had still not come to terms with the dual nature of a science that can both create and destroy.

Before commencing with chapter readings, it may be useful to explain why one specific genre of crime fiction—the penny dreadful—is not included within the analytical purview of this book. Although the vast majority of poisoners who appear in Victorian fiction are chemical criminals, not all are, particularly in penny dreadfuls. A good example of this is the Lady Edith Vandeleur from Mary Elizabeth Braddon's series of penny dreadful tales collectively known as *The Black Band, or the Mysteries of Midnight*. The Moriarty-like villain Colonel Oscar Bertrand gives Lady Edith, who desires to kill her husband, poison. He supplies her with a chemical that is "a mysterious essence of which only the science of the East holds the fatal secret" and that causes a "death which is mistaken by doctors for disease of the heart."[83] Although this passage has a passing reference to "the science of the East" and mentions that the poison mimics heart disease, it is not as insistent as contemporary texts in its representation of poisoning as a scientifically informed practice. Instead, its references to the East shroud the poison in Oriental mystery and the occult. There is no laboratory scene where the reader watches as the poison is distilled, nor does the poisoner, Lady Edith, have any specific scientific training. She simply "pour[s] one drop of the poison into her husband's champagne glass" and is immediately caught when her husband sees her actions reflected in a mirror.[84] *The Black Band*'s formulation of poisoning more as an occult than a scientific practice is typical of the ways that penny dreadfuls portray these crimes and explains why this book does not include these works within the scope of its analysis.

Braddon makes a specific choice not to feature chemical criminals in her more "lowbrow" works, while she does include scientific poisoners in her novels written for a more educated, middle-class audience. The novel *The Trail of the Serpent* (1860), for instance, follows the antiheroine Valerie de Cevennes, who is very similar to the later Lady Edith. Like Lady Edith, Valerie wants to poison her husband but needs help to acquire the poison. Unlike in *The Black Band*, Valerie's poison is from "a chemist who will one

---

83. Braddon, *Black Band*, 47.
84. Braddon, *Black Band*, 50.

day work a revolution in the chemical science."[85] Her visit to his laboratory to get the poison is described as "a lesson in chemistry," and the chemist's description of the drug is scientifically straightforward: "For a full-grown rabbit use the eighth part of what you have there; the whole of it would poison a man, but death in either case would not be immediate. The operation of the poison occupies some hours before it terminates fatally."[86] Valerie has no more formal scientific training than Lady Edith, but the scientific origins of her poison and her education at the hands of the chemist qualify her as a chemical criminal. Indeed, the novel displays the haunting anxiety that "our wives and daughters [will] learn how they may poison us without fear of detection"; in other words, fears about mixing women and science are a central concern of *The Trail of the Serpent* but are not present in her penny dreadful.[87] The lack of chemical criminals in penny dreadfuls can tell us much about the ways middle-class Victorians understood readers of lowbrow literature. It suggests that authors did not believe lower-class readers would enjoy (or perhaps understand) scientific crime. Science it seems, even in terms of crime, was something reserved for educated middle-class readers; therefore, this book focuses on those genres of crime fiction specifically written for these consumers.

---

85. Braddon, *Trail of the Serpent*, 151.
86. Braddon, *Trail of the Serpent*, 153.
87. Braddon, *Trail of the Serpent*, 161.

CHAPTER 1

"THE SCIENCE OF MURDER"

Educating the Female Chemical Criminal
in L. E. L.'s *Ethel Churchill*
and Bulwer's *Lucretia*

THE BODY OF THE POISONED WOMAN; OR, WHAT LETITIA KNEW

This chapter begins with the eerie coincidence between an author's death and her literary work. In 1838, the writer Letitia Elizabeth Landon, best known for the poetry published under the acronym L. E. L., died in Cape Coast Castle on the western coast of Africa. The early death of an Englishwoman living in the colonies was not unusual, but Landon's death caused a sensation that transcended even her status as a literary celebrity. The Victorian fascination with Landon's death has much to do with the sudden and mysterious nature of her last moments. On the morning of October the fifteenth, only four months after her marriage, L. E. L.'s servant found her lifelessly slumped on the floor. Landon's body reportedly smelled strongly of poison and her hand still clutched an empty bottle labeled "Hydrocyanic acid," a chemical more commonly known as prussic acid or cyanide. Despite her husband's attempts to revive her, Landon was already close to death and never regained consciousness. She was buried at night, without fanfare, in the parade grounds of the castle.

Almost as soon as the news reached England, questions arose about the suspicious nature of L. E. L.'s death. Was she the victim of a murder or did she commit suicide? Had her death been natural or just a terrible accident?

rationality of men. Forays into these masculine arenas can only have harmful effects on the female mind.

The public obsession with how much Landon knew, or did not know, about poison—in other words, if she was a kind of chemical criminal herself—also colored the literary afterlife of her novel. How she died became integral to interpretations of *Ethel Churchill*, and the initially positive reviews (*Tait's Edinburgh Magazine* called the novel "her most brilliant achievement") that praised her realism and attention to scientific detail shifted to a more uncertain tone.[10] In *Homes and Haunts of the Most Eminent English Poets*, William Howitt praises "the convictions of 'higher moral responsibilities and greater power,' which strike us so forcibly in the later writings of L. E. L.," but also wonders "what shall we say to the preparation of prussic-acid, and its preservation by Lady Marchmont" and "the evolution of scenes and characters in her last work, bearing such dark resemblance to those of her own after experience"?[11]

Landon's dead body had become an ambiguous signifier that was impossible to interpret definitively and confused ways of reading both her life and literary work. This is especially true in relation to how the reader should interpret women's scientific education in *Ethel Churchill*. Ironically, this novel asks the same questions about allowing women access to poisonous knowledge found in the interpretations of Landon's death: What is women's intellectual capacity? Can they engage in complex fields such as science? And if so, what should women learn (or be forbidden from learning)? Landon's answers to these questions are similarly complex, and she sets up an opposition between "masculine" and "feminine" intellectual pursuits that directly links Henrietta's mental decline and transformation into a chemical criminal to her masculine scientific education. But to argue that L. E. L. condemns scientific education for women because it gives them access to dangerous knowledge is too simplistic of a reading. Just as Landon's body becomes paradoxical once it is touched by poison, education in *Ethel Churchill* is a site of contradiction; Henrietta's chemical crimes prove that women have an intellectual capacity for science while also showing how scientific education can be a source of their corruption.

This chapter argues that L. E. L.'s inclusion of a female chemical criminal in her novel *Ethel Churchill* illustrates a reaction to contemporary discussions of female education that suggest women should be restricted from certain forms of scientific knowledge. Although the study of science corrupts her,

---

10. "New Novels," 745.
11. Howitt, *Homes and Haunts*, 441.

Henrietta's depiction as a brilliant scientist is progressive—even feminist—during a time when most female poisoners were not yet characterized as chemical criminals. Landon creates a sympathetic villain who collapses the male/female binary but cannot reconcile her gender hybridity, particularly in relation to the tension between her sensibility and rationality. Frustrated by the vapidity of life as an aristocratic woman, her yearning for emotional connection clashes with her intellectual ambition. Landon's framing of Henrietta as a paradox highlights the constriction of women's domestic lives and offers the pessimistic view that early Victorian society was not yet ready for the scientific woman.

By using poison to reveal the cracks in the façade of the sanctified domestic sphere, Landon far outstrips the genre conventions of the silver fork novel and predicts developments in later Victorian crime fiction, notably the Newgate novel and sensation fiction. This chapter inaugurates this book's interest in the chemical criminal's appearance at moments of generic innovation, and uses examples from real cases of poisoning women to trace how a paradoxical response to the issue of women's scientific education affects the development of early Victorian crime fiction. Examining how Landon develops the female chemical criminal allows this chapter to chart the influence of the silver fork novel on the development of the Newgate novel—a type of popular fiction that derived its source material from real-life crimes featured in the infamous *Newgate Calendar*. Silver-fork novels have not been critically categorized as crime fiction, and relatively little attention has been paid to their contribution to emergent crime genres, but works such as Landon's *Ethel Churchill* nonetheless illustrate that silver fork texts were deeply involved in shaping early Victorian representations of crime. In particular, this text, which frames the chemical criminal as a symbol of women's domestic unhappiness, is a landmark example of early Victorian crime fiction that specifically focuses on women's issues.

The influence of Landon's *Ethel Churchill* is best traced in the crime writings of her friend Edward Bulwer (later Lord Lytton). Bulwer became infamous as the author of several critically harangued Newgate novels, but he was also the only author to pen a Newgate novel featuring a female protagonist.[12] This 1846 work, *Lucretia; Or, the Children of Night*, draws heavily from Landon's *Ethel Churchill* for its characterization and themes. As Landon's close friend, Bulwer would have read *Ethel Churchill* and been well aware of the debates about Landon's final moments that avowed (or

---

12. W. M. Thackeray, of course, included a female criminal as the main protagonist of his novel *Catherine*, which included many Newgate themes. However, since Thackeray intended the novel to be a parody of the genre, I have not included it in this discussion.

denied) that her knowledge of poisons was a contributing factor in her death. Like *Ethel Churchill*, *Lucretia* shares the earlier novel's focus on an aristocratic, educated, and socially sophisticated chemical criminal driven to murder through social constraints and the abuse and neglect of men. In both Landon's and Bulwer's works, then, the discontent of the two women, and their eventual murderous impulses, are linked to their unusual educations and masculine ambitions. Writing after Landon's death, Bulwer also explores the paradox of a scientific education that can both empower and poison women and uses this tension to comment on the state of the Victorian domestic sphere. By examining *Ethel Churchill* and *Lucretia* together, this chapter illustrates that 1830s and 1840s crime fiction was deeply interested in issues such as female scientific education and women's domestic situations—a fact that has been previously neglected by scholars. In addition, it also reveals that the male-dominated crime genre of Newgate fiction reacted, and was deeply indebted, to a tradition of women's writing that has yet to be critically acknowledged.

SILVER FORK NOVELS AS CRIME FICTION

Since silver fork fiction is not usually included in surveys of Victorian crime fiction, I want to discuss briefly its generic characteristics and its kinship to Newgate fiction. Silver fork fiction developed slightly earlier than Newgate novels, but the two genres are largely contemporaneous, spanning a period from the 1820s to the end of the 1840s.[13] As critics have begun to point out, despite obvious generic differences there was a considerable cross-pollination between the two genres. For example, although silver fork novels tended to follow the general formula of featuring "the balls, the dinners, the hunts, the teas, the gossip, the electioneering, the opera, the theater, the clubs, the marriage settlements, the love marriages, the fashionable marriages, the gambling, and the dissipation" that characterized the lives of aristocratic characters negotiating the complexities of fashionable life, these novels increasingly featured the "crimes" of the rich—whether these transgressions took the form of social crimes, such as adultery, or legal crimes, such as dueling.[14] Silver fork fiction's increasing reliance on crime to spice up plots certainly reflects the growing popularity of Newgate fiction;

---

13. Although the earliest novels to be labeled "Newgate" fiction did not appear until the 1830s, Keith Hollingsworth notes that the "Newgate theme" was widely prevalent in 1820s literature.

14. Rosa, *Silver Fork School*, 62.

indeed, as the silver fork genre developed in the 1830s, it reacted to the craze for crime fiction by featuring just as many "murders, suicides," and "mysteries" as it did "dukes, silver-forks," and "kitchen stuffs."[15]

Silver fork novels incorporated the tactics of Newgate novels to satiate changing public tastes in literature, but contemporary critics were also quick to point out that the popularity of Newgate novels "was a natural and inevitable reaction of the public mind upon the fashion of the so-called silver-fork school."[16] Even before silver fork novels widely incorporated crime into their plots, the "vapid and languid insipidity" of the genre, as one nineteenth-century commentator wrote, had given the public "a morbid appetite in search of strong excitement" that naturally made them turn "to the coarse manners and vulgar crimes of low life" made available by Newgate novels.[17] But the influence of silver fork fiction on Newgate novels went beyond priming the pump. Although Newgate novels generally shifted narrative emphasis from "high" to "low" life, they retained the silver fork emphasis on aristocratic characters—criminals who are the long-lost children of peers, or highwaymen who comport themselves with aristocratic flair, often grace the pages of Newgate novels. There is a clearly a continuum between the egotistical silver fork dandy and the, as Thackeray described them, "dandy, poetical, rosewater thieves" of Newgate fiction.[18] Indeed, April Kendra's definition of "dandical" silver fork novels could also describe the Newgate novels *Jack Sheppard* or *Paul Clifford*:

> The dandy novel . . . records the adventures of a swaggering male protagonist whose experiences lead him to greater self-awareness and maturity while confirming his sense of superiority. Since the dandy is a man of sophistication, the dandy novel always has an urban setting, for it is only in the metropolis that the hero's powers can be fully displayed and appreciated. The action of the novel is largely episodic and centred on the hero.[19]

As a character already outside the pale of ordinary experience, the dandy-hero easily crosses boundaries—even the boundaries between "high" and "low" life. As Heather Worthington notes, this boundary crossing often served to highlight double standards in the legal system that harshly pun-

---

15. Manning, review of *Village Belles*, 471.
16. Morgan, review of *Jack Sheppard*, 803.
17. Morgan, review of *Jack Sheppard*, 803.
18. Thackeray, *Catherine.30*.
19. Kendra, "Gendering the Silver Fork," 26.

ished the poor while turning a blind eye to the transgressions of the rich.[20] Thus, the dandy figure's migration between Newgate and silver fork fiction illustrates the overlapping elements of the two genres and cements their shared concern with unfair legal systems and social prejudices.

While the literary influence of the dandy novel on early Victorian crime fiction is easily illustrated, the effects of other forms of silver fork fiction on the rise of the Newgate novel are less clear. As Kendra has convincingly shown, silver fork fiction is divided into two distinct subgenres: the masculine dandy novel and the feminine society novel. In contrast to "hero-centred" dandy novels written primarily by men, society fiction was usually produced by women and "includes a large cast of characters whose lives are clearly interdependent, frequent shifts of narrative focus to highlight these different characters (rather than telling the story through the perceptions of a single narrator or central consciousness), and emphasis on family and community relationships."[21] With their emphasis on everyday concerns and familial relationships, society novels present the female experience and prefigure the rise of Victorian domestic realism. Many of these works also explicitly address contentious issues facing early Victorian women, such as unhappy marriages and even divorce.

Written almost entirely by men, Newgate fiction features the glories of male criminal-heroes, which can perhaps explain the scholarly neglect of the links between these texts and feminine literary traditions. The amount of crime in many society novels makes this scholarly oversight apparent; in fact, works like Landon's *Ethel Churchill* describe crimes, including murder, that are just as brutal as any found in Newgate fiction. Thus, this chapter contends that feminine forms of silver fork fiction, like society novels, need to be included in histories of crime fiction because they affect the evolution of Newgate novels and also later sensation fiction. Many Newgate novels shared society fiction's concern about the effects of crime, not just on the individual, but on the wider community. These texts increasingly included "a large cast of characters whose lives are clearly interdependent" in order to highlight the interconnectedness of society and illustrate to the middle classes the necessity for legal and social reform. In addition, as the Newgate form developed in the late 1830s and 1840s, it began to examine the effect of crime on women and the domestic sphere. For example, Charles Dickens's Newgate novel *Oliver Twist*, which began serialization the same year that *Ethel Churchill* was published, examines both crime's effect on the middle-

---

20. Worthington, "Against the Law," 55–56.
21. Kendra, "Gendering the Silver Fork," 27.

class family (in the form of Oliver's parentage and his relationship to the Maylie family) and crime's looming presence in the domestic lives of poor women (as exemplified by Nancy and Bill's destructive relationship).

The Newgate novel that best illustrates the influence of feminine society novels is Bulwer's *Lucretia*, which adapted many of the concerns found in Landon's *Ethel Churchill*. Bulwer is known for both his Newgate novels and his "dandy" silver fork works, but *Lucretia*'s connection to *Ethel Churchill* reveals an interest in women's issues that also links him to the traditionally female-orientated society novel. Yet *Ethel Churchill* might not have been such an influence on Bulwer's work had it not already displayed some elements found in the emergent Newgate genre. Both works are concerned with crime and the sanctity of the domestic sphere, and Bulwer's re-visioning of *Ethel Churchill* is demonstrated through the two novels' shared depiction of women who trespass into the "masculine" realm of scientific education. Combining society fiction's interest in female education with Newgate's investigation of corrupt pedagogical practices, *Ethel Churchill* and *Lucretia* use the female chemical criminal to register anxiety about women's increasing access to scientific information; at the same time, however, they acknowledge women's intellectual potential and are critical of the restrictive cultural roles that make science and the domestic seemingly incompatible.

ETHEL CHURCHILL

L. E. L.'s contemporary reviewers situate her last novel, *Ethel Churchill*, within a tradition of silver fork literature and compare it favorably to other works within the genre such as Bulwer's *Pelham*.[22] Like many fashionable novels, *Ethel Churchill* follows the fate and fortunes of the aristocracy, simultaneously glorifying and harshly criticizing the frivolity of living the high life. Set in the 1720s and incorporating historical figures such as Alexander Pope, Lavinia Fenton, and Lady Wortley Montagu, *Ethel Churchill* does not strictly adhere to the silver fork formula of describing contemporary characters, but it does draw parallels between the aristocracy of the past and that of the present. The novel is also unusual because it features a crime (other than the "crime" of adultery) perpetrated by a female character—and still more unusual in that this crime is a chemical one, signaling the scientific sophistication of the murderer. This inclusion of historic characters and a pair of murders signals *Ethel Churchill*'s response to the growing popularity

---

22. "New Novels," 745.

of the Newgate novel, which often featured crimes committed by historical characters. Yet, by featuring a poisoning *woman*, *Ethel Churchill* moves murder away from low-life and male criminals that characterized Newgate fiction and instead situates it directly in the domestic sphere.

Historians have shown that men poisoned more frequently than women did, and yet, as George Robb notes, the "relatively few cases of wives murdering husbands" by poison caused much "greater alarm."[23] Poison's reputation as an equalizer of sorts—a way for weaker women to take advantage of physically stronger men—was one of the greatest anxieties associated with chemical weapons. Women's growing agency in the nineteenth century meant that the public often connected female poisoners with a transgressive agenda, as evidenced by the obsession with the relatively few sensational cases of women poisoning their husbands. Long before the sensational novels of Wilkie Collins and M. E. Braddon, L. E. L. figures poison as a literary symbol of nineteenth-century domestic discord. After all, Henrietta Marchmont turns to chemical crimes out of desperation: She murders her indifferent husband after he threatens to expose her infidelity (although she is innocent of his accusations) and kills her potential lover, George, after he cruelly manipulates her affections. The murders in *Ethel Churchill* combine the generic concerns of both society and Newgate novels. On the one hand, the chemical crimes violently illustrate the society novel's critique of arranged aristocratic marriages and emphasize, in Kendra's words, "the necessity of domestic affections and supportive communities."[24] On the other hand, the novel also incorporates the Newgate device of cultivating sympathy for criminals by framing Henrietta as a victim of cultural circumstances that necessitated her loveless marriage and the scientific education that kept her from developing these supportive structures. With these dual concerns, *Ethel Churchill* can be seen as a hybrid text that blends society fiction's interest in domestic structures and the formation of female characters with the Newgate novel's interest in the psychological development of criminality.

Landon situates the root of Henrietta's problems in the unusual education she receives. Central to Landon's exploration of the effects of education is the dichotomy between "masculine" and "feminine" pursuits she draws from early Victorian culture. Orphaned as an infant and raised by her uncle, Sir Jasper Meredith, Henrietta receives a peculiarly masculine education that raises her interests and ambitions above the sphere of domestic duty. Her uncle, a world-weary and morose man who lives as a recluse in his country

---

23. Robb, "Circe in Crinoline," 176–77.
24. Kendra, "Gendering the Silver Fork," 28.

mansion, has turned to several branches of scientific study, including chemistry, to occupy his time. Much of Henrietta's childhood is spent within the shadow of her uncle's studies: "I took you, Henrietta, when an infant, from your dying mother's arms. Your cradle was placed in my laboratory; and often have I closed the midnight volume to watch the fitful slumbers of your childhood."[25] Here, the scientific exploits of the laboratory are disturbingly grafted onto domestic scenes of the nursery and child-rearing; just as her uncle's memories of Henrietta's youth are bound to images of "the midnight volume," the association between Henrietta and scientific knowledge begins in her infancy. Significantly, Henrietta never grows out of this association. The opening conversation between Meredith and Henrietta occurs in the same laboratory where Henrietta has spent her infancy, and the reader learns that this space has been the setting for much of their familial interactions. Replacing the kitchen or family parlor, Meredith's laboratory is the domestic heart of the home, and Henrietta spends her entire domestic experience in an environment saturated in scientific pursuits.

This laboratory is clearly not meant to be a healthy environment for a young woman to grow up in. The reader is informed, "it was a large vaulted apartment, and had been once a chapel; but it was now half library, half laboratory."[26] That the hall used to be a "chapel" and now houses scientific apparatuses reflects the nineteenth-century fear that scientific study encouraged a materialistic and atheistic worldview. Indeed, the chamber's decoration illustrates humanity's separation from both nature and God:

> The arches were formed of black oak, hewn into all the fantastic shapes of Gothic imaginings; in which it was singular to note that all the natural imitations were graceful, while those of humanity were hideous. The oak-leaf and the garland mingled grotesquely with the distorted faces, that ever and anon peeped from among their wreaths.[27]

The careful contrast between the beauty of the "natural" decorative elements and the gruesome human forms on the laboratory's ceiling suggests humans' inherent corruptibility and even implies a form of divine judgment of the "unholy studies" happening in the room below.[28] Drawing a distinction between science and spirituality, Landon suggests that scientific and

---

25. Landon, *Ethel Churchill*, I: 5.
26. Landon, *Ethel Churchill*, I: 10.
27. Landon, *Ethel Churchill*, I: 8.
28. Landon, *Ethel Churchill*, I: 11.

materialist thought corrupts humanity and separates it from nature and divine knowledge.

If the chamber's carvings are "grotesque," the same can be said of Meredith's scientific collections. Meredith has amassed an amalgamation of exotic specimens that are crowded into display cases; yet unlike the carvings on the ceiling, the representation of Meredith's "natural" specimens are anything but "graceful": "Here was a grisly crocodile, its teeth white and sharp as when they glistened in the waters of the Nile; there, a massy serpent, knotted into huge and hideous contortions; while myriads of small snakes, lizards, and disgusting insects, were stored around."[29] The obsession with scientific collection and categorization has turned these once beautiful natural forms into artificial exhibits—revealing Landon's construction of science as unnatural. Metaphorically, these specimens also mirror the condition of Henrietta's mind, which, like the taxidermized animals, has been warped and deformed from its natural state. The association between reptiles and poison gestures toward the prussic acid that Henrietta will later manufacture in this room, but these "disgusting" exhibits also endow Meredith with a reputation for eccentricity and even sorcery. The "care" that Meredith puts into organizing his exotic collections gives him, "among his neighbours, the reputation of a magician, though they were but the sickly fancies of a heart ill at ease, that mocked itself in its pursuits."[30] While moving away from a description of Meredith's scientific experiments as "occult," Landon does affirm that these academic obsessions are "sickly fancies" that only lead to sterile and nonproductive knowledge.

The result of Henrietta's constant association with her uncle's weird science is that she is a paradox: Outwardly the epitome of womanly beauty, she has the rationality and ambition of a man. Yet, her gender hybridity means that she is ill-equipped to deal with the world outside of her uncle's laboratory:

> She knew more of the world than most women of her years; for her converse had been chiefly with her uncle, a man of remarkable endowments: and she had read an infinite variety of books—read them, too, with that quick perception which seizes motive and meaning with intuitive accuracy. Such, however, inevitably is half knowledge; and theory that lacks the correction of practice, is as the soul without the body.[31]

---

29. Landon, *Ethel Churchill*, I: 10.
30. Landon, *Ethel Churchill*, I: 10–11.
31. Landon, *Ethel Churchill*, I: 8.

The passage's emphasis on the phrase "the soul without the body" is a key for unlocking the tension that will ultimately lead to Henrietta's madness. Heavily trained in science and taught to despise feminine concerns such as love, she sacrifices soul for mind by repressing her sensibility in favor of cultivating her rationality. Henrietta is destined for marriage, and her training in the hard sciences cannot prepare her for traditionally female preoccupations such as "the science of society" or "*la haute science de la coquetterie*."[32] Although fashionable society worships her beauty, she chafes under the realization that women's ambitions have very few culturally acceptable outlets beyond marriage and social popularity. Bored and disgusted with the shallowness of upper-class society, Henrietta's only consolation from her education is the ability to manufacture liquid revenge.

This conflict between sensibility and rationality situates *Ethel Churchill* within contemporary debates about the nature of women's education, especially in relation to the field of science. Despite the progress furnished by the Enlightenment, in the 1830s scientific education for upper- and middle-class women, especially in areas like chemistry, was still relatively rare. For example, a review of Mary Somerville's 1831 book *Mechanism of the Heavens* suggests, "The higher branches of the mathematics are not among the recognised objects of female accomplishment; and accordingly the education of women is so directed, that they have rarely the means afforded them of acquiring even the elements of scientific knowledge."[33] The first half of the nineteenth century, however, saw a push for change and more opportunities for women to participate in the sciences. Mary Wollstonecraft famously advocated for women's education in *A Vindication of the Rights of Woman*, and subsequent writers, such as Maria Edgeworth, argued for an inclusion of science in the course of women's education:

> A girl who runs through a course of natural history, learns something about chemistry, has been taught something of botany, and who knows but just enough of these to make her fancy that she is well informed, is in a miserable situation, in danger of becoming ridiculous, and insupportably tiresome to men of sense and science.[34]

It is important to note that, as for Wollstonecraft, a central piece of Edgeworth's case for female scientific education is that eligible men will eventually find the artistic and showy "accomplishments" of women "tiresome."

---

32. Landon, *Ethel Churchill*, II: 124, II: 237.
33. The *Edinburgh Review*, unsigned review of *Mechanism of the Heavens*, 1.
34. Edgeworth, *Practical Education*, 144.

At least early in the century, it was common for writers to argue for women's increased access to science on the basis that it would benefit them in their domestic duties, especially as the caretakers of the family. Other writers recognized that the repetitive nature of women's domestic lives could be insipid and argued for scientific education to break the vacuity of their lives.

Ann B. Shteir notes that the century saw a vast increase in scientific writing aimed directly at women, who were particularly encouraged to study sciences like "geology, ornithology, and conchology."[35] Other branches of science, such as chemistry and medicine, however, were not fit material for women. As Pamela Gilbert has discussed, there was a general anxiety that "texts were potentially deceptive, slippery substances which could affect the reader without the reader's knowledge or consent, like a poison," and this fear only increased when the text in question was a scientific work.[36] Even Jane Marcet, whose *Conversations on Chemistry* was designed to introduce young women to chemical studies, was careful to "[draw] clear boundaries between professional and general appreciation of the discipline," argues Saba Bahar, perhaps out of a concern that professional knowledge should be carefully regulated.[37] In early editions of Marcet's work, the author is cautious about discussing the effects of chemicals on the body:

> CAROLINE: If this is the case, I have certainly been much mistaken in the notion I had formed of chemistry. I own that I thought it was chiefly confined to the knowledge and preparation of medicines.
>
> MRS. B.: That is only a branch of Chemistry which is called Pharmacy, and though the study of it is, no doubt, of great importance to the world at large, it belongs exclusively to professional men, and is the last that I should advise you to pursue.[38]

In a rather uncharacteristic move, "Mrs. B.," Marcet's mouthpiece, makes clear to her pupils that studying chemicals' effects on the body is best left to "professional men." Since many medicines were also poisonous, Marcet's hesitation in discussing pharmaceutical applications of chemicals could reflect a fear that this knowledge could be abused or turned to criminal applications. Scientific education for women, it seems, is positioned as a paradox; it could be beneficial to women's intellectual lives, but at the same

---

35. Shteir, "Elegant Recreations?," 237.
36. Gilbert, *Disease, Desire, and the Body*, 21–22.
37. Bahar, "Jane Marcet," 30.
38. Marcet, *Conversations on Chemistry*, 2.

time, it could lead to women having access to potentially dangerous information. During a period when feminist writers like Mary Wollstonecraft and Maria Edgeworth were advocating for women's scientific education by arguing that it could improve women's lives and intellectual satisfaction, *Ethel Churchill* suggests that certain forms of scientific knowledge are too dangerous for general consumption, and that until cultural gender expectations are reformed, women will receive little benefit from it.

Responding to this state of women's scientific education, Landon situates Henrietta as a paradoxical mixing of masculine and feminine parts that contribute to her tragic end because she lives in a society that rejects her. Her love life is evidence of this since she is secretly infatuated with Walter Maynard, a "poor and dependent" poet, despite her vow that she "is too quick-sighted for the delusions of love."[39] Walter, however, is not attracted to an intellectual woman but prefers Ethel, the novel's representative of conventional femininity. The sweet, purely domestic Ethel's "training had been widely different" from Henrietta's, and Ethel knows nothing of books "beyond her grandmother's cherished volumes of which a herbal was the study, and the Cassandra of Madame Scudori the recreation."[40] Henrietta's husband, Lord Marchmont, is obviously insecure about his wife's superior mental capabilities, and although Henrietta's wit contributes to her success in society, it does not guarantee her personal happiness. Henrietta's lover, George, who claims to be fascinated with her sharp mind, finds her intellect intimidating and mocks her by having his secretary write philosophical love letters to her. Henrietta's wit merely buys her a place in society, where she is "flattered, admired, and courted, but not loved."[41]

Henrietta's rejection by society suggests that Anne Mellor's argument that early nineteenth-century female writers "tended to celebrate . . . the workings of the rational mind," and located this rationality in "the female as well as the male body" needs to be modified.[42] Critics such as Glennis Stephenson have disagreed with Mellor, noting that Landon's works confirm a biologically essentialist model of womanhood:

> In her life Landon may often seem to come close to epitomising Wollstonecraft's revolutionary new woman, but in her poetry she quite explicitly rejects Wollstonecraft's revisionary definitions, and instead propounds a view of women that draws more upon the earlier construction of female

---

39. Landon, *Ethel Churchill*, I: 41, I: 3.
40. Landon, *Ethel Churchill*, I: 41.
41. Landon, *Ethel Churchill*, II: 319.
42. Mellor, *Romanticism and Gender*, 2.

gender as identical with sensibility, the very view that Wollstonecraft so passionately denounced in *A Vindication of the Rights of Woman*. For L. E. L., love, erotic passion, feelings—these are the principles that rule women's lives.[43]

Stephenson's thesis is applicable to *Ethel Churchill*, for "love, erotic passion, and feelings" eventually become the motives for murder; however, I want to add that Landon highlights the dichotomy between heart and science to shift the Victorian conception of women's biological capacities. Henrietta's erudition confirms that Landon believes that women are *capable* of highly rationalistic learning, even as she affirms the essentialist view that women cannot shuffle off their feminine sensibilities. Although the novel sustains the growing nineteenth-century feminist argument that women are intellectually equal to men, it also is hesitant to endorse scientific education for women. Challenging Edgeworth's argument, Landon positions the learned woman as unlovable. Landon recognizes that until men are willing to accept the erudite woman, the constrictions of the domestic sphere restrict intellectual engagements.

Henrietta's privileging of her masculine ambitions over her emotional needs means that she cannot have a happy ending. With the death of her uncle, Henrietta's sensibility erupts as emotional turmoil. Heretofore, Meredith had acted as a conduit for Henrietta's emotional needs: Much of the first and second volumes of the novel are Henrietta's letters to her uncle, where she shares her experiences, thoughts, and dreams for the future. When her husband ignores Henrietta's premonition that her uncle is ill and flippantly prevents her from attending his deathbed, she finally realizes that "she hate[s] her husband."[44] He sends Henrietta to Meredith Place in order to secure the money and estates, but she instead focuses on her intellectual inheritance—her uncle's laboratory—for revenge. In these passages about Henrietta's distillation of poison, Landon again underscores Henrietta's scientific training, reminding her readers that "from her childhood she had been accustomed to watch, and often aid, in her uncle's chemical experiments: she was, therefore, not at a loss, as a complete novice in the science would have been."[45] In a mockery of the domestic duties of cooking and baking that Henrietta was taught to despise, she constantly refers to one of her uncle's "huge volume[s]" of chemistry for her poison recipe.[46] Far more

---

43. Stephenson, *Letitia Landon*, 2.
44. Landon, *Ethel Churchill*, II: 320.
45. Landon, *Ethel Churchill*, II: 326.
46. Landon, *Ethel Churchill*, II: 327.

deftly than she could have read a cookbook, Henrietta is able to comprehend the complicated scientific process necessary to create the prussic acid. What follows is a highly scientific description of the poison-making that Landon must have carefully researched, since Bohn's discovery that prussic acid could be distilled out of almond kernels was a recent one, found only in specialized periodicals and books.[47] Following Bohn's methodology, Henrietta takes the almonds, which she has "crushed together, and placed to simmer over the furnace," and makes certain to protect herself from the noxious fumes by using "a glass mask, and some strongly aromatic vinegar."[48] Once the countess has finished placing the newly distilled prussic acid into vials, she locks them in "a small casket" and places "the little key on a chain that she always wore of her uncle's hair" that she wears near "her heart."[49] By placing the key on a chain of Meredith's hair, Landon symbolically connects the poison to Meredith's tutoring of Henrietta; the chain represents the link between Henrietta's chemical crime and her distorted domestic upbringing.

Henrietta's combination of out-of-control sensibility with calculating rationality makes her monstrous. In the laboratory scene, Landon heightens the narrative tension by gothicizing Henrietta, whose state of mind is reflected in her "wandering to and fro like a disturbed spirit" throughout the "scattered" room.[50] When she ventures out into the foggy night to collect the bitter almonds she needs to produce her poison, she seems more like a specter than a human woman:

> Any one who had seen her, might have been pardoned for believing, from that hour, in supernatural appearances. Her tall figure was wrapped in a loose white robe, and her long black hair hung down to her waist, already glistening with raindrops. The moonlight fell directly on her face, whose features seemed rigid as those of a statue, while the paleness was that of a corpse; but the large gleaming eyes, so passionate and so wild, belonged to life—life, racked by that mental agony, life, and human life, only knows.[51]

Here, Henrietta figuratively becomes a living corpse that will leave death in her wake; and indeed, the sensibility that Henrietta has long denied is reanimated into a monstrous form of intellectual madness. Like a vengeful Medea, Henrietta too is like one of "the sorceresses of old, bending over

---

47. Thomson, *System of Chemistry*, 8.
48. Landon, *Ethel Churchill*, II: 326.
49. Landon, *Ethel Churchill*, II: 328–29.
50. Landon, *Ethel Churchill*, II: 324.
51. Landon, *Ethel Churchill*, II: 326.

herb and drug, to form their potent spells."⁵² Unsurprisingly, Henrietta's monstrous transformation is fully realized on the night she murders her husband:

> There were no ornaments on the neck and arms; indeed, Lady Marchmont had used up the principal of hers to form the curious head-dress of the picture. The hair was formed into one thick braid, which went round and round the head: amid the folds of this was wound a serpent of precious stones, whose head, formed of rubies and diamonds, rose out of the knot behind, and made a sort of crest.⁵³

Dressed in an elaborate costume for a party, Landon presents Henrietta as a living Lamia—a half woman, half poisonous snake. The Lamia reference hearkens back to the images of the grotesque snakes found in her uncle's laboratory, and the bejeweled snake's position on Henrietta's head—the seat of her rationality—also suggests that Henrietta's mind is figuratively poisoned. Indeed, Henrietta's murder of her husband and lover marks the moment when her rationality and sensibility collapse into insanity. By transforming the chemical criminal into a supernatural creature, L. E. L. suggests that the confluence of science and femininity is strange, unnatural, and dangerous. Fully transformed into a Lamia and pushed to the brink of her emotional capacity, the educated woman is now a monster capable of murder.

Henrietta's knowledge of science, which is clearly a factor in her downfall, also marks a significant moment for representations of female criminality. When Landon wrote *Ethel Churchill*, most female poisoners were not yet marked as chemical criminals, but the same was not true of their male counterparts. Thomas Griffiths Wainewright, who was suspected of poisoning his niece in 1830, had limited education in scientific matters, yet the public credited him with being a methodical chemical criminal who kept "a diary in which he carefully noted the results of his terrible experiments and the methods that he adopted."⁵⁴ When the servant Eliza Fenning attempted to poison her employer, Robert Turner, and his family with a plate of arsenic-laced dumplings in 1815, she was represented very differently. Noting that "the quantity of arsenic mixed in the dumplings must have been very considerable," one of the doctors who attended the family wrote that the Turners all survived only because she had inexpertly given them too much arsenic. The large dose had immediately acted as a "powerful emetic and

---

52. Landon, *Ethel Churchill*, II: 328.
53. Landon, *Ethel Churchill*, III: 173.
54. Wilde, "Pen, Pencil and Poison," 50.

purgative," causing the afflicted family members to expulse the majority of poison from their systems—a reaction that the ignorant Fenning did not take into account.[55] A case that would have been more recent in the memory of Landon's readers, the 1834 poisoning of Clara Ann Smith by Mary Ann Burdock, also presented an unskilled female poisoner. There was not only a witness to Burdock putting a powder into the gruel of Smith, but her choice of poison turned the food "a nasty *red* color." Noting the imprudence of using realgar, or red arsenic, for murder, the *Magazine of Popular Science* called Burdock a "fool-hardy" criminal.[56]

By characterizing Henrietta as a scientific criminal, Landon departs from depictions of real-life female poisoners and instead aligns her character with male chemical criminals. Even though *Ethel Churchill* sets up a binary between proper masculine and feminine intellectual pursuits and suggests that there should be limitations on women's access to scientific study, Lady Marchmont's capacity for chemical crime can also be read as a feminist move. These conflicting viewpoints demonstrate the paradox of scientific education for women in *Ethel Churchill*. The novel argues that women *can* excel at science, but also perhaps that they should not study it—at least not until cultural attitudes toward women change. Chemical crime allows Landon to explore early Victorian attitudes toward women and their natural or proper roles, revealing that Henrietta's tragedy is not caused by her scientific education, but rather by a restrictive society that does not allow her to fulfill her feminine role while still having a proper outlet for her immense mental capacities. Landon comes to the pessimistic conclusion that there is no place for women like Henrietta (and perhaps herself) in early Victorian society.

Recognizing Landon's feminist argument about women's intellectual restraint, reviewers of *Ethel Churchill* nonetheless largely read Henrietta as a sympathetic character. Comparing Henrietta to her husband, the critic for the *Athenaeum* wrote that the "Countess of Marchmont, whose character of a gay, beautiful leader of fashionable life, full of wit, and with a recklessness of manner which fails to hide even from herself the pangs of a too sensitive heart—stands in admirable contrast with the stiff, pompous, and self-conceited nothingness of her lord and master."[57] Similarly, one of L. E. L.'s Victorian biographers felt undisturbed by Lord Marchmont's death: "We leave him after this, without regret, to his fate; sympathy is alike unnecessary

---

55. Marshall, Five Cases of Recovery, 4, 20.
56. "Prevention and Detection," 377.
57. The Athenaeum, unsigned review of *Ethel Churchill*, 713.

and impossible."[58] In situating Lord Marchmont as the villain (who deserved his fate) and Henrietta as a figure of sympathy, *Ethel Churchill* draws from the Newgate tradition of encouraging audience identification with and empathy for the criminal-hero. Like many Newgate heroes, she is "exhibited as a symptom of social evil" rather than as an inherently evil character.[59] Similarly, Landon borrows from the Newgate tradition with her carefully drawn psychological portrait of Henrietta—a tactic that further encourages the reader's identification with the countess and serves as a justification of her crimes. Finally, Henrietta's downward spiral into madness, which finally subsides into a "hopeless," "miserable," yet "gentle" form of mental disease, provides both an appropriately horrific punishment for the chemical criminal while also sympathetically maintaining her image as a gifted and beautiful woman broken on the wheel of an uncaring world.[60] This mixture of the society novel and Newgate fiction found in *Ethel Churchill* demands that we reconsider works like this in the historiography of crime fiction and demonstrates the extent to which female authors, women's issues, and explorations of science participated in shaping early Victorian crime fiction.

If *Ethel Churchill* draws heavily from the Newgate genre, then why did the novel escape the harsh criticism usually lobbed at this type of crime fiction? *Ethel Churchill* is also a clear precursor to sensation fiction, so why did reviewers empathize with Henrietta when they heavily criticized later female chemical criminals of sensation fiction (such as Lydia Gwilt), especially when they could also be read sympathetically or raised feminist concerns? Why, if Landon evoked poison within her text, was the natural progression not to consider the novel toxic and capable of spreading both beneficial and dangerous knowledge to its primarily female audience? I argue that these contradictions exist because women were not yet depicted as chemical criminals in the 1830s. Female poisoners were represented as lower-class, ignorant blunderers, allowing readers to interpret Henrietta as a figure purely of the imagination. A rational scientific female murderer was a fantastical creature in 1837—but this view of the female poisoner would not last long. When Bulwer wrote *Lucretia* in 1846, women who poisoned were beginning to be depicted as chemical criminals. Bulwer responded to this change by situating women's scientific education as a Newgate theme and treated the subject very similarly to the way Landon did, but his novel got a very different reaction from the public and became one of the most abused Newgate novels ever published.

58. Sheppard, *Characteristics*, 117.
59. Hollingsworth, *Newgate Novel*, 14.
60. Landon, *Ethel Churchill*, III: 327.

LUCRETIA; OR, THE CHILDREN OF NIGHT

The relationship between L. E. L. and Bulwer, and her influence on his work, is complex. Having first met when they were both young writers, Landon and Bulwer mutually encouraged each other's work—both privately and publicly. Landon, for example, included a favorable portrait of both Bulwer and his wife Rosina in her 1831 society novel *Romance and Reality*. The same year, she wrote a very flattering account of Bulwer in *New Monthly Magazine*'s series on "Living Literary Characters." In the piece, Landon not only defends Bulwer's works against his critics but also labels Bulwer as "the first-rate talent of our time" and compares him favorably to Byron and Wordsworth.[61] Bulwer was eager to repay the favor. In a review of *Romance and Reality*, Bulwer applauded Landon's prose and revealed his early admiration for her poetry. After declaring "the author of these volumes is a lady of remarkable genius," he reminisces about his "rush every Saturday afternoon for 'The Literary Gazette,' and an impatient anxiety to hasten at once to that corner of the sheet which contained the three magical letters of 'L. E. L.'"[62]

Bulwer calculated his review to increase sales of the novel, yet its anecdote about Landon's poetry also reads as genuinely heartfelt. Since L. E. L.'s literary career was well established before Bulwer became a professional writer, this passage also confirms that Bulwer was interested in and inspired by Landon's work.

Unfortunately for both Landon and Bulwer, this exchange of flattery did not go unnoticed. Soon after Bulwer's review, *The Age* published the following "skit":

N.: Child of love and Muse of Passion
Pretty Letty—that is you.
L. E. L.: Ned, in all *you* lead the fashion,
Neddy mine, indeed you do.[63]

The Age's skit implies a subtext to Landon and Bulwer's exchange that went far beyond mutual career boosting; the "Pretty Letty" and the "Neddy mine" suggest an intimate, rather than professional, relationship. Although there is no reliable evidence to dispute the platonic nature of their friendship, their interactions nevertheless sparked salacious speculation. Through-

---

61. Landon, "Living Literary Characters," 443.
62. Bulwer, "Romance and Reality," 546.
63. Quoted in Sadleir, *Bulwer: A Panorama*, 415.

out her career, Landon weathered a series of scandalous rumors that linked her sexually to Bulwer and several other men, including literary figures such as William Jerdan and William Maginn.[64] It was perhaps enough for the gossips that Landon "was certainly in the habit of visiting Bulwer and Rosina [his wife] at home, and was observed to be somewhat flirtatious in her manner," but the rumors came from a much more "reliable" source.[65] Always eager to blame Edward for any indiscretion, Rosina Bulwer accused Landon of "intriguing with my infamous husband."[66]

Whether or not Bulwer was sexually involved with Landon is uncertain, but it is clear that the two writers remained friends even in the face of damaging rumors. When Landon's engagement to John Forster was broken off, Bulwer supported L. E. L. and even attempted to reconcile the pair. Although this romantic project failed, Bulwer was ready to facilitate Landon's next engagement and gave away the writer at her wedding to George Maclean. According to one account of Bulwer's life, he was so moved at her wedding feast that during a toast he accidentally called her his "'daughter' in allusion to the part he had borne at the marriage ceremony," and then, overcome with emotion, he "rushed home with tears in his eyes, shut himself in his cabinet, and wrote persistently till the gray dawn crept through the window-shutters."[67] Bulwer was also one of the last of Landon's English friends to see her alive, and upon receiving news of her death, "the friend of her youth and young womanhood hastened to raise a subscription, which he himself headed with a generous amount, to support her widowed, poverty-stricken, and desolate mother."[68] Unsurprisingly, Bulwer and Landon's relationship has been characterized, both during their lives and after their deaths, as "constant, sensible, and sincere."[69]

Although there is no direct evidence that Bulwer had *Ethel Churchill* in mind when he began writing *Lucretia*, his familiarity with both Landon's life and her works perhaps explains the similarities between the two novels and *Lucretia*'s repeated use of motifs and themes from the earlier novel.[70] For instance, the characterization of Bulwer's eponymous character is highly reminiscent of Landon's Countess Marchmont: At the opening of the novel,

---

64. Leighton, *Victorian Woman Poets*, 53.
65. Leighton, *Victorian Woman Poets*, 53.
66. Rosina Bulwer Lytton, *Unpublished Letters of Lady Bulwer Lytton*, 127.
67. "Reminiscences of Bulwer-Lytton," 267.
68. "Reminiscences of Bulwer-Lytton," 267.
69. "Reminiscences of Bulwer-Lytton," 267.
70. F. J. Sypher even posits that Bulwer finished Landon's last novel, *Lady Granard, or, Keeping up Appearances*, which Landon only completed part of before her death. This claim has been contested, however. See Sypher's introduction to *Lady Anne Granard*.

Lucretia is an intelligent, socially ambitious, upper-class woman living in relative isolation with her aristocratic uncle, Sir Miles St. John. Lucretia is Sir Miles's presumed heir, and he grooms her to inherit the vast estate of Laughton. Despite the similarities in the two antiheroines, the plot of *Lucretia* differs in significant ways from Landon's work: Lucretia, unlike the Countess Marchmont, follows her heart and becomes surreptitiously engaged to William Mainwaring—a young man decidedly lower on the social scale than his fiancée. Her uncle discovers the engagement and reacts violently, expelling her from his home and disinheriting her. Abandoned by Mainwaring, who prefers her half-sister, Lucretia rashly marries her morally corrupt tutor, Oliver Dalibard. He brings her to France, and Lucretia barely escapes his attempts to poison her by arranging his political assassination. She returns to England, marries again, and has a son. Lucretia is again deceived into a bad marriage and dispatches her second husband with poison—but not before he hides their son from her. Years later, and now a full-fledged chemical criminal, Lucretia masterminds a plot to regain her lost fortune with the help of her stepson, Gabriel Varney. Together, they search for her son and plot to poison the relatives that stand in the way of her lost inheritance.

Bulwer's reliance on the Newgate tactic of fictionalizing the biographies of real-life criminals explains the plot differences between the two novels. Not only does Bulwer draw from histories of his character's namesake, Lucretia Borgia, for his plot, but he also includes the details of more modern poisoning cases.[71] In the preface to the novel, he writes,

> I became acquainted with the histories of two criminals, existing in our own age;—so remarkable, whether from the extent and darkness of the guilt committed—whether from the glittering accomplishments and lively temper of the one, the profound knowledge and intellectual capacities of the other—that the examination and analysis of characters so perverted became a study full of intense, if gloomy interest.

The first poisoner he mentions is Thomas Griffiths Wainewright, who was suspected of (although never charged with) poisoning his niece for life insurance money. Wainewright, whom Oscar Wilde called "a subtle and secret poisoner almost without rival in this or any age," was depicted as a chemical criminal in the printed accounts of his life, but Bulwer's reimagining of him in the form of Gabriel Varney is a very tepid reproduction of the

---

71. Lucretia's murder of her own son draws heavily from the legends of Lucretia Borgia that contend she accidentally poisons her illegitimate son. Victor Hugo fictionalized this legend in his 1833 play *Lucrèce Borgia*.

original.[72] Varney's part in the novel is to assist the schemes of the novel's true chemical criminal: Lucretia Clavering. I argue that Marie Lafarge is the second of the two poisoners Bulwer mentions, and she provides the pattern for his realistic psychological portrait of a female chemical criminal.[73]

Marie Lafarge was a Frenchwoman of aristocratic antecedents found guilty of murdering her husband, Charles Lafarge, with arsenic in 1840. As a young woman, the orphaned Marie was apparently hustled into a hastily arranged marriage with Charles by her aunt and uncle. Her new husband had represented himself as wealthy and landed, but when Marie traveled to her new home, she found that he had greatly misrepresented his financial status. This caused an immediate rift between the two, with Marie "declar[ing] her hatred of her husband." Charles worked to repair his marriage and their relations somewhat improved over the next few months; nevertheless, when he became ill his family immediately suspected Marie of poisoning him. At her trial, her behavior and appearance came across as sympathetic and innocent, but the prosecution brought out some of the best chemists in France to prove that Charles had ingested arsenic and convict her of his murder.

Her case caused a sensation not only in France but also in England, where a deeply divided public debated her innocence or guilt. One of the chief factors of interest in the case, in addition to her class status, was her level of intelligence. Accounts of her life and trial agree that Marie was unusually bright. Her intelligence was used as evidence in her favor as well as to her detriment. An example of the former is Dr. Lynch's discussion about the claim that Marie had been seen mixing a powder into her husband's food. He writes "that Mad. Lafarge evinced upon the trial the possession of good sense and great presence of mind, a circumstance tending to prove her innocence, for if guilty, so intelligent a woman would not have acted (as she did on several occasions) in a way calculated to insure her conviction."[74] The *Edinburgh Review,* however, noted, "throughout [the trial], the plan of the prosecution was to represent her as a person endowed with extraordinary ability—who, by the force of her intellect, was placed above the common follies or weakness of her age and sex; obeying steadily, indeed, the dictates of a depraved and wicked spirit, but pursuing her objects with an unerring sagacity."[75] Much like in the speculation about Landon's death,

---

72. Wilde, "Pen, Pencil and Poison," 41.
73. Keith Hollingsworth suggests the second poisoner is Wainewright's wife, based on a statement made by Bulwer's grandson. See Hollingsworth's *Newgate Novel.*
74. Lynch, "Analysis of Madame Lafarge's Trial," 19.
75. "Trial of Madame Lafarge," 378.

Marie's intelligence and educational background were interpreted in contrasting ways and evaded easy analysis.

By 1847, the good feeling of the English public toward Lafarge was apparently dwindling, most likely because of the occurrence of several other very similar poisoning cases. Fears began to spread that the heavy reporting on Marie's trial had caused a "diffusion of criminal ingenuity" that encouraged others to copy her crimes.[76] Reflecting these anxieties, the author of "On the Increase of the Crime of Secret Poisoning" claims that "no well-ascertained instance of slow poisoning had been brought to light in England until subsequently to the trial of Madame Laffarge [sic]"; after the trial, however, "criminals are now becoming quite acquainted with the slowly destructive effects which comparatively small doses of arsenic . . . and are beginning to employ these means to the exclusion of those less guarded measures."[77] Plainly assuming Marie's guilt, this passage also presents a new facet in discussions about her suspected guilt, for it endows her with a scientific adeptness that is missing from earlier accounts. This new version of Lafarge does not present her as a potentially bumbling poisoner who mixed chemicals into her husband's food in front of witnesses, but as one who worked through small doses and over time in an attempt to avoid detection. In other words, Lafarge had transformed from a poisoner into a sophisticated chemical criminal who used scientific knowledge to commit murder—in fact, she is the first female poisoner positioned as a chemical criminal in the English press.

Interpretations of Landon's novel are colored by her death, and opinions on Marie's accountability in the death of her husband similarly changed once other comparable crimes occurred. What is consistent in all these accounts, however, is an interest in, as the sympathetic editors of her autobiography put it, how "the vice of an education ill-directed" factors into Marie's case.[78] The second half of this chapter analyzes how Bulwer grafts the Lafarge case onto the pattern of the female chemical criminal that Landon establishes in *Ethel Churchill*. L. E. L.'s novel is also interested in the mental development of its murderer, but Bulwer utilizes the Newgate form to focus more deeply on the psychological formation of criminality for his work by drawing from Lafarge's case. Bulwer himself was very vocal in declaring education to be his object of study in *Lucretia*. In the preface to the 1853 edition of the novel, Bulwer wrote that "the moral design" of *Lucretia* was to examine

---

76. "On the Increase of the Crime," 192.
77. "On the Increase of the Crime," 192.
78. Chapelle, *Memoirs of Madame Lafarge*, xviii.

the effects of "evil . . . early circumstance and training."⁷⁹ Again, in a letter to John Forster, Bulwer insisted that it was through [Lucretia and Varney's] *cultivation* that I thought to trace the phenomena of their crimes."⁸⁰ Similar to the concerns of *Ethel Churchill*, what is at stake are questions about women's education: What can women learn, and what should they learn? *Lucretia* maintains a comparable approach to education as *Ethel Churchill* through Bulwer's careful distinction between masculine scientific knowledge and a more traditionally feminine education. Through Lucretia, who paradoxically combines feminine beauty with a masculine acuteness, Bulwer confirms women's capacity for rational thought while maintaining an essentialist view of female sensibility. Accordingly, Lucretia struggles with the same social rejection and constriction as Henrietta, and an examination of chemical crime in the novel exposes Bulwer's conflicted approach to women's education and its implications for the domestic sphere.

It is with this educational theme that we can most productively trace the influence of Landon's work and the Lafarge case on Bulwer's novel. Bulwer spends considerable time early in the novel outlining Lucretia's unusually sharp intellect and her advanced education. Like Landon's Countess Marchmont, from her early childhood "a superior mind developed itself in the young Lucretia" and her "quickness defied even that numbing ordeal" of being "set methodically to study."⁸¹ Lucretia also learns the particularly "masculine studies which her erudite tutor opened to a grasping and inquisitive mind."⁸² Like *Ethel Churchill*, *Lucretia* makes a distinction between what are properly female and male spheres of learning. Instead of exclusively learning "what ladies generally know—French and Italian, and such like," Lucretia undergoes an educational regimen more fit for a man than a future wife and mother.⁸³ As Laura Ciolkowski notes, "like an eldest son heir to the wealth and position of the St. John family, Lucretia is provided with all the trappings of masculine power"—including an education seemingly designed for a politically ambitious young man.⁸⁴ Her tutor tells her, "I saw,

---

79. Bulwer, *Lucretia* (1866), xi.
80. Victor Bulwer Lytton, *Life of Edward Bulwer*, 88.
81. Bulwer, *Lucretia* (1846), I: 47. There are some differences between the first volume of *Lucretia* and subsequent volumes printed during or after 1853, mainly relating to the ending. In the first edition, Lucretia successfully kills Helen, but public outcry caused Bulwer to revise this ending and extract some passages (especially those that outlined Lucretia's criminal plotting in detail) that could be construed as providing guidance to would-be criminals. Except where noted, all references are to this 1846 edition.
82. Bulwer, *Lucretia*, I: 48.
83. Bulwer, *Lucretia*, I; 37.
84. Ciolkowski, "The Woman (in) Question," 81.

or fancied I saw, in you a mind congenial to my own—a mind above the frivolities of your sex—a mind, in short, with the grasp and energy of a man's."[85] Continuing, he stokes her ego by noting, "Have I not given to your intellect the strong food on which the statesmen of Florence fed their pupil-princes; or the noble Jesuits, the noble men who were destined to extend the secret empire of the imperishable Loyola?"[86] Lucretia, whose mind is like "a man's," has had the same training as powerful and politically great men, such as the "statesmen of Florence" and "the noble Jesuits." As with the Countess Marchmont, Lucretia is taught to despise traditionally female concerns of love and nurturing (the so-called "frivolities of [her] sex") in favor of masculine ambitions. Yet Lucretia realizes, to an extent, that her education has been a form of corruption or poison. Although she deeply values her superior intellect, Lucretia also has some serious misgivings about the nature of her training. In speaking to Dalibard, she admits:

> "You gave me the taste for knowledge rare in my sex, I own," answered Lucretia, with a slight tone of regret in her voice; "and in the knowledge you have communicated I felt a charm that, at times, seems to me to be only fatal. You have confounded in my mind evil and good, or, rather you have left both good and evil as dead ashes, as the dust and cinder of a crucible. Of late, I wish that my tutor had been a village priest."[87]

A number of shallowly submerged concerns appear in this passage. To begin, Bulwer affirms that there is a causal link between Lucretia's academic pursuits and her moral corruption, and he foreshadows the eventual "fatal" criminal applications of this education. The confusion Lucretia feels—particularly about the distinction between good and evil—reveals that her purely intellectual approach to the world has left her morally bereft, without feminine sensibility to guide her. Lucretia even begins to "wish" that, like her sister, she had received a more spiritual, limited, and properly feminine education at the hands of the local clergyman.

In keeping with Victorian ideas about physiognomy, Lucretia's paradoxical gender hybridity is mirrored in her physical attributes, transforming her body into a site where we can read the internal conflict between competing feminine and masculine traits. In descriptions that are highly evocative of Henrietta's appearance, Bulwer reveals Lucretia to be a strange, and eerily seductive, blend of masculine and feminine physical traits. He begins with

---

85. Bulwer, *Lucretia*, I: 17.
86. Bulwer, *Lucretia*, I: 17.
87. Bulwer, *Lucretia*, I: 17.

illustrating her body as perfectly feminine—"a figure more perfect never served for model to a sculptor"—yet with one flaw: the hand.[88] Lucretia has "more the hand of a man than a woman; the shape had a man's nervous distinctness, the veins swelled like sinews, the joints of the fingers were marked and prominent. In that hand, it almost seemed as if the iron force of the character betrayed itself."[89] Instead of the soft, white, and delicate hands of a young aristocratic woman, Lucretia's strong, sinewy hands bespeak her tremendous mental power. As Bulwer suggests, these are the hands of a scholar, not the hands of a properly idle young woman.

Despite this one flaw, Lucretia still has "the form of Agrippina," but she also has the "head of Augustus." Bulwer leads the reader to muse on Lucretia's face to grasp fully her gender ambiguity. For example, Lucretia's hair, which is worn "clustered in profuse curls over the forehead," still cannot "conceal a slight line or wrinkle between the brows; and this line, rare in women at any age, rare even in men at hers, gave an expression at once of thought and sternness to the whole face."[90] Here, Bulwer suggests that Lucretia's hair, a symbol of her womanhood, cannot disguise the physical markings of her manly "thought[fulness] and sternness." Therefore, throughout the text, Bulwer presents Lucretia as an inherent contradiction: She has a feminine body and sensibility but a masculine mind and ambition. In the words of Laura Ciolkowski, Lucretia "is a problem subject whose feminine beauty codes her as a woman but whose disdain for the protected field of the home and whose desire for power in the public sphere of politics codes her as a man."[91]

Unfortunately for Lucretia, her masculine mind cannot save her from the social inequities facing women. Unlike Landon's Countess Marchmont, who for a time maintains a belief that she can find fulfillment in society, Lucretia is barely of age before she realizes that her ambitions can have very few proper outlets. When her cousin and suitor Charles Vernon teases Lucretia and suggests she could find her "empire" in London, she responds: "You forget that I am not a man. Man, indeed, may hope for an empire. It is something to be a Pitt, or even a Warren Hastings."[92] When he suggests that "a woman has an empire more undisputed than Mr. Pitt's, and more pitiless than that of Governor Hastings," she tersely replies that "a woman's empire over gauzes and ribbons, over tea-tables and drums, over

---

88. Bulwer, *Lucretia*, I: 59.
89. Bulwer, *Lucretia*, I: 60.
90. Bulwer, *Lucretia*, I: 60.
91. Ciolkowski, "The Woman (In) Question," 81.
92. Bulwer, *Lucretia*, I: 65.

fops and coquettes, is not worth a journey from Laughton to London."[93] Lucretia knows that only through a man—either a husband or son—can she have access to the power that she desires. If she had found a "happy and well-placed love" with a strong and sympathetic mate, then "her ambition might have had legitimate vents."[94] Thus, Helen Small is correct in asserting that *Lucretia* gives its heroine "a capacity for criminal cunning which it denounces as masculine and, ultimately, monstrous, yet it insists on making a bid for sympathy by alluding sentimentally to the woman she would have been if not for the loss of her first lover and the corrupting tutorship of Oliver Dalibard."[95] Perhaps taking a lesson from Landon's tragic life, Bulwer understands that society cannot accommodate an ambitious, intelligent woman unless she operates through a man.

Lucretia is doomed not to marry a man who will soften her heart and productively funnel her talents. As with Landon's Henrietta, Lucretia's intellect makes her unlovable. Even after Lucretia sacrifices her inheritance and social position for Mainwaring, he rejects her in favor of her half-sister—a more conventionally feminine woman who will never challenge his intellectual superiority. Under emotional duress, she makes the mistake of wedding Dalibard. Her tutor-turned-husband completes Lucretia's transformation into a chemical criminal by introducing her to "experiments in chemistry," his avowed "favorite study."[96] Having found his wife engrossed in reading a book of historical poisonings, Dalibard suggests that "it might be amusing to a chemist to learn exactly what were the compounds of those ancient poisons" and offers to teach her.[97] A short time after this conversation, the reader is informed that "Lucretia stood by her husband's side" in his secret attic laboratory.[98] Bulwer chooses not to show her in the laboratory, yet there is no doubt that Lucretia is just as scientifically formidable as Henrietta is. After her training she readily understands the nature of the poisons she studies and, with the help of a manuscript entitled "Philosophical and Chemical Inquiries into the Nature and Materials of the Poisons in Use between the 14th and 16th Centuries," she too is able to manufacture her own poisons.[99] She learns not only how to "kill by a flower, a pair of gloves, a soap ball" but also about "some most marvellous application of

---

93. Bulwer, *Lucretia*, I: 65.
94. Bulwer, *Lucretia*, I: 50.
95. Small, *Love's Madness*, 148
96. Bulwer, *Lucretia*, I: 195.
97. Bulwer, *Lucretia*, I: 199.
98. Bulwer, *Lucretia*, I: 199.
99. Bulwer, *Lucretia*, I: 221.

noxious gases to the art of death, which inhaled only at night and in sleep, kills rapidly (yet not too suddenly) the victim, and dispenses with all aid from drug and mineral."[100]

Despite Lucretia's introduction to "the science of murder," Bulwer attempts to gain sympathy for her by placing her into circumstances where she has little power or choice.[101] While still married to Lucretia, Dalibard finds a wealthy widow who will better serve his political ambitions than his wife, and he begins to poison Lucretia. Forewarned by her stepson, Lucretia is on guard when "a dull torpor creeps over [her]—she feels the taint in her veins—the slower victory is begun."[102] Unlike the stereotype of the passive Victorian wife, she refuses to submit to her death and is able to escape by helping Dalibard's enemies assassinate him. As one reviewer writes, at this point in the novel "my sympathy, at least, now passes to Lucretia. Demon against demon, a young she-demon ought to be preferred to the middle-aged demon of the other sex who has perverted, betrayed, and ruined her."[103] But, as the reviewer goes on to note, "it is a very serious defect in the artistic composition of the novel, viewed as a work of art, that our sympathy is permitted at this point to rest so strongly with [Dalibard's] executioners."[104]

As the novel continues and Lucretia transitions from the poisoned to the poisoner, many readers found it more and more difficult to sustain empathy for her. Lucretia's next foray into crime is when she uses Dalibard's teachings to poison her second husband, Braddell. Their marriage and its end closely mirror accounts of Marie Lafarge's crimes. After a hurried marriage, Lucretia discovers that "though ostensibly in a flourishing business, he was greatly distressed for money to carry on operations which swelled beyond the reach of his capital" and he "had knowingly deceived her as to his worldly substance" because "his fingers itched for the sum which Lucretia had still at her disposal."[105] Like Lafarge, Lucretia learns that her husband has grossly misrepresented himself and that he is in reality small-minded, hypocritical, and deceitful. A new mother, she realizes that "the low-born, groveling father had the sole right over that son's destiny," and she initially tries to take her infant and flee from him. But Braddell discovers her hiding place, and during the ensuing argument he "lost all self-possession, and

---

100. Bulwer, *Lucretia*, II: 178.
101. Bulwer, *Lucretia*, I: 199
102. Bulwer, *Lucretia*, II: 178.
103. Bayne, "Studies of English Authors," 329.
104. Bayne, "Studies of English Authors," 330.
105. Bulwer, *Lucretia*, II: 149, II: 148.

struck her to the ground."[106] Despite his physical violence, "there was no resisting the power which all civilised laws give to the rights of husband and father" and Lucretia returns to his home. The word "civilised" is ironic here, as Bulwer is referring to the laws that gave husbands exclusive child custody and the right to enforce cohabitation—even when the man was corrupt and cruel. Legally, at least, Lucretia is powerless against her husband, and she experiences firsthand the unfair cultural and legal codes that dictate women's lives. She has a remedy for this problem—one which Bulwer has explicitly linked to feminism. Earlier in the novel, Dalibard tells Lucretia about a poisoning epidemic that occurred in Italy specifically because

> husbands were, indeed, lords of the household: they married mere children for their lands; they neglected and betrayed them; they were inexorable if the wife committed the faults set before her example. Suddenly the wife found herself armed against her tyrant. His life was in her hands. So the weak had no mercy on the strong![107]

Lucretia's murder of Braddell for the same reasons women have historically killed their domineering husbands invites the reader to link the patriarchy of ancient Rome with the legal inequality of Victorian women.

To kill Braddell, Lucretia uses the same poisoning technique that Lafarge supposedly used: slow poisoning with small quantities rather than using a single, lethal dose. Lady Marchmont is mad when she murders her lover and husband and therefore has no care for her own safety. Lucretia's object is not only to kill but also to get away with murder—which she hopes to effect by using poisons that mimic natural disease and (to avoid the fate of Lafarge, whose conviction rested on forensic tests) cannot be traced by toxicology. Her poisons act as "counterfeits of natural disease" and[108]

> aimed at creating, by artificial means, the maladies that might seem the most commonly incidental to our human infirmities;—fever, in especial, in all its gradations, form the slow and wasting to the rapid and devouring; here, too, for more immediate purposes, were the ingredients to strike the heart, produce the *aneurism*, or destroy at once, by the sudden spasms of the *angina pectoris*; here were the prescriptions which teach to simulate the effects of passion and emotion, which send the blood to the brain, call the laugh from delirium, bid the surgeon moralize on the connexion between

---

106. Bulwer, *Lucretia*, II: 151.
107. Bulwer, *Lucretia*, I: 198.
108. Bulwer, *Lucretia*, II: 179.

criminals could makes audiences identify too strongly with the characters. The subtext to this fear is that the reading audience would then recreate the crimes of their favorite literary antiheroes. After the Lafarge case, reviewers of *Lucretia* were unconvinced that a "useful end" could be derived from a work that went about "feeding the fancy" with ideas of murder only to attempt to counteract the damage with the weak "moral, that if the reader should seek to poison his nearest relatives to get at their property, he may possibly end his days in a madhouse, or find himself chained to a grave stealer in Norfolk Island."[116] As this review of *Lucretia* indicates, it was particularly when crime narratives were "decorated by the false lustre which the imagination of a romance writer can throw over things in themselves the most disgusting, that the details of offenses of this kind become first endurable, then interesting and exciting, and in the end too frequently suggestive of crime to the ill-regulated minds of weak and unprincipled readers."[117] Critics were particularly worried that the "weak and unprincipled," or, in other words, women and the lower class, would emulate these fictional criminals. Ironically, Bulwer suggests the same fear within the pages of his novel. Lucretia's imagination is first tempted by poisonous thoughts after she reads a historical text about "that singular epoch of terror in Italy, when some mysterious disease, varying in a thousand symptoms, baffled all remedy, and long defied all conjecture—a disease attacking chiefly the heads of families, father and husband—rarely women." Quickly realizing the "disease" is poison, Lucretia devours "the anecdotes, the histories, the astonishing craft brought daily to bear on the victim, the wondrous perfidy of the subtle means, the variation of the certain murder—here swift as epilepsy—there slow and wasting as long decline." So "absorbing" is her reading that Lucretia starts "when she heard Dalibard's voice behind; he was looking over her shoulder."[118]

That Lucretia feels a guilty pleasure in reading this passage is evident by her embarrassed reaction when she realizes Dalibard has been watching her read. He cryptically warns her, "*Enfan,* play not with such weapons," but the passage, which details a plan for getting away with murder, nonetheless becomes deeply impressed on her imagination.[119] Years later, Lucretia will reproduce the story of the Italian poisoners when she uses knowledge gleaned from this book and slowly poisons her second husband. Furthermore, the revolutionary aspect of the text, which illustrates that women have

---

116. Review of *Lucretia*, 618.
117. "On the Increase of Secret Poisoning in This Country," 106.
118. Bulwer, *Lucretia*, I: 197.
119. Bulwer, *Lucretia*, I: 197.

(and possibly should) free themselves from domestic tyrant-husbands, further incites Lucretia to commit murder.

Despite Bulwer's suggestion in *Lucretia* that certain kinds of literature can become weapons in the hands of immoral readers, reviews of the novel accusing the book of being a poisonous text shocked him. Many critics found *Lucretia* to be "in two senses . . . busy with poison," since it both dealt with poisoning on a textual level and became a poisonous influence on a metatextual one.[120] A typical reaction to the novel declared that "the extremely suggestive character and peculiarly dangerous tendency of these works . . . has, in many recent instances, been the result of the clear, though indirect, lessons which the literature of the day too amply afford to the weak and the criminal."[121] Here, the reviewer directly charges Newgate fiction with not only inspiring real-life crime but also teaching would-be criminals how to do their villainous work more effectively.

Bulwer quickly responded to negative reviews of *Lucretia* in a pamphlet entitled "A Word to the Public." In this text, Bulwer attempts to justify his works by situating them within a long tradition of literary portrayals of crime. Moreover, he argues that since crime is everywhere in real life, fiction can become a deterrent because these narratives can "demonstrate [crime's] causes, portray its hideousness, and insist on its inevitable doom."[122]

Even though Bulwer's avowed purpose in writing *Lucretia* was to demonstrate the danger of certain types of educational systems, his critics charged him with writing one of many "convenient hand-books of poisoning, for the guidance and instruction of the public."[123] In fact, the *London Medical Gazette* was so concerned about *Lucretia*'s impact on the public that it published a flurry of articles warning medical practitioners about the dangers of such literature. These articles declared that works like *Lucretia* actually taught potential criminals how to commit murder and were directly responsible for "occasioning the late frightful increase of assassinations by poison."[124] The particular problem with *Lucretia* is that the novel was too scientific and too inventive with its criminal schemes, or, in the words of the *London Medical Gazette*, this novel "is deserving of censure for having recalled to the notice of men facts which should have been allowed to slumber in oblivion."[125] The irony here is that these critiques of the novel fail

---

120. Review of *Lucretia*, 177.
121. "'A Word to the Public'—The Art of Secret Poisoning," 248.
122. Bulwer, "A Word to the Public," 723.
123. "On the Increase of Secret Poisoning," 106.
124. "On the Increase of the Crime," 191.
125. "'A Word to the Public'—The Art of Secret Poisoning," 243.

to recognize that *Lucretia* also examines the nature of education and who should have access to potentially "dangerous" forms of knowledge. This seems to be lost on these reviewers, and in the eyes of periodicals like the *London Medical Gazette, Lucretia* is a symptom of a much larger trend of allowing nonspecialists access to science. In addition to faulting the novel, the article also takes offense at other avenues for disseminating knowledge, such as open scientific lectures. The writer "regrets" to report that "mixed London audiences have recently been indoctrinated in the elements of toxicology," including "the entire detail of the nature and powers of hydrocyanic acid."[126] This writer's shock at the "mixed" audience, consisting of "ladies and non-professional gentlemen," reveals exactly who the *London Medical Gazette* feared would criminally benefit from this knowledge.[127] The *London Medical Gazette* comes to the same conclusion as Bulwer does in *Lucretia*: Certain populations should be barred from learning dangerous forms of scientific knowledge. This article declares "that scientific men should exercise the most conscientious vigilance in guarding against the promulgation of destructive knowledge among the community at large."[128] Only doctors could protect the public from dangerous, poisonous reading materials, the journal claimed, forming a judgment that ultimately confirms Bulwer's point that Victorian society was not yet ready to admit women into certain areas of knowledge.

Bulwer was so mortified at these reactions to *Lucretia* that he eventually rewrote the ending to accommodate public taste. In the 1853 edition, Helen no longer dies at the hands of Lucretia but lives to marry her distant cousin and become mistress of Laughton. Despite these changes, which softened critics toward the novel, Bulwer was so discomposed that he never again ventured into crime fiction, turning his literary interests to more critically acceptable forms of literature. Bulwer felt that the reaction against *Lucretia* was unfair, and in many ways, he was correct. After all, he had drawn from an earlier (and acceptable) literary tradition for his approach to crime and education, even if the Newgate form allowed him to pepper his narrative with more violence and sensation than Landon's. What these strong reactions to Bulwer's novel demonstrate is that in between the publication of *Ethel Churchill* and *Lucretia*, cultural opinion changed. With Landon's death, the dead body of the *poisoned* woman engrossed the public; with *Lucretia*, the focus (and sympathy) had shifted to the dead bodies left in the wake of the

---

126. "Suppression of the Crime of Secret Poisoning," 284.
127. "Suppression of the Crime of Secret Poisoning," 284.
128. "Suppression of the Crime of Secret Poisoning," 284.

poisoning woman. As Landon recognized (although her reviewers did not), the transformation from a poisoning woman to a female chemical criminal was an overtly feminist act. Bulwer did not realize that the Lafarge case solidified the transgressive power of the female chemical criminal, and the reception of his work consequently suffered.

THE VICTIMS OF THE POISONING WOMAN; OR, WHAT SARAH LEARNED

I began this chapter examining the strange coincidence between Landon's death and the events in her novel, and I will end by discussing another literary coincidence: the fact that Lucretia shares her last name with Clavering—a village in Essex that became a household word synonymous with "poison" after a series of sensational murder cases.[129] While Bulwer was busy finishing the manuscript of *Lucretia*, there occurred the first inquest into what would later be known as the "Essex Poisoning Club." According to news accounts of the trials of Sarah Chesham (1847 and 1851), Mary May (1848), and Hannah Southgate (1848), women in the county of Essex were trading tips about how to rid themselves of troublesome children and husbands. The first woman tried, Sarah Chesham, was accused of poisoning three children. All three victims had taken ill suddenly, and the analysis of the stomachs of the deceased by the toxicologist Alfred Swaine Taylor easily found large amounts of arsenic still lining the stomach. He estimated that one of the victims ingested enough of the poison to "destroy the lives of from three to six adult persons."[130] Despite the forensic evidence, the jury acquitted Chesham

---

129. There is a chance that this was not a coincidence at all, as Mary Mulvey-Roberts ("Fame, Notoriety and Madness") and Ayse Naz Bulamur (*Victorian Murderesses*) both claim that Bulwer changed his character's last name when news of the poisoning case came to light. This is speculation, and neither of these critics offers concrete evidence that Bulwer made this change. I believe that it would have been very last-minute indeed if Bulwer altered his manuscript, as reporting on the first of the Clavering cases—Sarah Chesham's 1847 murder trial—was only beginning to pick up steam at the end of September 1846 and Bulwer's novel was released a little over a month later, in November 1846. Moreover, it would have been extremely prescient on Bulwer's part to recognize in the fall of 1846 the degree of interest that Chesham's spring 1847 trial would garner, and impossible for him to predict that she would be tried again in 1851—or that two more women would also be tried. I will also add that Bulwer had previously used the name "Clavering" in his unpublished and unfinished *Greville: A Satire upon Fine Life*, which he was writing in 1829, and it is far more likely this is a case of name recycling, not a specific homage to these crimes.

130. "Poisonings in Essex," 7.

at her first trial, freeing her (it was widely believed) to become the hub of a poison-ring of women who shared information about how to undetectably poison troublesome husbands and other unwanted family members. But how did the lower-class and uneducated Sarah, who had so spectacularly overdosed her previous victims, ever get access to specialized knowledge about how to poison undetectably? In order to explain this discrepancy and demonstrate how Sarah had morphed from a sloppy poisoner into a chemical criminal, the *Times* wrote:

> On her first trial a medical witness detailed at some length the deleterious properties of arsenic, and its effects when administered under given conditions and circumstances. The woman, then in peril of her life, stood quietly at the bar, listened, and *learnt*. No sooner was she discharged than she availed herself of her lesson. She had previously poisoned her people out-of-hand after a coarse and unscientific fashion of proceeding, but she now put her arsenic into a bag of rice, and mixed up the whole with such care that every single grain of rice was saturated with as much poison as it would take. She then gave it to her husband at intervals and in small doses, consuming him by slow tortures, and leaving him at last, after six months' suffering, with so little arsenic in his body that its presence was scarcely discoverable by the most searching tests of chymistry.[131]

Sarah Chesham is another example of how dangerous forms of knowledge can transform a woman from a poisoner into a chemical criminal, but, unlike the fictional Henrietta and Lucretia, Sarah did not keep this information to herself. The cases that followed her initial 1847 trial suggest that Essex women were banding together and creating poisoning communities:

> A woman in the village of Clavering tired of her husband's companionship, and, it appears, acquainted her gossips with the fact. In Clavering, that seemed to be not an uncommon thing, and the remedy popular in Clavering was suggested—one lady hinting that it might be advantageously administered by means of a pie: it might have been, and really appeared to be, that experience had taught her this. At any rate, some such method was resorted to to bring peace to the heart of the unhappy wife—and her husband died.[132]

---

131. *Times,* March 8, 1851, 4. Emphasis mine.
132. Paget, "Philosophy of Murder," 173.

By swapping recipes for death through informal oral networks, the women of Clavering were committing a feminist act that threatened to undermine the patriarchy and the structure of the Victorian family. These murders once again reveal the extent to which education (in this case, direct woman-to-woman webs of instruction) was perceived as a contributing factor to the increase in poisoning crimes, and just as in L. E. L.'s and Bulwer's novels, poison becomes a tool to reveal the problems of the home.[133] The fears of Bulwer's critics ostensibly came true, as poisonous knowledge was apparently seeping outside the pages of his novel and English communities were becoming "thoroughly infected with the abomination."[134] Landon's death changed the way that critics read her novel, and these subsequent poisoning cases similarly affected the way that the public approached Bulwer's work. Bulwer's depiction of a female chemical criminal who poisons husbands and dependents within the home touched an area of the Victorian psyche that was growing increasingly sensitive, and he felt the backlash.

The backlash, in this case, is specifically *Lucretia*'s designation as a Newgate novel, despite the fact that it seems in many ways an awkward fit for Newgate fiction. My examination of genre in this chapter shows how science, education, and poison were integral in shaping early Victorian crime fiction by arguing that silver fork fiction's contribution to crime fiction should be reevaluated because of its influence on the development of the Newgate novel. Having noticed the female criminality, domestic crime, and household mysteries featured in the novel, readers may be wondering why these novels are not more properly categorized as early sensation fiction. I believe there is a good argument for making this classification, and that *Lucretia* and *Ellen Churchill*'s combination of society fiction's interest in domestic structures and the formation of female characters with the Newgate novel's interest in the psychological development of criminality presents the same rich tapestry of domestic discord that informs sensation fiction—it is the formula that much sensation fiction is patterned upon. The reason I have not made this argument myself is that this chapter has been deeply interested not in how we could reclassify Bulwer's novel, but in how his contemporaries classified it. Why was Bulwer's novel widely panned and marked with the label "Newgate"—the severest form of condemnation critics could lob at a work of fiction at the time—while Landon's was not? The answer is that after the Clavering cases, the focus shifted from Lucretia's tragic education to the

---

133. They also eerily reproduce the confederation of poisoning women in Renaissance Italy that Lucretia reads about in Dalibard's book.

134. Paget, "Philosophy of Murder," 173.

potentially tragic consequences of what *Lucretia* could teach its readers. The generic classification of *Lucretia* as a Newgate novel relies not so much on its adherence to the rules of the genre, but rather on historical events over which Bulwer had no control.

CHAPTER 2

MEDICAL BLUEBEARDS

Gothic Medicine and the Poisoning Doctor
in the Fiction of Ellen Wood

IN "THE ADVENTURE of the Speckled Band," Sherlock Holmes cryptically remarks to Watson, "When a doctor does go wrong he is the first of criminals. He has nerve and he has knowledge. Palmer and Pritchard were among the heads of their profession."[1] Many of Sherlock's late-century readers would have implicitly agreed with his assumptions about doctors who "go wrong." By the 1892 publication date of "The Adventure of the Speckled Band," the British public had endured a series of high-profile criminal scandals involving doctors that spanned a period of fifty years. Throughout the nineteenth century—from the body-snatching outrages of the 1820s, which linked prominent medical schools to illegal corpse theft, to the *fin de siècle* speculation that Jack the Ripper was a surgeon—medical professionals were persistently associated with sensational crimes. The nineteenth century seemed to witness an "epidemic" of poisoning doctors. The chemical criminals that Holmes refers to, William Palmer (1856) and Edward Pritchard (1865), were just two of a surprisingly large fraternity of medical men who used their specialized knowledge to commit murder. Along with Palmer and Pritchard, the list includes James Cockburn Belany (1844), Thomas Smethurst (1859), Alfred Warder (1866), George Lamson (1882), Philip Cross

---

1. Doyle, "Adventure of the Speckled Band," 257.

(1888), Thomas Neill Cream (1892), and George Chapman (1903).[2] Their trials were so widely followed that they became household names and convinced the public that they were facing a fearsome new chemical criminal.

Like the writer for the *Saturday Review*, the Victorians were increasingly concerned with how the "patient and physician—these, the closest and most sacred relations of domestic and civil life, are said to have been violated by the drugged draught."[3] The medical practitioner's expertise in medicine and chemicals meant that the poisoning doctor was regarded as one of the most potent and anxiety-provoking chemical criminals of the nineteenth century. As one commentator noted:

> Give a medical man motives for getting rid of his patient, and it is clear that he had the man at his mercy. Without a metaphor, your medical man can always poison you if he chooses; and unless he is very clumsy—unless he fails to calculate the effect of the *negative* symptoms, he can poison you without detection.[4]

After all, "what [is] more easy" for a doctor "than to make up poison into two pills—some powerful poison that acts suddenly?"[5] The "drugged draught" became a potent gothic symbol for the suspect relationship between doctors and the home, revealing what Andrew Smith notes as the public belief that "medicine represented conflicting impulses; the desire to help, but also the desire to do harm."[6] As both a healer and a murderer, the medical chemical criminal is an inherent paradox that fueled fears about how doctors were applying their specialized knowledge. Although the profession successfully weathered these scandals and increased its influence and prestige throughout the century, the poisoning doctor nevertheless persistently appears in Victorian fiction, raising significant concerns about the increased influence of medical practitioners.

Since the poisonous doctor signaled that something might be rotten in the state of institutional medicine, it is unsurprising that Victorian authors

---

2. This list only includes poisoning doctors who were British or who killed in Britain (Cream had spent much of his life in America, although he was Scottish by birth; George Chapman was a Polish émigré who lived and killed in Britain). There were several more American and Continental doctors who poisoned in the nineteenth century, such as J. Milton Bowers, who are not included on this list although their trials and executions were heavily reported on in the British press.
3. "Poisoning in England," 134.
4. "Poison in the Prescription," 1224.
5. "Poison in the Prescription," 1224.
6. Smith, *Victorian Demons*, 11.

use this figure to examine the rise and professionalization of the medical field. For the Victorians, the villainous doctor would be a familiar figure from gothic literature, but the burst of real-life poisoning doctor cases at mid-century caught the attention of authors of the emergent genre of sensation fiction. Gothic sensibilities run deep throughout sensation fiction, and this chapter specifically examines medical chemical crime in sensation to explore this genre's indebtedness to the "medical" or "clinical" gothic tradition. Although no scholar has yet undertaken the task of extensively defining the medical gothic, the term has been used to broadly describe works that reveal the human costs of medical progress—particularly in relation to experimentation or medical innovation—and the clash between a romantic and materialist worldview. Meegan Kennedy notes that "these novels thrive on the energy produced by revealing a secret history, and the unexpected presence of a repressed Other—the monstrous in medicine, the curious in the clinic, the romance in realism."[7] In concrete terms, this gothic form typically reimagines traditional gothic tropes into modern scientific settings, transforming the moldering castle and dank dungeon into the laboratory or grafting supposedly "low" criminality onto the socially or academically elite.[8] Oftentimes, the medical gothic resides at the intersection between occult and materialist science and highlights the dangers of successfully harnessing these combined powers.

As a gothic form that responds to scientific innovations, the medical gothic is particularly sensitive to new developments and current debates, which often becomes the focus of its critique of nineteenth-century medicine. Due to the resurgence of the gothic in the latter part of the century, most Victorian scholars have focused a critical examination of the medical gothic on late-century texts, including Robert Louis Stevenson's *The Strange Case of Dr. Jekyll and Mr. Hyde* and H. G. Wells's *The Island of Dr. Moreau*. This approach, however, leaves a considerable gap between the publication of the first nineteenth-century medical gothic novel—Mary Shelley's 1818 *Frankenstein*—and these *fin de siècle* texts. Several critics, such as Tabitha Sparks, Laurence Talairach-Vielmas, and Meegan Kennedy, have begun to fill in this critical oversight, and sensation fiction, in particular, is a rich site for exploring Victorian literature's ongoing engagement with the medical gothic. Sensational authors took a deep interest in how outside social issues influenced the domestic sphere, often using their texts to explore the wide-ranging effects of cultural movements. Since one of the major social and sci-

---

7. Kennedy, "Ghost in the Clinic," 345.
8. Talairach-Vielmas, *Wilkie Collins, Medicine, and the Gothic*, 21.

entific advancements of the nineteenth century was the growing influence of the medical field, sensational authors thus transformed the most representative figure of medical practice—the doctor—into a fictional villain in order to highlight the effects of disturbing medical developments on the home.[9]

Chemicals are a common motif of the medical gothic, and as William Hughes notes, in this genre "pharmaka are at once a cure and its opposite."[10] In the medical gothic, chemicals implicate the profession that puts them to use. Hughes writes that the medical gothic frames "the discourse of medicine" as "a paradoxical institution" with the power to both harm and heal.[11] This chapter argues that medical chemical crime best illustrates the breadth of sensation fiction's incorporation of the medical gothic because this crime most visibly represents the paradox of Victorian medicine to both heal and harm and its potential impact on the home. As Tamara Wagner points out, "Drawing on a medical understanding . . . sensation novelists represented poisoning in the Victorian home as a particularly revealing part of the genre's rupture of middle-class ideologies of domesticity," and chemical crime, in particular, provides a convenient way to fuse sensation fiction's domestic preoccupation with medical crime.[12] An examination of the poisoning doctor in sensation fiction, then, illustrates the extent to which the domestic concerns of sensation fiction are shaped by the medical gothic's concerns about scientific abuse.

To exemplify just how fully the medical gothic assimilates into the narrative fabric of sensation fiction, this chapter examines the works of Ellen (Mrs. Henry) Wood. Wood's engagement with medical issues has received little scholarly attention, despite the regular appearance of doctors, illness, and injury in her texts (and the author's own struggles with a debilitating spinal affliction).[13] This scholarly oversight is especially surprising given the tendency for critics to focus on sensation fiction's rather antagonistic relationship to medicine, for Wood devotes considerable space within her

---

9. Throughout this chapter, I will use masculine pronouns when referring to medical professionals. This decision is based on several considerations: Most doctors during the Victorian period were male, all convicted or suspected poisoning doctors during the period were men, and all the poisoning doctors in Wood's fiction are male. I should also point out that fictional female doctors are an exception to the conclusions about sensational doctors that I draw in this chapter.

10. Hughes, "Medicine and the Gothic," 439.

11. Hughes, "Medicine and the Gothic," 439.

12. Wagner, "Clinical Gothic," 30.

13. The exceptions are Andrew Mangham's *Violent Women and Sensation Fiction: Crime, Medicine and Victorian Popular Culture* and Anne-Marie Beller's "Suffering Angels: Death and Femininity in Ellen Wood's Fiction."

texts to outlining the dangers of Victorian medicine. Throughout her body of work, Wood consistently engages with contentious medical issues; from her first novel, *Danesbury House*, which features a drunken nurse and the near-fatal overdose of an infant, to medical malpractice in *Oswald Cray*, Wood often relies on medical mistreatment to sensationalize her novels. Wood's most direct engagement with medical abuses, however, appears in her 1857 sensational short story "Mr. Castonel" and her 1864 full-length work *Lord Oakburn's Daughters*, which both employ the figure that most immediately represents medical abuse at mid-century—the poisoning doctor. This chapter demonstrates that sensational authors like Wood "capitalized on the ambiguous status of practitioners" and refigured the doctor as the modern gothic villain in order to explore the growing tension between doctors and women over control of the home.[14]

MEDICAL BLUEBEARDS

To highlight the potential danger of male medical power in the home, Wood draws inspiration from real cases of criminal doctors, but she also evokes the gothic villain of the fairy tale "Bluebeard."[15] The repetitive cycle of marriage and murder, the domestic secrets and forbidden spaces of "Mr. Castonel" and *Lord Oakburn's Daughters* all signal that these stories are a reinterpretation of the "Bluebeard" myth set in the middle-class Victorian home. In the most widely circulated version of this *Märchen*, the rich and powerful Bluebeard murders a long line of successive brides who disobey him by opening a forbidden closet that holds the corpses of all his previous wife-victims. He murders each new wife and places her body in the bloody closet until his final wife has her brothers cut off his head. By mid-century, most Victorian readers would have been familiar with "Bluebeard," as the story was included in the widely published *Perrault's Fairy Tales*.[16] With the rise

---

14. Talairach-Vielmas, *Wilkie Collins, Medicine, and the Gothic*, 8–9.
15. Several studies have established the gothic nature of the Bluebeard fairy tale. In particular, see *The Bluebeard Gothic: Jane Eyre and Its Progeny* by Heta Pyrhönen and *Art of Darkness: A Poetics of Gothic* by Anne Williams.
16. In this version of the tale, the rich and powerful Bluebeard requests to marry one of two sisters. Despite his strange appearance and the mysterious disappearance of his previous wives, the younger sister agrees to marry him. Shortly after the marriage, Bluebeard announces that he needs to leave his castle on business. He leaves his young wife in full charge of the home, with the caveat that she not open a certain small closet. Once her husband is gone, Bluebeard's wife cannot contain her curiosity and opens the closet, only to find the bodies of all of Bluebeard's previous wives (who also disobeyed

of sensation fiction at the end of the 1850s, Wood's use of "Bluebeard"—a fairy tale that highlights abusive male power and the dangers of domestic secrets—is especially timely. Like the surviving wife in the "Bluebeard" fairy tale, sensation fiction is primarily concerned with revealing the skeletons in (particularly middle-class) closets. Wood is interested in just how much mid-century science is complicit in putting those skeletons in those closets and uses her medical Bluebeards to explore the growing intrusion of medicine in the home. She therefore refigures Bluebeard's "bloody closet" into the home laboratory, where, away from the prying eyes of women, deadly doctors hide the relics of their crimes—small vials of deadly gray powder or incriminating letters—within "dummy drawers" or iron safes. If, as Anne Williams notes, Bluebeard's "secret room" symbolizes "the structure of [masculine] power that engenders the action within this social world," then having the laboratory be the site for the transformation of Bluebeard's cutlass into the doctor's poison bottle effectively links science to brutal domestic crime.[17]

Wood's inclusion of the Bluebeard motif means that the approach her works take toward medical abuse differs from that of other sensation writers. While villainous doctors appear throughout sensation texts, the medical practitioners in Wilkie Collins's novels have come under the greatest critical scrutiny. Perhaps this is because Collins's novels so often feature suspect medical men: *The Woman in White* features Fosco wrongfully incarcerating Laura Fairlie in an asylum; *Armadale* is haunted by the plotting of Dr. Downward; and Collins's later work *Heart and Science* critiques the heartless Dr. Benjulia's scientific practice of vivisection. Recognizing that Collins was writing at a historical moment that saw the increased professionalism of medicine, Tabitha Sparks writes:

> Thus, by way of the representational currency that is Collins's most sustained achievement, his novels map not only controversies in Victorian culture but their evolution. In this vein, the representation of doctors in the Collins canon encapsulates medicine's fraught rise to authority. Collins attests to the emergent mindset that fostered scientifically based medicine, and that both marginalized and elevated the work of the doctor, conferring

---

him by looking into the closet). Horrified, she drops the key, which becomes stained with blood. Upon Bluebeard's return, he demands the key and discovers the condemning stain. He sentences his wife to death, but her brothers appear just in time to save her by cutting off Bluebeard's head.

17. Williams, *Art of Darkness*, 41.

a considerable power that would increasingly be interpreted as suspicious and even sinister.[18]

Both Talairach-Vielmas and Sparks see Collins's representation of doctors as a reaction to the changing dynamics of mid-century medical professionalism. Although neither of these critics engages with Collins's last novel, *Blind Love*, the poisoning doctor in this work perhaps best exemplifies "the conflict between a moral vision of the world and a dispassionate, scientific one" that both critics claim is at work throughout Collins's oeuvre.[19] In *Blind Love*, the doctor Vimpany, a "member of the English College of Surgeons," induces Lord Harry Norland to fake his own death in order to perpetrate a life-insurance fraud.[20] In a plot that has obvious similarities to *The Woman in White*, Vimpany procures a sickly patient named Oxbye who bears a striking resemblance to Lord Harry, and then poisons the man in order to pass his body off as the nobleman's. In the novel, poor Oxbye's body becomes merely a commodity used to procure insurance money. As Vimpany tells the doomed man, "You are not Oxbye, you are a case; it is not a man, it is a piece of machinery that is out of order."[21] Vimpany's emphasis that the patient ("it") is not a human being, but only a machine, speaks to a dangerous permutation of scientific detachment that views all patients as "cases" instead of individuals. Vimpany's depersonalized view of Oxbye shows how scientific detachment can be perverted into a worldview that sees patients as only subjects for furthering medical knowledge, or worse, as commodities for personal enrichment.

These analyses of Collins's work provide a useful starting point for examining Wood's texts because there are distinct similarities between Wood's configuration of doctors and those of other sensational writers. Like Collins, Wood is clearly reacting to cultural movements that gave doctors more social and professional authority, and she shares Collins's concern that professional detachment can erode into a form of scientific objectivity that commodifies human bodies. Wood's poisoning doctors, however, tend to pose a greater threat to domesticity than do Collins's villains. Although the Victorians fretted about doctors poisoning their clientele for personal aggrandizement, Wood realized that the medical chemical criminal was far more likely to poison those close to him: siblings, in-laws, children, and (most commonly) sexual partners. Tellingly, while Collins's poisoning doc-

---

18. Sparks, *Doctor in the Victorian Novel*, 87.
19. Sparks, *Doctor in the Victorian Novel*, 89.
20. Collins, *Blind Love*, 358.
21. Collins, *Blind Love*, 405.

tors plot to poison male strangers in order to promote complex financial schemes, Wood's medical men employ their clinical detachment to murder their wives and children within the supposed safety of the home. If Victorian domesticity was considered to be a haven from the troubles of the outside world, then situating these types of murders within domestic spaces suggests not only that the private sphere was becoming less isolated but also that the modern depersonalization of the public world was intruding into the home. Wood suggests one vehicle for this depersonalization was the Victorian doctor—a figure who regularly traversed the two spheres and brought his public authority into the private realm of the home.[22] If "Wood essentially utilizes the conventions of domestic realism but also employs seemingly anti-realistic devices rooted in the Gothic in order to convey a darker vision of the home—a place of secrets, lies and cruelties of all kinds," then in "Mr. Castonel" and *Lord Oakburn's Daughters* Wood uses the gothicized medical poisoner to demonstrate medicine's complicity in domestic corruption.[23]

Like Collins, Wood frames poison as being able to dissolve boundaries and reveal hidden truths. Wood recognizes that the professional realm of medicine and the domestic sphere of the home have been framed as binary opposites with competing interests: Women have a cultural mandate to manage the home (indeed, it is the only sphere where they have power), yet the field of medicine is insisting on more authority over family management. Wood understands these two worlds cannot exist separately but believes that medicine is overstepping its bounds. As many critics have shown, during the nineteenth century doctors gained a larger command over women's health, particularly in the fields of gynecology and obstetrics.[24] The ascendance of the doctor's power was not uncontested: Cultural wrangling over medical innovations such as man- midwives suggests a resistance on the part of women to male professional control.[25] For Wood, the numerous cases of poisoning doctors became symbolic for medicine's increased encroachment into the home. In Wood's fiction, criminal doctors invade idyllic country towns and insinuate themselves into genteel homes—all while using their medical authority to gain access to and murder their female victims.

---

22. It should be noted that most sensation authors used the poisoning wife and mother to comment on this cultural shift. Wood, however, does not feature a single poisoning woman in her works. See chapters two and five for more on the poisoning woman.

23. Liggins and Maunder, "Introduction: Ellen Wood," 151.

24. Moscucci, *Science of Woman*, 42–74. See also Furst, *Between Doctors and Patients*.

25. Moscucci, *Science of Woman*, 42–74.

Wood uses the paradoxical symbolism attached to the poisoning doctor—his association with healing and murder—to undermine arguments for scientific management of the home by showing just how harmful domestic medicine could be.

The presence of these death-dealing doctors in the domestic sphere certainly questions the increased presence of medical men in the Victorian home and the challenge they presented to women's authority and power. According to Andrew Mangham, Wood's works "allowed readers a glimpse of the ethical issues that haunted the shadowy recesses of medical science."[26] The ethical issue at stake for Wood, as John Kucich points out, is "the threat professionals posed to the moral power of women, particularly within the private sphere."[27] In positioning certain medical practices as antithetical to female morality, Wood highlights the need for women to retain their domestic authority and offers several remedies to her readers to prevent medical intrusion. Wood realizes that many in the field of medicine desire a one-way street of influence over the home, expecting obedience but not reciprocating when it comes to women's intimate (albeit unprofessional) knowledge of their families. In response, Wood highlights the necessity of women carefully managing their domestic health practitioners. In order to defend the home against perverted medical influence, Wood instructs her female readers to have a more active and progressive role in choosing and overseeing medical practitioners and features her heroines carefully choosing their practitioners and defying medical authority in order to assert their domestic rights.

"A DRAUGHT OF POISON": WOOD'S EARLY FICTION AND THE BELANY CASE

Wood's first uses of chemical crime to reveal the dangerous intermingling of home and medicine were in two linked short stories written for *Bentley's Miscellany*. "A Draught of Poison" and "Another Passage in a Dark Story" (which were later integrated into her 1890 novel *The House of Halliwell*) were published in September and October of 1855.[28] The stories deserve brief mention, as they help demonstrate the development of Wood's engagement with crime, medicine, and domesticity. In "A Draught of Poison," the narrator, Hester, is visiting her sister, who is recovering from her parturition and the death of her infant. Mary Goring is married to a country doctor and has

---

26. Mangham, "Life after Death," 290.
27. Kucich, *Power of Lies*, 158.
28. Wood, "Draught of Poison," 266–80; Wood, "Another Passage," 388–401.

recently hired a governess, Miss Howard, to instruct her daughters. Hester immediately dislikes the governess, based on Miss Howard's inappropriate flirting with Mary's husband, Matthew. She convinces the Gorings to dismiss Miss Howard, but before her month's warning is up Mrs. Goring is dead, poisoned by strychnine. An inquest is held, and while it is clear the poison came from Dr. Goring's surgery, the murderer remains unidentified. Many of the townspeople blame Matthew for the crime, but Hester is convinced that Miss Howard has singlehandedly murdered her sister in the hopes of marrying the widower. In the subsequent story, Matthew Goring refuses to heed Hester's warning and makes Miss Howard his second wife. When he returns from his honeymoon he is mysteriously changed; he is brooding and unhappy, and dies a short time after his return home. Before he dies, he promises Hester that his will provides "justice" and publicly slights his second wife by leaving her only a hundred pounds. Hester believes that through a "chanced word," Matthew discovered Miss Howard "was indeed the willful instrument of Mary's death" and that the shock of the revelation kills him.[29]

In these early short works of sensation fiction, Wood rejects criminalizing her doctor and instead takes the sensational sexual threat offered by the governess to the extreme, creating an evil, ambitious woman willing to do anything to replace the mistress of the home. This does not mean that the medical field escapes Wood's pen unscathed, since the murder is still a chemical crime at least enabled (even if it is not orchestrated) by Dr. Goring. Locked out of the medical profession, Miss Howard can still find a way to research her murder weapon. In one telling scene, Hester overhears a clandestine *tête-à-tête* between Miss Howard and Dr. Goring that takes place in his home surgery:

> "I shall soon become a chemist if you bestow these pains upon me," she was saying, with her soft insinuating accents, false as she was. . . . "That little bottle, up there, labelled "Poison'—it is always kept by itself in that same place, I observe—is it prussic acid?"
>
> "No; but a poison quite as deadly. It is a preparation of strychnia."
>
> "How is it administered?"
>
> "A very minute portion, taken in water, would destroy life. Shall I try it upon yours?"
>
> "*Would* you?" she murmured, with an affectation of submissive tenderness. "I will give you leave to do so if you wish."

---

29. Wood, "Another Passage," 401.

"My darling girl," he replied, "you know I would rather try it on my own."

Then came a silence, and I pushed open the door: but may I never speak truth again, if I did not first hear a sound like a kiss."[30]

The scene reveals exactly who is the naïve one. Playing the part of a pleasingly submissive and innocently curious girl, Miss Howard skillfully tricks Dr. Goring into teaching her how to murder his own wife. This scene demonstrates how easily dangerous medical knowledge can sneak out of the surgery, slink up the stairs, and eventually settle into the glass on the bedside table.

By providing both the motive and means for the murder, Goring, and by extension the medical profession, is implicated in his wife's death. These stories' focus on the tension between medicine and the domestic inaugurate two themes that highlight Wood's incorporation of the medical gothic. The first of these themes is the vulnerable wife, whose susceptibility is directly tied to her status as a patient. As William Hughes notes, "the powerlessness of the patient is a consistent feature of medical Gothic," and in her later works, Wood will meditate on how the practice of medicine places women into vulnerable positions.[31] The second theme is that of the morally suspect doctor, who is often oversexed. Fears about doctors becoming overly familiar with their female patients surfaced repeatedly in the nineteenth century, and while Miss Howard is not Goring's patient, his flirtation with her (while his wife is upstairs recovering from her delivery) is unseemly. When his sister-in-law points out, "Your behavior to Miss Howard, and especially hers to you, is unbecoming in itself and a disgrace to both of you," he initially argues that married men's flirtations are merely "nonsense" that offer "no disloyalty to our wives."[32] Yet Miss Howard interprets his actions much differently, and poisons his wife on the prospect of becoming the next Mrs. Goring. Indirectly, at least, Wood begins exploring the dangerous combination of doctors, lust, and crime.

The wife-victim and morally lax doctor of Wood's medical gothic both blur the division between medical practice and the domestic. These two spheres should be separate, but Wood recognizes how easily they bleed into each other. As in the case of her later fiction, this binary collapse is at the root of the chemical crime: If not for Dr. Goring's home laboratory—the most obvious symbol of the intermingling of hearth and vial—Miss Howard

---

30. Wood, "Draught of Poison," 269.
31. Hughes, "Victorian Medicine and the Gothic," 197.
32. Wood, "Draught of Poison," 270.

would not have the knowledge of or access to her murder weapon. At the same time, if Mary Goring had not been rendered vulnerable by a medical condition, she would not have been victimized so easily. "A Draught of Poison" and "Another Passage in a Dark Story" are the first of Wood's fiction to question having a medical practice in close proximity to the home, but they are not the last.

Wood often recycles plots, and her scheming governess seems like good fodder for further pieces of sensation fiction, but when she revisits chemical crime two years later in "Mr. Castonel," her focus had changed from the poisonous stepmother to the medical Bluebeard. "Mr. Castonel" is another early piece of her fiction, and it first appeared in *Bentley's Magazine* in 1857, was republished posthumously in *The Argosy* in 1895, and was even released as a novella under the title *Gervase Castonel; Or, the Six Gray Powders*. The novella relates the story of a young doctor, the titular Mr. Castonel, who moves to the village of Ebury and begins treating patients as a general practitioner. Despite his contemptuous treatment of the town apothecary and the rumors about his connection to Lavinia, a mysterious woman who follows him to Ebury and lives on its outskirts, Mr. Castonel manages to gain favor in the town. Having garnered a successful practice, he soon begins wooing the three town beauties, Caroline Hall, Ellen Leicester, and Frances Chavasse, who in fairy-tale fashion are each more lovely than the last. He marries them one by one, and each dies of strange convulsions about six months after their marriages. Suspicions that Mr. Castonel is a poisoner come to a head after the deaths of his third wife and a local infant (supposedly his illegitimate child), and a formal investigation is launched. Before Castonel is brought up for charges, however, he is found dead in Lavinia's home. Lavinia claims to have married Mr. Castonel before he moved to Ebury, and explains that he accidentally poisoned himself while trying to murder her.

So why does Wood decide to shift her focus from the murderous governess to the medical Bluebeard? The answer most likely has to do with the appearance of real-life poisoning doctors in the interval. Perhaps the William Palmer case (previously discussed in the introduction), which occurred the year before she wrote "Mr. Castonel," reminded her of the 1844 trial of the doctor James Cockburn Belany, who was accused of killing his young wife. Belany was a Scotsman who moved to the small town of North Sunderland and began practicing medicine as a surgeon. He soon became acquainted with the town beauty (and heiress) Rachel Skelly, who "was well to do" and "fair as the day and sweet as summer flowers."[33] They married early in

---

33. "The Belaney [sic] Poisoning Case," 356.

1843 and, by all appearances, the doctor seemed pleased with his wife; "no discord or angry word was ever known to pass between" them, and "a happier couple could not have been found in the countryside."[34] Mrs. Belany had previously miscarried, but an advanced stage of pregnancy still did not prevent the couple from traveling to London on a pleasure trip, early in the summer of 1844. She fared the trip rather well and began shopping and visiting the theatre. Oddly, Belany wrote to friends upon his arrival that his wife was ill and attended by two medical men, a move that *The Age* called "a subtle and evident" way "to prepare the minds of his wife's relatives for the news of her death."[35] She really would be ill and dying from prussic acid poisoning two days later. Belany sometimes took prussic acid for a stomach complaint, and allegedly broke the neck of the poison bottle while measuring out a dose. He placed the contents of the broken bottle in a glass, which he left in his bedroom. According to Belany, when he was out of the room his wife awoke from a nap and, either thinking the medicine was intended for her or not realizing the poison was in the glass, drank all the prussic acid. He reported that she cried out and told him she had taken the poison. She died a short time later.

The subsequent inquest revealed several pieces of evidence that pointed to murder. It seemed dubious that his wife would not notice the distinctive smell of a drug her husband took regularly, and impossible that she could get back into bed and tell her husband about the accident after drinking it. Dr. Belany "administered to her nothing whatever in the shape of antidote" even though the medical witness (Dr. Henry Letheby of London Hospital) declared "in 90 cases out of 100" the patient could be saved "by strong exertions on the part of the practitioner."[36] He delayed calling in another doctor and did not mention the prussic acid, instead suggesting that she had hereditary heart disease and was in a fit. After her death, he did not immediately notify her friends and relatives, writing that she was "dangerously ill" with "premature labor" complicated by a diseased heart.[37] The autopsy disproved his claims of heart disease, and he later admitted he was so "ashamed of my awful neglect in having left the acid for a moment in such a situation" that he did not initially disclose his wife's poisoning.[38]

Despite the evidence against him, the jury returned a "not guilty" verdict. One factor that worked in his favor, as suggested by the *Examiner*, is

---

34. "The Belaney [sic] Poisoning Case," 357.
35. *A Full Report*, 16.
36. *A Full Report*, 7.
37. *A Full Report*, 11.
38. *A Full Report*, 50.

that "he belonged to the class of the respectable, which juries are very apt to regard as impeccable."[39] His wife's fortune allowed Belany to live as a gentleman, writing treatises on falconry and rubbing shoulders with the aristocracy. Before sensational journalism and fiction began exposing criminality within the middle classes, Belany's respectability evidently worked strongly to acquit him. The primary exculpating circumstance, however, was the "entire absence of all motive or inducement to commit so horrible a crime."[40] Everyone who knew the couple described the marriage as happy and there was no evidence of affairs. It is true that Belany inherited wealth from the death of his wife, but also true that he already had complete financial control of Rachel's estate. No plausible motive was offered at trial, but the public might have found one. Noting local dissatisfaction with the verdict in North Sunderland, the *Tyne Mercury* wrote, "The public also seem desirous of knowing something about the 'miscarriage' in 1843, and what became of the child, &c., in order that the real facts of both cases may be properly and fully investigated."[41] This cryptic remark, couched as it is in the language of Victorian propriety, proposes a link between Rachel's earlier miscarriage and her poisoning death; in fact, it seems skeptical that a natural miscarriage actually took place. Poisons such as prussic acid were known abortifacients, and the implication is that Belany had performed an abortion on his wife in 1843. It raises the possibility that Rachel's death was a second, botched abortion attempt or perhaps that Belany killed his pregnant wife to avoid having children.

Recalling the details of the Belany case, Rachel's pregnancy and death may have first suggested the idea of a medical Bluebeard to Wood. That the original of Bluebeard was a wife-killing medieval ruler of Brittany was in circulation around mid-century. An 1871 *Notes and Queries* article notes this first Bluebeard "was fond of matrimony, but was not desirous of being troubled with the consequences; so whenever his wife gave signs of being likely to become a mother, he made away with her."[42] As we shall see, pregnancy and childbirth herald the murders of all the female victims in "Mr. Castonel" and *Lord Oakburn's Daughters*. Indeed, in Wood's fiction the prospect of a new child seems to take the place of discovering the bloody closet in "Bluebeard," since both Castonel and Carlton become murderous when their wives reproduce. For Wood, the Belany case emphasized the power

---

39. *A Full Report*, 9.
40. *A Full Report*, 42.
41. *A Full Report*, 14.
42. MacCulloch, "Bluebeard," 29.

doctor-husbands can wield over their wives—particularly in relation to their bodies and reproduction.

GOTHIC VILLAINS: "MR. CASTONEL"

Castonel is not a typical gothic villain. He lives in a house "with a stone balcony and green verandah"; not a castle.[43] It contains no locked rooms filled with hanging bodies, only lumber closets where the possessions of previous wives collect cobwebs. While rather unattractive, there is no blue tinge to his beard. Yet Castonel has the uncanny ability to spread death and domestic discord throughout the homes of Ebury. This is because the very presence of Castonel—whose name is evocative of the deadly castor seed—is poisonous. He encourages each of his three wives to defy their parents (or guardians) to marry him, and each time their actions result in misfortune or death.[44] His expertise in chemical crime gives him a power, that while all too real, seems supernatural. The original Bluebeard had to deal with hiding the bodies of his previous wives; Castonel can murder out in the open, using poisons that circumvent forensic identification. Even other doctors have difficulty "detect[ing] the nature of the poison; it was indeed rare and subtle, leaving, where it should be imbibed, but little trace after death."[45]

Despite some obvious differences from his fairy-tale counterpart, Castonel is undoubtedly a Bluebeard whose use of "subtle and deadly" poisons highlights the dangers of institutional medicine's growing presence in the home.[46] Castonel preference for the vial over the cutlass effectively aligns brutality with scientific knowledge, but at first glance, Wood's decision to transform her Bluebeard into a medical poisoner may seem to humanize

---

43. Wood, "Mr. Castonel," 295. All subsequent references are to the 1901 MacMillian edition, which is based on the 1895 version of the text republished in *The Argosy* after Wood's death. The story was originally published in Bentley's in five parts: "The Passing Bell" (May 1857), "Ellen Leicester" (June 1857), "The Six Grey Powders" (July 1857), "A Midnight Dream," (August 1857), and "Beech Lodge" (September 1857). There are some minor textual variants from the 1857 *Bentley's* stories, such as the change in the apothecary's name from "Winninton" to "Winnington" in the later version. However, as the variations are minor, I have chosen to cite the more widely available 1895 version of the story.

44. Both Mr. Winnington (Caroline's uncle and guardian) and the Rev. Leicester (Ellen's father) take a great disliking to Castonel and die from heartbreak after their children marry him. Mrs. Chavasse is paralyzed from a stroke after she receives news of Frances's death.

45. Wood, "Mr. Castonel," 421.
46. Wood, "Mr. Castonel," 421.

or "soften" her villain. After all, poison has a long-standing reputation for being less violent and more humane than other forms of death (such as throat-cutting). The Victorian suicide's overwhelming preference for opiates confirms this chemical's reputation for providing a relatively painless mode of self-destruction, but it also suggests that other varieties of poison were not so gentle. Indeed, other common poisons, such as arsenic, caused excruciating pain. Katherine Watson richly describes the effect of arsenic on the body: "Imagine stomach pains so sharp that it seems like rats are gnawing at your insides. The pain is accompanied by a thirst almost impossible to quench, with loss of bowel control and violent vomiting and retching."[47] While poisoning is not as gory or barbaric as slitting throats, Wood clearly equates the effects of the doctor's chemicals with a brutal death. In "Mr. Castonel," the type of poison used is never established, but each wife dies in torturous spasms, "writhing on the bed in awful agony, screaming and flinging [their] arms about."[48] Castonel's other victims, his bastard child and Gaffer Shipley, have similar reactions to his powders: "[Gaffer] can't hold himself still on the bed for screeching. And the babby's a dying and screeching."[49] These victims' tortured screams and uncontrollable writhing definitively mark their deaths as not only painful, but brutal. Wood thus positions Castonel as a modernized (and not less brutal) version of his fairy-tale counterpart, highlighting the destructive potential of his modern medicines.

While the women's painful deaths most readily testify to the brutality of medical science, the extent to which this Bluebeard has biophysical control over his wives' reproduction further emphasizes the threat male science poses to female patients. In her reading of Bluebeard motifs in Wilkie Collins's novels, Laurence Talairach-Vielmas notes that the use of this fairy tale "displays a picture of women's lives in marriage as endless repetition, as sterile and oppressive reproduction."[50] Certainly Talairach-Vielmas's analysis also holds true in "Mr. Castonel," not only because each wife becomes a repetition of the one that comes before her but also because each marriage ends in reproductive sterility and death. In "Mr. Castonel," the doctor-husband's threat to the female realm of reproduction is revealed by the unusual timing of each of his wives' deaths. Six months after their marriages, all three wives are struck by a mysterious ailment that brings them close to death. Each seems well on the way to recovery when they relapse into fatal convulsions. The first attacks are significant, not only because they

---

47. Watson, *Poisoned Lives*, 1.
48. Wood, "Mr. Castonel," 403.
49. Wood, "Mr. Castonel," 360.
50. Talairach-Vielmas, *Wilkie Collins, Medicine, and the Gothic*, 162.

reveal that Castonel is repeatedly poisoning his wives, but also because each one apparently results in a miscarriage: The "nature" of Ellen's first attack "was such as to destroy the hope that had sprung up in her heart," while Frances's "symptoms were the same as those which had attacked Mr. Castonel's first and second wives, *destroying prospects of an heir.*"[51] Significantly, Castonel becomes murderous when each of his wives nears her third trimester, suggesting that each murder is a reaction to a rapidly approaching birth. Based on the Belany case, it would be tempting to label the women's deaths as failed abortion attempts, but Castonel supplies the fatal dose *after* each miscarriage—indicating that he first intends to terminate the pregnancy before death. Each wife experiences sorrow and pain from the loss of her fetus before Castonel gives her the fatal dose.

Castonel's manipulation of his wives' reproduction, then, reveals that his actions are not only murderous but also specifically misogynistic. Wood frames his repeated cycle of marriage and murder as a symbolic struggle for the sexual conquest and control of his wives' bodies, and Castonel becomes a (albeit monstrous) symbol for the increased control doctors in Victorian culture were exerting over women's bodies. Even before the Contagious Disease Acts passed in 1864, mid-century doctors were gaining power over Victorian women's health. Mary Poovey identifies the 1840s and 1850s as a time when doctors began "reducing all women to a socially undifferentiated, reproductive body," which "foregrounded the biological difference between man and woman in such a way as to authorize male-dominated medical expertise."[52] Many scholars have documented the medicalization of midwifery in the nineteenth century and have outlined how male physicians actively sought to replace "untrained" female midwifes.[53] By mid-century, "it was widely accepted that keeping up a practice without any midwifery was impossible," and doctors (particularly rural general practitioners) were jealously guarding this lucrative practice from interlopers.[54] One of the central arguments doctors used to justify their monopolization of obstetric practices was their superior scientific training. Using a doctor for the birthing process was promoted as a safer and more sanitary option than relying on traditional midwives. By imagining a male doctor who murders pregnant women instead of safely delivering them, Wood challenges the growing presence of medicine in the female realm of reproduction. Casto-

---

51. Wood, "Mr. Castonel," 339, 390. Emphasis mine.
52. Poovey, *Uneven Developments*, 44.
53. For example, see Moscucci.
54. Moscucci, *Science of Woman*, 59.

nel's deadly and abortive drugs reveal the potential dangers of conceding too much power to male practitioners.

The need to keep clear boundaries between the domestic and the professional world of medicine is further emphasized by the sexual predations of Castonel. As "a reflection of the sexism of Victorian institutional medicine," the medical gothic frames "the presiding physician as invariably male, and his power over his prone female victims in particular may gain a suspiciously erotic imperative."[55] Wood borrows fears about doctors using their authority to molest or rape female patients from the medical gothic and paints Castonel as a manipulative womanizer who takes advantage of his privileged access to private homes in order to seduce his victims. Throughout the story, Castonel is described as a "general admirer" of women, and his list of sexual conquests is long.[56] For example, while he is married to all three of his Ebury wives, Castonel continues to visit Lavinia (his legal wife) at night; nor is his interest in women limited to just the middle-class ladies of Ebury. The rector sarcastically remarks that "amongst the poor," Castonel "is more warmly welcomed by the daughters than the parents."[57] The Castonel housekeeper voices similar concerns, when she admits both that Castonel "is out much in an evening" and that the old apothecary, Mr. Winnington, never "had these evening calls upon his time."[58] More direct evidence of Castonel's infidelities comes in the form of the lower-class Mary Shipley's bastard child; after much prevaricating, Mary finally admits that Castonel is the father. The doctor gains access to all his paramours through his profession; as a medical man, he has the freedom to enter a variety of homes (even at unusual hours) without suspicion. His sexual exploits confirm fears about doctors' insatiable sexual appetites and suggest that doctors have too much freedom in their access to the private sphere.

"Mr. Castonel" inherits the medical gothic's anxiety that scientific training divorces doctors from common human emotion. William Hughes points out that a regular feature of the medical gothic is "the overwhelmingly materialist—rather than simply secular—attitude to the patient."[59] Wood highlights the moral deficiencies of her fictional doctor and his unfeeling approach to his patient-victims. In many ways, Castonel seems devoid of religious belief or normal emotions. For example, he is variously described as "impenetrable" or "unfathomable"; he has a "passionless face," and his

---

55. Hughes, "Victorian Medicine and the Gothic," 440.
56. Wood, "Mr. Castonel," 302.
57. Wood, "Mr. Castonel," 305.
58. Wood, "Mr. Castonel," 345.
59. Hughes, "Victorian Medicine and the Gothic," 197.

emotions are always "so completely under control."[60] This description of Castonel is eerily evocative of the ways in which the Victorian press characterized other medical chemical criminals, like William Palmer, who was usually described as some variant of "cool, cautious, and sober," retaining his "self-possession," "profound composure," and "perfect equanimity" even during his trial.[61] Nothing, seemingly, can move Castonel either, and his ability to emotionally detach develops into outright cruelty. When his third wife, Frances, realizes that she had fallen into the same deadly path as his two previous wives, she begs Castonel for her life: "Oh, Gervase, save me! what will you do without me? Save me, save me! Let not this terrible fate be mine!"[62] Castonel is apparently completely unmoved by her piteous cries, and Frances dies by his hand a few days later.

What enables this emotionlessness is a detached mind-set cultivated by medical training. A. J. Youngston notes that "most doctors before 1850 . . . simply did not observe or think scientifically," but this had begun to change by the time Wood was writing "Mr. Castonel."[63] Doctor training began specifically addressing the development of clinical detachment. But viewing humans as organic machines whose parts could be individually examined and treated threw into question doctors' relationship to their patients. The feminist Frances Cobbe expressed concern that too many medical men were entering the profession, not from "the motive of pure *Humanity*," but from "*Scientific interest*" alone.[64] The problem Cobbe identifies with the latter motive is that it degrades the doctor-patient relationship: The "patient is to a doctor what a rock is to a geologist, or a flower to a botanist—the much coveted *subject of his studies.*"[65] Even if a man enters the medical profession from benevolent motives, the work requires such "great callousness" that "a year in his profession would suffice to blot from the mind all beauty of the world, and to spoil the charm and sanctity of the sweetest mysteries of human nature."[66] Cobbe's fear is that medical training can create a perverted scientific worldview that devalues individual human life. She declares that each patient has a right to know their doctor's moral qualifications just as they have the right to know their scientific qualifications. For Cobbe, only

---

60. Wood, "Mr. Castonel," 378.
61. *Illustrated Life and Career of William Palmer*, 34; Dickens, "The Demeanour of Murderers," 505.
62. Wood, "Mr. Castonel," 391.
63. Youngston, *Scientific Revolution in Victorian Medicine*, 17.
64. Cobbe, "The Medical Profession and Its Morality," 301. Both Pritchard and La Pommeray were poisoners.
65. Cobbe, "The Medical Profession and Its Morality," 302.
66. Cobbe, "The Medical Profession and Its Morality," 304.

religious feeling can combat the dehumanizing process of medical training; if it is lacking, then a murderous physician like "a Pritchard or a La Pommeray—handsome and gentlemanly"—has "as a doctor, unparalleled facilities for the commission and concealment of crime."[67] Despite the many rebuttals of Cobbe's argument (mostly written by medical men), her views were by no means singular.[68] An earlier commentator anticipates Cobbe's point that the man of science must have either religious or deep philanthropic feelings:

> Man can co-operate in the laws of the CREATOR, which give life; he can carry out the secondary laws which destroy life; and if unguided by a sense of religious responsibility he will use the destruction at his pleasure. There is, as we observed lately, one other influence to paralyse crime—it is affection. The babe is at the mercy of its mother, who can stifle it at any moment; the son can poison his father; the wife her husband; the physician his patient. It is natural instinct which makes us feel terror at the idea of death—anxiety to preserve the life of our fellow creatures.[69]

As the poisoning doctors of the nineteenth century proved repeatedly, these commentators' fears were not unfounded. Displaying little concern for the sanctity of human life or their professional obligations, and dehumanized by their cold scientific thinking, criminal doctors seemed to pose a serious threat to Victorian society.

What could a typical Victorian woman do to protect herself and her family from these abuses of medical power? How could she ensure a reasonable separation of home and doctor? The pile of dead bodies in "Mr. Castonel" does not seem to offer much assurance that this can be achieved, yet Wood does offer her readers some advice: Choose your medical attendant very carefully (your life may depend on it). She begins this process by focusing on the tension Mr. Castonel's arrival brings to homely Ebury. At the opening of the story, Mr. Winnington, the apothecary, is the only source of medical advice in the town. Although Winnington is a practical and able practitioner, the town immediately flocks to the new doctor, Castonel. Castonel's chief attraction seems to be his reputation as a "fashionable doctor"; the town is enamored with his "stylish cab with a tiger behind it" and his flashy zinc-

---

67. Cobbe, "The Medical Profession and Its Morality," 306.
68. Several rebuttals were printed, such as "The Medical Profession and Its Morality" in *The Medical News*, "The Medical Profession and Its Morality" in *The Student's Journal and Hospital Gazette*, and "A Critic's Morality(?)" in *The Lancet*.
69. "Poison in the Prescription," 1224.

plated sign.⁷⁰ Unlike Winnington, who gives his patients unfiltered professional advice, Mr. Castonel purposely sets out to gain clients by appealing to their petty conceits. The new doctor's initial consultation with Mrs. Major Acres demonstrates his underhanded method of obtaining new clients:

> He sympathized so feelingly with her ailments; but assured her that in a little time, under his treatment, she would not have a symptom left. That horrid Winnington, she confided to him, had told her she wanted nothing but walking and fasting. Oh, as to Winnington, Mr. Castonel rejoined, with a contemptuous curl of his wire-drawn, impenetrable lips, what could be expected of an apothecary? He (Mr. Castonel) hoped soon to leave no patients to *his* mercy.⁷¹

The passage has a satirical tone; although Winnington has given good advice to his gouty and obese patient, Mrs. Major Acres's insulted vanity balks at the apothecary's direct discussion of her weight. Mrs. Major Acres is ridiculously conceited, and Castonel is a skillful manipulator. As Mrs. Acres is at the head of Ebury's fashionable society and an inveterate gossip, the rest of the town is quickly convinced to follow her lead and abandon Winnington for Castonel. The story repeatedly states that there is more than enough work in the growing town for two medical men, but Castonel is not satisfied with his share. Greedy for a lucrative practice, he makes good on his threat to leave no patients to Winnington. Through a combination of artful manners and flashy persona, within "six months not a patient remained with Mr. Winnington," even though "in reality" Castonel is "less skilled than" his rival.⁷²

The danger inherent in Castonel's monopolization of Ebury's medical practice is, of course, that it allows him to undertake his illegal and immoral activities without interference. Indeed, Wood uses the return of a medical rival, Mr. Ailsa, to highlight this fact. Having heard of the friendless Mary Shipley's seduction (at the hands of Castonel), Ailsa "declares that, had he been in Ebury at the time, he should have taken it upon himself to bring Mr. Castonel to the justices for it."⁷³ It is also implied that Dr. Ailsa might have been able to save Frances's life. When Frances first becomes ill, her mother insists she be attended by another doctor, declaring "You have lost two wives; it may have been through negligence in not having good advice. . . .

---

70. Wood, "Mr. Castonel," 296.
71. Wood, "Mr. Castonel," 297.
72. Wood, "Mr. Castonel," 298.
73. Wood, "Mr. Castonel," 388.

Not an hour shall go over without further advice."[74] She requests Ailsa, but Castonel replies: "Call in any medical man you please, except Ailsa."[75] Mrs. Chavasse allows Castonel to override her desire to consult Ailsa, and an inferior doctor, Mr. Wilson, is called instead. Castonel is able to keep Ailsa out of the sickroom and the reader is left wondering: If Mrs. Chavasse had persisted in consulting with Ailsa, would Frances have died?

Influenced by the Belany case and the medical gothic's tendency to feature powerless female victims, "Mr. Castonel" is pessimistic. The story gives the doctor-husband-turned-gothic-monster total power of the home and suggests his female victims can only escape by chance. In between the publication of "Mr. Castonel" and *Lord Oakburn's Daughters,* additional cases of doctors poisoning their wives gave greater urgency to the need for reform, and Wood's later fiction demonstrates that perhaps, if properly managed, the medical chemical criminal can be foiled.

GOTHIC HEROINES: LORD OAKBURN'S DAUGHTERS

Wood's 1864 novel *Lord Oakburn's Daughters* shares a number of important similarities with "Mr. Castonel." Like the earlier novella, *Lord Oakburn's Daughters* is also a variant on the Bluebeard tale, focusing on the uxoricide committed by Dr. Lewis Carlton. This crime opens the novel and continues to haunt the narrative; the dead wife's fate is relayed through dreams and "buried" writing that, true to the Bluebeard tale, are excavated by the murderer's subsequent spouse. The novel deals with two seemingly separate mysteries: the suspicious death of a young mother, Mrs. Crane, and the equally suspicious disappearance of Clarice Chesney, the daughter of Lord Oakburn. The novel therefore immediately foregrounds the dangers Victorian medicine can pose to women by introducing a premature death and a medical mystery. The story opens with the arrival of a young, beautiful, and pregnant woman calling herself "Mrs. Crane" in the rural town of South Wennock. Mrs. Crane immediately goes into labor, and (to the surprise of her landlady) requests the attendance of the newest medical practitioner in town, Mr. Carlton. Carlton, however, is out of town, and Dr. Stephen Grey instead safely delivers her baby. Shortly after the birth, Mrs. Crane sends her baby away with a stranger named Mrs. Smith and continues to convalesce under the care of Grey. Once Carlton returns, Mrs. Crane insists that he take

---

74. Wood, "Mr. Castonel," 390.
75. Wood, "Mr. Castonel," 390.

over her case, yet almost immediately after his arrival, she gives "an awful cry of alarm and agony" before lapsing into convulsions and finally death.[76] During the ensuing inquest, Carlton blames the medication made by Grey for her death. Grey is officially cleared during the inquest, but the skeptical people of South Wennock drive him out of town (despite this setback, Grey moves to London and prospers so much in his new practice that he is knighted). Just as the inquest fails to identify the murderer of Mrs. Crane, it also fails to establish her real identity or the location of her infant; nameless and without family or friends to claim her, "Mrs. Crane" is buried in the local cemetery and, for a time, forgotten by South Wennock. Carlton cannot forget her death, however, as a misshapen and ghostly man who accuses him of murdering Mrs. Crane periodically haunts him. Despite the frightening apparition, Carlton remains in the town and eventually elopes with Laura Chesney, the daughter of the aristocratic, albeit poor, Lord Oakburn.

The rest of the novel follows the fate of the Oakburn family, which consists of the ageing Lord Oakburn, his second wife, and four daughters: Jane, Laura, Clarice, and Lucy. The Oakburn family is involved in a mystery because Clarice, who changed her name and went into service as a governess so as not to be a financial burden on her family, has disappeared. Her fate remains unsolved until Laura, jealous and suspicious of her husband's fidelity, goes into his laboratory and searches through a secret safe. She discovers a letter that reveals not only that Clarice is the mysterious Mrs. Crane but also that she was secretly married to Lewis Carlton (although at the time he was not aware of her real identity). A servant, Judith, who accidentally saw Carlton adulterate Clarice's medicine, finally tells her story and admits that she has been "haunting" Carlton by dressing as the ghostly man. With the evidence mounting against him, Carlton admits that he murdered his first wife in order to marry Laura. He dies (likely from poison "of too subtle nature to be discovered") before he can be brought to trial.[77]

Lord Oakburn's Daughters features only one wife-murder, not three as in the earlier short story, but Carlton is still a Bluebeard whose crimes are enabled by his moral deficiency and scientific detachment. Wood writes, "Perhaps few men living were more inclined by nature to transgress social laws than was Mr. Carlton. He had been lax on his notions of morality all his life; he was lax still."[78] Significantly, Wood directly ties Carlton's ambivalent morality to the lack of female guidance in his upbringing:

---

76. Wood, *Lord Oakburn's Daughters*, I: 98.
77. Wood, *Lord Oakburn's Daughters*, II: 330.
78. Wood, *Lord Oakburn's Daughters*, II: 313.

His father, who was in the same profession as himself, a surgeon, in large practice in a populous but not desirable quarter of London, lying eastward, had been rather given to sins and recklessness himself, and no good example had ever been placed before the boy, Lewis. Had his mother lived, as he remarked to Captain Chesney, things would have been widely different.[79]

Here, Wood creates a chain of moral delinquency that is linked from father to son and is connected through ties of blood and profession. Carlton has inherited not only his father's "sins" but also a profession that provides the mind-set and opportunity to commit those sins. Thus, Carlton's moral ambivalence leads to a disturbing worldview that hierarchically categorizes human life into a continuum of value. In describing the events surrounding his wife Clarice's death, Carlton declares:

I never knew her but as Clarice Beauchamp; I never knew that she had claim to a higher position in life than that of governess. She was always utterly silent to me on the subject of her family and connections, and I assumed she was an orphan.[80]

Carlton's confession suggests that had he known Clarice was the daughter of an aristocratic family (not an orphaned and friendless governess), she would not have been disposable. While this certainly is a commentary on the precarious position of governesses in Victorian society, it also reveals that Carlton believes some lives are worth more than others are—a dangerous precedent for a medical man to have.

If medicine and the domestic must meet, then Wood insists that medicine adhere to the superior morality of women. She reveals this viewpoint through the reintroduction of the curious heroine. In the "Bluebeard" fairy tale, the machinations of the gothic villain are circumvented by what scholars have termed "the curious heroine": the final wife who discovers her husband's crimes and arranges for her brothers to chop off his head. The curious wife is central to the resolution of the original fairy tale because she represents the drive to discover the secrets of the home; only through exposure can Bluebeard be brought to justice for his murders. In *Lord Oakburn's Daughters*, Lady Laura most closely adheres to the pattern of the traditional curious heroine. Angered by her belief that Carlton is committing adultery, Laura obtains a skeleton key and sneaks into her husband's laboratory in

---

79. Wood, *Lord Oakburn's Daughters*, I: 72.
80. Wood, *Lord Oakburn's Daughters*, III: 313.

order to rifle through his safe. There she finds a letter from her missing sister and the first clue to unraveling the mystery of Clarice Chesney's disappearance. Wood swaps the bloody closet for the locked safe, and while Laura does not find an actual body, she does find the literary remains of her sister. Thus, although the fairy tale and novel both highlight the dangers of female curiosity, that curiosity is also integral to outing Bluebeard and bringing him to justice.

In "Mr. Castonel" Wood completely dispenses with the curious heroine. Castonel's wives are aware of their predecessors—and their mysterious deaths—but not a single one probes deeply into her husband's secrets. Lavinia survives because she accidentally catches a glimpse of Castonel dosing her wine in a mirror and tricks him into drinking his own poison, not because she solves the mysterious deaths. The failure of these women to discover Castonel's secrets suggests just how powerful medical authority had become. Each time doubts are raised regarding the women's deaths, Castonel answers that the cases are "perfectly satisfactory to medical men" and shuts down any opposition.[81] The danger, Wood suggests, is not only that the Castonel wives will not question their husband, but that (even if they did challenge him) they cannot effectively contest his scientific authority.[82] Castonel has more power over his wife-patients than Bluebeard could ever dream of, and Wood purposefully dispenses with the curious heroine of the original fairy tale in order to highlight the power and influence of medical authority at mid-century.

This chapter suggests that the reemergence of the curious heroine in Wood's later work is a direct response to increasing cultural concern about the medical profession's relationship to women. While still highlighting anxieties about medical science, Wood also offers a model of female domestic management that counteracts the dangers of the gothic chemical criminal. She does this not only by incorporating the curious heroine back into her modern version of Bluebeard but also by presenting this figure in a variety of forms. At different points in the novel, Laura Carlton, Lady Oakburn, and Lady Jane are all positioned in the role of the curious heroine. Their efforts are responsible for exposing Carlton's crime as well as the medical misdeeds of other doctors. In the case of Lady Oakburn and Jane, their insistence on having information and participating in the masculine world of doctoring allows them to use their moral superiority to reestablish a balance between the two worlds of medicine and domestic.

---

81. Wood, "Mr. Castonel," 339.

82. The only person who does challenge Castonel's scientific authority is Mr. Ailsa, another doctor who returns to Ebury toward the end of the novella.

The introduction of the curious heroine into Wood's 1864 novel probably arises from the continued appearance of real-life poisoning doctor cases. The 1859 case of Thomas Smethurst, in particular, seems to have prompted Wood to revisit and revise "Mr. Castonel" into a longer work. Unlike the Belany and Palmer cases, the death of Isabella Bankes Smethurst did include a curious heroine of sorts—the dead woman's sister, Louisa. Working with doctors, Louisa was able to get her sister away from her supposed poisoner; although Isabella still died, Louisa demonstrates that a persistent woman could potentially foil the plans of even such a powerful murderer as a poisoning doctor.

THE SMETHURST CASE

The similarities between the Smethurst case and her own fiction must have given Ellen Wood a shock when she opened her morning paper and read about his supposed crimes. Here was yet another poisoning doctor accused of murdering his pregnant wife. And, like her own Castonel, Smethurst had bigamously married his victim. Smethurst was a general practitioner, a licensee of the London Apothecaries Hall, and held a doctor of medicine degree from Erlangen University.[83] His troubles began in 1858, while he was living in a boarding house at Bayswater. At the time, Smethurst had been retired from his medical practice for six years and had recently returned from living on the Continent. He had married a woman twenty years older than himself when still quite a young man, and his marriage was childless. While living at Bayswater, Smethurst became friendly with a fellow lodger, Isabella Bankes. Bankes was in her early forties and apparently responded warmly to Smethurst's advances—so warmly that the landlady evicted Bankes for improper conduct with the doctor. The eviction did not end the relationship, and on the ninth of December, 1858, Smethurst left his wife at the boardinghouse and bigamously married Bankes. They moved to Richmond and began living together as husband and wife.

Unfortunately for the couple, the honeymoon period did not last long. At the end of March, the new Mrs. Smethurst began suffering from a recurring illness that resembled dysentery, consisting mainly of diarrhea and vomiting. Smethurst did consult with partners Drs. Julius and Bird, "the most eminent practitioners in Richmond," but he never "allowed [them] to

---

83. The account of Smethurst's life and trial are compiled from Sir James Fitzjames Stephen's *A History of the Criminal Law of England* and Richard Altick's *Victorian Studies in Scarlet*.

be alone with their patient."[84] The two doctors were puzzled by the case, particularly because the medicines they supplied Isabella, many of which were mild, "had a directly contrary effect to what they were intended."[85] On April 18, Smethurst wrote to Isabella's sister, Louisa Bankes, and requested she come make her ailing sister a visit. The two sisters had been somewhat estranged by Isabella's decision to live with Dr. Smethurst (unmarried, as Louisa thought), but Louisa nonetheless was an affectionate sister and concerned for Isabella's health. During her visit, she offered several times to make invalid foods for Isabella, but Smethurst dissuaded her each time. The next day, she received a letter from Smethurst stating that Isabella had become overexcited from the visit and that her doctors forbade any future visits. Louisa continued to receive letters from Smethurst over the next two weeks, which often put her visits off or sent her on long errands to pick up medicines. Fears of overexcitement, however, did not keep an attorney from visiting the sickroom, and Isabella signed a will that disinherited her family and left all her assets to Dr. Smethurst.

Isabella knew she was very ill, and several times "expressed a wish for further medical assistance."[86] Smethurst complied, calling in Dr. Todd. Todd agreed with Julius and Bird that "the patient was suffering under unfair treatment," and therefore had her evacuations tested and notified authorities about his reservations.[87] Louisa, who was undeterred by Smethurst's strange behavior and persisted in trying to gain access to her sister, was at the house when the police took Smethurst into custody on suspicion of poisoning. After Louisa and a hired nurse took over Isabella's case, "she did not vomit on any one occasion. She also asked for some tea, and that was also retained on her stomach."[88] But by then Isabella was feeble from weeks of illness, and she died the next morning.

The autopsy confirmed that the cause of death was suspicious and also revealed that Bankes was in the early stages of pregnancy. The trial was a scandalous affair, not only because of the salacious details of Smethurst's bigamy but also because the prosecution witnesses significantly bungled the evidence at the trial. The most famous "poison hunter" of the Victorian period, Dr. Alfred Swaine Taylor, testified at the inquest that he had discovered traces of antimony and arsenic in only one sample taken from Bankes's body. By the time of the trial, however, Taylor admitted that his

---

84. "The Richmond Poisoning Case," 343.
85. "The Richmond Poisoning Case," 343.
86. "The Medical Evidence," 202.
87. "The Richmond Poisoning Case," 344.
88. "Trial of Thomas Smethurst," 707.

testing apparatus was contaminated and that he could find no definitive proof that poison was present in the second Mrs. Smethurst's body. The prosecution countered this blow by arguing that "the prisoner was a medical man, possessed of considerable skill," who "had availed himself of this knowledge to administer the poison to this unhappy lady in such a manner . . . to render its discovery in the body very difficult."[89] The Crown's argument that Smethurst was a skilled chemical criminal able to defy forensic testing worked. Despite the lack of physical evidence, Smethurst was still convicted of the crime. The verdict caused an immediate sensation, and the home secretary eventually had the case reviewed by the presiding judge and the eminent doctor Sir Benjamin Collins Brodie. Their report determined that the evidence at the trial did not conclusively prove Smethurst's guilt, and the condemned man was granted a pardon. The chief baron could not resist from offering "a conjecture" that, like Belany, "SMETHURST administered poison to Miss BANKES not for the purpose of murder, but of procuring abortion."[90]

Despite the pardon, many observers of the trial maintained that the doctor was guilty and painted him as a gothic villain who treated Bankes's death like "a scientific experiment."[91] In many ways, Bankes's story—her late marriage to a wealthy doctor, illness, and subsequent mysterious death—seemed ripped from the pages of an eighteenth-century gothic novel. Commentators were fascinated by gruesome aspects of Bankes's death because

> it implied cool and deliberate experimentalising in poison, upon a person whom the prisoner professed to love, who loved him, and who was with him, hour by hour, while he administered the means of torture, and she died slowly, hour by hour, under that torture, done with such cruel hypocrisy that through all the moments of the nights and days of that month in wretchedness, he had to maintain the profession of love, with such demoniacal art that through them all he could meet the observations of ordinary practitioners; and, not satisfied with that danger, he invited the presence of gentleman believed to possess more than ordinary skill.[92]

This passage argues that Smethurst is a ghoulish criminal who manipulates his position as husband-doctor to carry out murder. Note that the language of the passage, particularly the use of the words "torture," "cruel hypoc-

---

89. "Richmond Poisoning Case," 344–45.
90. "Ought There to Be a Criminal Court of Appeals?," 122.
91. "The Case of Thomas Smethurst," 248.
92. "Circumstantial Evidence," 550.

risy," "wretchedness," and "demoniacal," specifically evokes the gothic and highlights the disparate power dynamic between Smethurst and his victim. Smethurst's murder of his bigamous wife both makes a mockery of the sacred institution of marriage and raises fears about the growing power of medical men to manipulate the bodies of their patient-victims. Presenting Smethurst as a gothic villain highlights the power the Victorians accorded chemical crime, giving the horrible impression that science had replaced magic in its ability to create invisible forms of murder. At every opportunity, the reports of the trial emphasized Smethurst's medical training and he was continuously referred to as "Doctor."[93] The Smethurst case was particularly damaging to the profession because of the corrupted evidence. Not only did the evidentiary problems shake trust in forensic science, but since the cause of death was never satisfactorily determined, it also suggested that doctors were finding ways to outsmart the celebrated poison hunters.

CURIOSITY SAVES

The Smethurst case, particularly the failure of Louisa Bankes to save her sister, had a profound effect on Wood's revision of "Mr. Castonel" into *Lord Oakburn's Daughters*. As a poisoning husband-doctor, Smethurst symbolized the erosion that was occurring between the carefully delineated professional and domestic realms. As M. Jeanne Peterson notes, in the eighteenth and early nineteenth centuries, patients had the power of choice, and many viewed their medical practitioners as employees rather than authority figures.[94] Around mid-century, however, this mind-set began to change, and by the *fin de siècle*, medical men were "the new priesthood, ministering to the physical and psychic needs of patients."[95] In *Lord Oakburn's Daughters*, Wood registers the shifting power dynamic between doctors and women, and she is especially concerned that the doctor's increased role in the home was an erosion of female management and domestic authority. She uses chemical crime to collapse the boundaries between the professional and domestic

---

93. The link between doctors and poisoning murders was becoming so entrenched that medical journals felt compelled to disassociate men like Palmer and Smethurst from the profession: "There may be some consolation, however, to those who follow out their Profession to its legitimate objects, in the reflection that both [Palmer and Smethurst] had long wandered from the ordinary paths of Medical life. Palmer took so early to the turf that he can scarcely be said to have practised; and Smethurst diverged into Hydropathy." Quoted in "The Smethurst Case," 214.

94. Peterson, *Medical Profession*, 134.

95. Peterson, *Medical Profession*, 285.

and transform the home into a space of both domestic virtue and horrid crime. She productively uses the tension created by this collapse to pose a question about who should have control over the health of the home. The answer Wood offers is nuanced, suggesting that the professional and the wife must work together. Doctors should be deferred to, but women do not have to offer their unquestioning obedience to medical authority. She therefore bucks the tradition of the medical gothic by reimagining the curious heroine of the Bluebeard fairy tale into a modern Victorian woman who does not uncritically follow medical advice. The curious heroine is proactive in her medical management, and Wood urges her (primarily female) readers to think carefully about how and why they choose their medical men.

Like "Mr. Castonel," *Lord Oakburn's Daughters* also begins by highlighting the importance of making wise medical decisions. The novel opens with Mrs. Crane's (Clarice Chesney's) insistence on her parturition being attended by South Wennock's newest practitioner, Mr. Carlton, and the fatal results of this choice. Clarice's death frames the narrative structure of the novel, emphasizing the danger certain doctors pose to naïve and trusting women, yet *Lord Oakburn's Daughters* also features women who successfully challenge suspect medical authority. In the novel, Wood remodels the curious heroine into women who refuse to be kept in ignorance by medical men and assert their own rights as patients and domestic managers. In the characters of Lady Eliza Oakburn and Lady Jane Chesney, the reader is shown a model of Victorian womanhood that both takes an active role in making medical decisions and continues to conform to the requirements of proper feminine behavior.

One of the most significant scenes for this process is another moment of birth and death: Lady Eliza Oakburn's recovery from the birth of her son and the almost simultaneous death of her husband. Lady Oakburn clashes with her doctors when they impress upon her their medical paternalism; the doctors make decisions for the "good" of Lady Oakburn without fully informing her about the realities of the case. As Lord Oakburn colorfully points out, it is all in a doctor's "day's work to go about deceiving people . . . telling them they are getting their sea-legs on again, while all the while you know before the eight bells strike they'll be gone down to Davy Jones's locker."[96] His words quickly become prophetic: The doctors ban together in order to keep the "delicate" Lady Oakburn from knowing that her husband is dying. Despite remonstrance from Lady Jane, the doctors refuse to enlighten Lady Oakburn:

---

96. Wood, *Lord Oakburn's Daughters*, II: 218–19.

> "Is it right to keep it from the countess?" asked Jane, her tone, as she put the question, betraying that she thought it was wrong. Dr. James heaved up his physicianly hands and eyes. "Right to keep it from her, Lady Jane! I would not for the world allow it to reach her ladyship in her present state of health; we don't know what the consequences might be. My reputation is at stake, my lady."[97]

As Wood makes apparent, the doctor's decision to keep the countess in ignorance of her husband's terminal condition is in a large degree based on his desire to preserve his reputation, and he ignores the moral guidance provided by Jane. Even worse, Dr. James's deceit goes beyond simply hiding the truth; he actively lies to Lady Oakburn and convinces her that the earl was "taking a renewed lease on life."[98]

Lady Oakburn's fears that she will be kept from a final meeting with her husband are realized: The doctors are successful in their ruse long enough to prevent a last interview between the husband and wife. Suspicious that she is being misled, the countess leaves her bed to discover that Lord Oakburn expired only moments before. Contrary to the doctor's warning that the news will be disabling, Lady Oakburn resumes active management of the home—which includes the dismissal of the treacherous Dr. James. The triumphant scene is worth quoting at length:

> She had done it, as she did most things, in a quiet lady-like manner, but one entirely firm and uncompromising. Dr. James had by stratagem, *by untruth*, prevented a last interview between her and her husband, and she felt that she could not regard him with feelings unallied to vexation and anger: it was better therefore that they should part. Dr. James urged that what he had done, he had done for the best, out of concern for her ladyship's welfare. That, her ladyship did not doubt, she answered; but she could not forget or forgive the way in which it had been accomplished: in her judgment, Dr. James should have imparted to her the truth of her husband's state, and *then* urged prudence upon her. It was the deceit she could not forgive, or—in short—countenance.[99]

This passage is revealing in several ways. First, it underscores why Dr. James's paternalistic approach to medicine is flawed and presents a more

---

97. Wood, *Lord Oakburn's Daughters*, II: 227–28.
98. Wood, *Lord Oakburn's Daughters*, II: 222.
99. Wood, *Lord Oakburn's Daughters*, II: 248–49.

morally responsible model for medicine (he "should have imparted to her the truth") that privileges the informed family. Second, by emphasizing the "stratagem," "untruth," and "deceit" inherent in the doctor's practice, Wood challenges medicine's purported professionalism. By lying to Lady Oakburn in order to protect his reputation, Dr. James reveals that he is not a disinterested professional working primarily for the good of his patient, but rather that his self-interest outweighs his patient's wishes. Finally, Wood offers her female readers a template for actively managing their health care without compromising their femininity. She demonstrates that a "firm and uncompromising" management of the home can be achieved while maintaining feminine and lady-like behavior.

That Wood intends for Lady Oakburn's behavior to be a model for other women is apparent from a subsequent scene between her daughter-in-law, Jane, and Dr. Carlton. While Jane's ward Lucy is on a visit to her sister Laura Carlton's home, she begins to feel ill. In fact, Lucy has contracted a dangerous fever that has been sweeping the town, and Carlton quickly recognizes the symptoms of the disease—yet he keeps Lucy at his home rather than sending her back to Jane. This move is prompted by Carlton's desire to "bring Lucy through the illness himself," thus ingratiating himself with his sister-in-law. Lady Jane has had an aversion to Carlton ever since one of her prophetic dreams suggested that the doctor was involved in the disappearance of her sister Clarice. Trusting to her intuition and suspicious about his actions, Lady Jane makes inquiries and a competing doctor admits that "he saw no reason why [Lucy] should not have been taken home at first."[100] Jane immediately realizes that Carlton must have ulterior motives; prompted by her fears and schooled by Lady Oakburn's experience with Dr. James, Jane takes firm control of the situation. Despite Lucy's confinement within Carlton's house, Jane insists on her sister being attended by Dr. Grey. When Carlton angrily protests, Jane "put[s] him down with calm self-possession":[101]

> Sir, it is true that my sister is your wife; but I beg you not to forget that I am Lady Jane Chesney, and that a certain amount of respect is due to me, even in your house. I do believe you to be as efficient as Mr. Grey; that your skill is equal to his; but that is not the question. *He* is my medical attendant, and I would prefer that he take the case.[102]

---

100. Wood, *Lord Oakburn's Daughters*, III: 113.
101. Wood, *Lord Oakburn's Daughters*, III: 108.
102. Wood, *Lord Oakburn's Daughters*, III: 108.

Just like Lady Oakburn, Jane takes a firm, yet calm, approach to dealing with Carlton. Through this strategy Jane is successful in her request, and gains control over the medical situation.

Jane's success in establishing Dr. Grey as Lucy's doctor may not just be a moral victory, and Wood hints that she may have unwittingly saved Lucy from being the victim of a chemical crime by taking her out of Carlton's care. Indeed, at this point in the novel the reader has a legitimate reason to wonder (as Judith does) if Carlton is keeping Lucy "to poison her on her sick bed" in order to get revenge against the Chesney family for refusing to accept him as a son-in-law.[103] Cryptically, while recovering from her illness, Lucy experiences symptoms of poisoning, including "a hot disagreeable sensation in [her] throat." Another doctor notices that Carlton has been dosing Lucy with "two small white papers" filled with powder (similar, indeed, to Castonel's gray powders) and instructs the young woman not to take any more medications from Carlton.[104] Lucy does not have the same fate as Isabella Bankes, whose sister was barred from seeing her and whose doctors had suspicions for weeks that Smethurst was poisoning her but did nothing. Jane's assertion of her own authority and insistence that Dr. Grey attend her perhaps saves Lucy (who, significantly, looks the most like her deceased sister Clarice) from becoming another of Carlton's victims.

While showing how Wood used the poisoning doctor to critique Victorian medicine's increasing influence in the home, this chapter is also mindful, as Lawrence Rothfield notes, that "a negative view of medicalization" can occlude differing representations of doctors "since it defines all forms of power as equally bad and equivalent in operation."[105] This analysis of Wood's work would be remiss if it suggested that she views the whole of the medical profession with skepticism; to the contrary, doctors in her novels are often necessary collaborators in maintaining the happiness and health of the home. The emphasis on collaboration is paramount. Both Lacy Oakburn and Jane rely on Sir Stephen Grey for their medical care, and a "close and lasting friendship" exists between the women and their doctor.[106] In several scenes, Wood depicts Sir Stephen rightfully overruling the behaviors of the two women, particularly in regard to the "coddling" of the young heir. Yet it is precisely because Sir Stephen is practical, honest, and willing to work with his patients that the two women bow to his authority. Despite the negative view of the medical profession that Wood's use of the poisoning doctor implies, Wood realizes the two worlds of medicine and home must

---

103. Wood, *Lord Oakburn's Daughters*, III: 109.
104. Wood, *Lord Oakburn's Daughters*, III: 155.
105. Rothfield, "Medical," 178.
106. Wood, *Lord Oakburn's Daughters*, II: 299.

interact and so constructs an ideal relationship built on trust and mutual consideration.

By advocating for this particular form of patient (or woman)-doctor relationship, Wood goes against contemporary medical advice. *The Lancet* advised that the doctor "ought not to be the intimate of his female patients" and should ensure "a certain sanctity" by presenting himself as a "priest of Hygeia ministering health in the family."[107] If he is friendly with his female clients, it erodes his authority and makes it impossible to do his job correctly. An article entitled "Doctors and Patients," originally published in *Ladies Companion*, is more explicit about the necessity for a stark divide between doctors and women. Displaying exasperation for women who want an active role in the medicalizing of their families, the article prompts women to ask themselves, "What is my duty to my doctor?"[108] It imagines a "poor practitioner" who has to deal with "the conceit, the timidity, the carelessness, the ignorance, and, what is worse, the half-knowledge" of female patients.[109] The article completely rejects the idea that women could bring any useful information to a doctor, snidely remarking, "If she is a theorist, and chooses to give him proof of her superior discernment, she will, perhaps, provoke him to prove her at fault, at some small abatement of his own straightforwardness."[110] Offering advice, in this context, is akin to challenging the authority of the doctor.

The poisoning doctor shows how dangerous it could be to passively obey medical guidance. Wood's rejection of contemporary medical advice and inclusion of women willing to challenge their doctors signals that her works may be less conservative than scholars have previously thought. Critics have argued that Wood's heroines "are at the mercies and whims of unscrupulous, complacent, predatory men" and that "transgressive, excessive female figures are usually condemned."[111] This reading of *Lord Oakburn's Daugh-*

---

107. "Medical Practitioners and Their Female Patients," 1009.
108. "Doctors and Patients," 44.
109. "Doctors and Patients," 44.
110. "Doctors and Patients," 44.
111. Liggins and Maunder, 151. True to her source material, Wood compares the beneficial "interference" of Lady Oakburn and Jane to the curious "prying" of Laura. The narrator repeatedly emphasizes that Laura is participating in improper behavior by snooping into her husband's secrets: "Laura! Laura Carlton! what are you about to do? To pry into your husband's private affairs, into things which he deems it fit and right to keep from you? Take you care; secrets sought out dishonourably, rarely benefit the seeker" (III: 175–76). Laura's spying ultimately leads to the arrest and imprisonment of her husband for Clarice's poisoning, an outcome that, while necessary to the resolution of the plot, Laura still must be forgiven for. Thus, while Laura's subversion of her husband's authority is positioned as improper behavior, Lady Oakburn's and Lady Jane's subversion of medical authority are situated as necessary.

ters and "Mr. Castonel" adds a new layer to this critical assumption. Even though the majority of critics view Wood's sensationalism as more "conservative" than her peers' work, medical crime is such a pressing topic that she sets her usual conservatism aside and writes works that rival those of more "subversive" authors, such as Wilkie Collins.

The inclusion of assertive women also signals Wood's deviation from the medical gothic. While the medical gothic obviously heavily influences her writing, this genre rarely features women who are able to subvert the power of medical men. Wood's fusion of the medical gothic with sensation fiction perhaps suggests that we need to reevaluate the way we understand the latter genre. There is an argument to be made that by moving the clinical gothic's concerns about medical abuse into the home, and specifically by exploring medicine's impact on intimate relationships, works like Wood's should perhaps be read within a subgenre of medical sensational fiction. The works of other scholars, such as Andrew Mangham, Tabitha Sparks, Meegan Kennedy, and Laurence Talairach-Vielmas, on the many cross-influences between sensation and medicine suggest that such a reevaluation may help us more productively understand this rich and varied genre of crime fiction.

CHAPTER 3

CHEMICALIZED BODIES AND CRIMINAL INTENT

Unruly Bodies and the
Limitations of Forensic Science
in Early Detective Fiction

IT IS STRIKING, even paradoxical, that many examples of detective fiction—a genre built upon rational scientific deduction and the revelation of truth—often feature the mysterious and unpredictable effects of drugs and poisons. Strange reactions to chemicals arise particularly in early detective fiction; for example, opiates, confused identities, and altered states of mind are central to the plot of Wilkie Collins's 1868 novel *The Moonstone*. The novel's protagonist, Franklin Blake, must prove that he did not *intend* to steal the titular diamond, although he undoubtedly did so while in an opium-induced trance. Most scholars of Victorian crime fiction regard *The Moonstone* as the first English detective novel, but an earlier claimant to the title also features the bizarre effects of chemicals: Charles Warren Adams's *The Notting Hill Mystery*.[1] Julian Symons first brought attention to this work's

---

1. The novel was originally published under the pseudonym "Charles Felix," and William Buckler first identified the author as Adams in *PMLA* in 1952. Yet somehow Buckler's identification of Adams slipped through the scholarly cracks, and critics generally continued to believe that the author was unidentified. Recently, Paul Collins claimed that he had discovered that Charles Warren Adams was the real identity of Charles Felix. Collins is mistaken, of course, that the identity of the author was not previously established, but he does offer more conclusive proof than Buckler that Adams actually is the pseudonymous author (although he is mistaken that Adams was a lawyer). Based on both Collins's and Buckler's scholarship, and my own biographic work on Adams, I also conclude that Felix is Adams's pseudonym, and have named him as the author of *The*

place in the historiography of detective fiction by proclaiming, "There is no doubt that the first detective novel, preceding Collins and Gaboriau, was *The Notting Hill Mystery*."[2] This novel, serialized in *Once a Week* from 1862 to 1863, shares many similarities with the later *Moonstone,* including a complex crime and confusion about criminal intent; a professional detective; its structure of interwoven, multivocal, documentary narratives; and its use of altered states of mind in the commission of crime.[3] In *The Notting Hill Mystery,* however, bodies are altered not only through poisons but also through mesmerism, and unlike in *The Moonstone,* the crimes in this novel are never fully explained or resolved. The evidence presented by Ralph Henderson, the detective and editor of the collected narratives, suggests that the mesmerist Baron R** poisons two women, Gertrude Bolton Anderton and her twin sister Rosalie (who also has claims to several other names, including Madame R**, Catherine Bolton, and Charlotte Brown). Since Rosalie was stolen by gypsies as an infant, the baron is the only one who realizes the true kinship between the two women and marries Rosalie to gain a stake in the family inheritance. The Baron R** then manages to poison Gertrude Anderton by manipulating the strong mesmeric link between the twins. According to Henderson, the baron doses Rosalie with antimony, which causes both her and Gertrude to sicken simultaneously. Mrs. Anderton's weaker constitution causes her to die first, and the baron later dispatches his wife by putting her in a mesmeric trance (which mimics somnambulism) and forcing her to drink poison.

Despite *The Notting Hill Mystery*'s earlier publication date and its employment of the narrative strategies of later detective fiction, most scholars have been slow to recognize it as the first British detective novel or to even include it in discussions of early detective fiction. This chapter argues that one of the main reasons for *The Notting Hill Mystery*'s exclusion is that it uses chemical crime to question whether or not forensic science can assign guilt—a move that seems antithetical to the ideological foundations of detective fiction. According to Ronald Thomas, *The Moonstone* achieves the distinction of being "the first and best of *modern* English detective novels" precisely because "it is the first novel of any kind to demonstrate in a compelling way the emergence of the modern field of forensic science and its growing importance to a new science called criminology"; in other words,

---

Notting Hill Mystery in this chapter. See Buckler's article "Once a Week" or Paul Collins's "Before Hercule or Sherlock."

2. Symons, *Bloody Murder,* 52.

3. Both Symons and Maurice Richardson (and some contemporary reviewers) note Adams's indebtedness to Wilkie Collins's *The Woman in White* for the narrative structure of *The Notting Hill Mystery.*

Thomas proposes that a work of fiction must legitimate forensics in order to be classified within the detective genre.[4] Thomas's argument downplays the contribution of novels that challenge forensic authority to the development of detective fiction. Excluding these works is problematic because it limits our understanding of the complex ways the Victorians responded to the rise of forensic science. By examining how *The Notting Hill Mystery* uses chemical crime to challenge the scope of forensic science, this chapter also works to resituate this novel within the historiography of the detective novel.

Acknowledging the role Adams's novel plays in the creation of detective fiction also allows us to reevaluate Thomas's claims about *The Moonstone*'s relationship to forensic science. The fact that both of these novels use poison and altered states of mind suggests that detective fiction is deeply imbued with, as Srdjan Smajic puts it, "the anxiety that generic purity is unattainable; that the supposedly rational genre . . . is everywhere contaminated by the supernatural, occult, or irrational; that the epistemological principles and investigative procedures that define detective fiction's characteristic modality are deeply implicated in what the genre insists on condescendingly treating as 'rubbish.'"[5] Instead of being built solely on the analytic foundations of forensic science, novels like *The Notting Hill Mystery* and *The Moonstone* show that the rise of detective fiction is, paradoxically, equally indebted to an inclusion of the strange and unpredictable drawn from a tradition of gothic irrationality rather than realist rationality.

At the heart of the failure of forensic science in *The Notting Hill Mystery* is the destabilizing force of chemical crime. The novel uses chemical crime to expose some of the weaknesses of midcentury toxicological testing, particularly forensic science's inability to deal with what I term "unruly" bodies—those that do not conform to standardized medical norms or that the conscious mind cannot control. The strange, unpredictable bodies found in the novel significantly disrupt the work of the detective because "at the center of virtually every detective story is a body upon which the literary detective focuses his gaze and employs his unique interpretive powers."[6] The detective's goal is to use his specialized knowledge to read the history of the crime from the various bodies—of victim, witness, or suspect—that he encounters. In order for him to effectively use his detective skills, these bodies must react homogenously to a set of predetermined rules that are derived from an anatomical or standardized way of understanding the human body. Victorian medical practice originated the idea of the standard-

---

4. Thomas, *Detective Fiction*, 67.
5. Smajic, *Ghost-Seers*, 3.
6. Thomas, *Detective Fiction*, 2.

ized body through observations gleaned from autopsies and dissection; it posited that all bodies are essentially similar and operate on a predictable basis. For the purposes of criminal detection, the standardized body allows for the invention of new technologies, such as fingerprinting and photographic mug shots, that rely on the stability of bodies over time.

Forensic science's reliance on the standardization of bodies results in a blind spot when it comes to the issue of abnormality, creating a potential loophole for savvy criminals. If bodies fall outside the boundaries of standardization, or if the body cannot be controlled by the mind, then how can criminal guilt be effectively resolved? Henderson's theory of the crime, which depends on Mrs. Anderton's and Rosalie's unusual reaction to mesmerism, reflects this problem. As it turns out, his theory is only as stable as the bodies he is responsible for interpreting—which is to say, not very stable at all. The novel uses the transformative power of poison, since poisons are, after all, unruly chemicals, to expose the unruliness of seemingly normal bodies; in turn, these poisoned bodies confound the forensic processes of parsing normal death from murder, guilt from innocence. Henderson cannot concretely determine if Mrs. Anderton was poisoned, nor can he grasp Rosalie's complicity—or lack thereof—in Mrs. Anderton's death and her own suicide. Instead of showing the effectiveness of early forensics, *The Notting Hill Mystery* raises questions about what happens if a chemical criminal can manipulate unruly bodies to leave no identifiable traces of poison in the body, or when the project of detection can track a body, but cannot provide evidence of criminal intent.

Unruly bodies are important not only for understanding how *The Notting Hill Mystery* probes the limits of forensic science but also for understanding this work's legacy to later detective fiction. Collins's more famous novel also features the unruly body of Franklin Blake, who unconsciously steals his cousin's diamond while in an opium-fueled hypnotic trance. Just as the poisons in *The Notting Hill Mystery* draw attention to the strange bodies of Rosalie and Mrs. Anderton, the opiates in *The Moonstone* demonstrate the unexpected ways that bodies coded as normal can behave after ingesting chemicals. *The Moonstone* also questions the limitations of forensic science, even if it does not offer as strong a critique as does *The Notting Hill Mystery*. Ezra Jennings's experiment, which reproduces Blake's somnambular wanderings, has long been hailed as evidence of Collins's sanctioning of forensic technologies, but this chapter complicates the assumption that science could completely, in the words of Thomas, "read the secret truth of the past in the bodies of the victims and perpetrators of crime."[7] The experi-

---

7. Thomas, *Detective Fiction*, 3.

ment only reveals a relatively small part of the investigative puzzle, and the very unscientific method of personal testimony corroborates the evidence it exposes. Jennings's reproduction of the night of the theft is meant to address the problem of determining criminal intent that *The Notting Hill Mystery* raises. It exonerates Blake, but only because Jennings—a figure who is literally on the social and scientific fringe—recognizes the paradoxical nature of Blake's body and resorts to an experiment that acknowledges this strangeness. Collins makes essentially the same argument as Adams when he suggests that a forensic science dependent upon standardization will fail when confronted with unruly bodies, except that Collins offers a version of science that acknowledges this ambiguity. Collins sees forensics as possibly being able to accommodate the strange—but only if it embraces the ambiguity of poison and unruly bodies.

POISON, GUILT, AND CRIMINAL INTENT

Both *The Notting Hill Mystery* and *The Moonstone* question the foundations of forensics, even such concrete assumptions as the expectation that the poisoned body is the victimized body. Unruly bodies mystify the detective figure's project of assigning innocence or guilt because their poisoning seems to implicate, rather than exonerate, them. As we have seen in previous chapters, before the 1860s victims of chemical crimes were usually the innocent prey of progressively more sophisticated criminals. After mid-century, however, poisoned bodies came under profound suspicion, a result of the idea that the act of *being* poisoned is a corrupting process. As Piya Pal-Lapinski notes, nineteenth-century "poison inscribed the bodies of both poisoner and victim with a dangerous sense of receptivity to infiltration."[8] Several cultural changes happening in concert caused this shift. First, the spate of high-profile cases in the 1850s (William Palmer and Madeleine Smith's cases being the most notorious) resulted in an increased stigma against poisoning crimes. According to the *London Medical Gazette*, poisonings are "great and increasing evil," and a perusal of the *Times* during this period shows an increase in autopsies and inquests on suspicious (and not very suspicious) deaths.[9] The Arsenic Act of 1851, a reactive bill that required purchasers of

---

8. Pal-Lapinski, *Exotic Woman*, 37.
9. "On the Increase of the Crime," 194. The *Times* reported many instances of autopsies being performed on persons who were later declared to have died naturally. The fear of secret poisoning was so intense that people began to suspect it even in cases of natural death.

arsenic to sign a registry and only receive dyed chemicals, assumed that every sale of poison had the potential to evolve into crime. Poison was such an abhorred crime that its presence, even in the bodies of victims, could suggest guilt.

The unresolved death of Charles Bravo in 1876 reflects the idea that chemical ingestion could potentially criminalize the victim's body. Bravo, a seemingly healthy, happy, and newly married man in his thirties, suddenly collapsed after declaring to a member of his household that he had taken poison. He did not expire immediately but lingered between life and death for three days, refusing during his lucid moments to say who poisoned him or how he was poisoned.[10] Despite the inquest's focus on Mrs. Bravo and the disaffected housekeeper for the murder, much suspicion rested on Bravo himself. Theories that he committed suicide, or accidentally dosed himself with the poison he intended for his wife, demonstrate the degree to which his body became a site to read shifting beliefs in his innocence or guilt.[11] In the end, the inquest could not determine if Bravo had been murdered at all. It was clear that he ingested an amount of antimony "sufficient to have killed ten persons," but who had done the dosing remained unsolved.[12] Forensic science could establish that antimony was in Bravo's body, but no science could reveal how it got there. Only Bravo's own testimony, which he persistently withheld, could have cleared up the mystery. The Bravo case demonstrates one of the key features of the problematic detective process in *The Notting Hill Mystery* and *The Moonstone*, namely the increasing difficulty of parsing guilty from innocent bodies, especially when those bodies are manipulated by poison or when the chemical criminal can subvert forensics.

The other issue the two novels raise concerning detection is the determination of criminal intent. Poisoning, especially chemical crime, has a special relationship to criminal intent. In Alfred Swaine Taylor's work on medical jurisprudence, he notes that in poisoning cases the intent of the accused is paramount for determining a guilty verdict. Writing, "It would seem that the proof of the crime of poisoning should rest upon the *intention* with which the substance is administered and on the effects produced, or on satisfactory evidence that it is capable either of destroying life or of causing injury to health," Taylor acknowledges that poison's inherent paradoxical nature insists that intent be established when determining guilt, since many dangerous chemicals were used for beneficial purposes.[13] Critics such as Lisa

---

10. "Bravo Inquiry," 204.
11. "Theory of Suicide," 207.
12. "Bravo Case," 651.
13. Taylor, *On Poisons*, 8.

Rodensky have shown the importance of determining criminal intent in Victorian culture, and in poisoning cases especially there was a sharp divide about whether or not a poisoning crime could be committed impulsively.[14] There are few weapons more closely associated with premeditation than poison, especially when used slowly, repeatedly, and in small doses. The decisive acts of planning, obtaining, concealing, and dispensing poison to the victim all suggest willful execution. Poison is often grouped as a class apart from other kinds of crimes that could admit mitigating factors:

> The murder by the hand of violence is bad enough, but such murders may be sometimes as much the effect of accident as of design—a hasty blow, not meant to kill, a violent passion under irritation, a momentary madness, not excusable because not controlled, but still raising some regret—not sympathy—for the committer, that he had not thought, reflected, cooled his temper, had not forborne. But the poisoner has been hated in all ages—and there is *no* security from his malice, his revenge.[15]

Passion, this writer suggests, has no place in poisoning crimes. Poison's reputation as a premeditated murder that required a certain amount of planning and skill made it difficult to accept that the insane, hypnotized, somnambulant, or hysterical could commit this type of crime. Even murders by large, single doses of poison were usually attributed to the criminal's ignorance and not factors like passion or insanity, which would mitigate premeditation. The link between poisoning and conscious premeditation was so strongly established that some doctors flatly refused to believe that a person in an altered state of mind could commit such a crime. A physician who worked thirty years at a lunatic asylum testified in one poisoning trial that he had never encountered an insane man "giving poison in small and repeated doses. Insanity to take away life by poison is rare."[16]

Until the 1850s, the prevailing legal opinion was, "of all species of deaths, that by poison has been considered as the most detestable, because it can, of all others, be least prevented by manhood or forethought. It is a deliberate act, necessarily implying malice, however great the provocation may have been." However, this position would receive several challenges at mid-century.[17] The issue of intent ranks high among three poisoning cases that all asserted the innocence of the accused by reason of insanity. In his

---

14. Rodensky, *Crime in Mind.*
15. "Poisoning Case," 527.
16. Stephen, *A General View,* 398.
17. Russell and Greaves, *A Treatise on Crimes,* 507.

chapter on "unconscious poisoning," Joel Peter Eigen outlines these cases—the murder trials of William Newton Allnutt (1847), William Dove (1856), and Ann Vyse (1862)—and their defense strategy of claiming that they were "morally" unconscious of their crimes. The legal defenses for all three claim that their defendants were laboring under uncontrollable impulses to murder. In only one of these cases, that of Ann Vyse, was this defense successful. Vyse was charged with killing her two children with a single large dose of Battle's Vermin Killer as a result of severe depression occasioned by the natural death of a third child. Vyse's suicide attempt, along with her open admission of guilt and her strange arrangement and display of her daughters' bodies, gave jurors enough probable proof of her insanity to find her not guilty.

That Ann Vyse had nothing to gain from her children's deaths went a long way toward her favorable verdict, but the jury did not think the same could be said for William Allnutt. The twelve-year-old Allnutt was convicted for poisoning his grandfather, Samuel Nelme. The investigation of Nelme's death and the sudden illness that also affected his wife and daughter discovered that Allnutt—the only member of the household who had not sickened—had stolen several of his late grandfather's effects. Subsequent chemical tests proved that "a large quantity of arsenic had been mixed with some pounded sugar" and Allnutt knew well that his grandfather liked "to eat the pounded sugar with baked apples"; he later admitted to the crime as he was awaiting trial.[18] Allnutt clearly was guilty, but there were several factors that made an insanity defense plausible, including his age ("hardly twelve years old") and the possibility that he had inherited mental disease from a father who had died insane.[19] His mother's testimony about an early childhood head injury, his "walking and talking in his sleep," and his complaints of "hearing voices in his head" provided even more legitimacy to Allnutt's claim that he had "not the moral sense of distinguishing between right and wrong so as to make him responsible for his actions."[20] Eigen argues that Allnutt's defense "raised the specter of persons oblivious to the moral nature of their transgression—pitiable rather than punishable" and notes that the judge, uneasy about the potential Pandora's box of insanity defenses that could spring from Allnutt's case, warned the jury to rely primarily on common sense rather than medical testimony.[21] The jury accordingly found him guilty.

18. "Poisoning of a Grandfather," 144.
19. "Poisoning of a Grandfather," 144.
20. "Central Criminal Court, Dec. 15," 205.
21. Eigen, *Unconscious Crime*, 118.

William Dove was also unsuccessful in his insanity bid, which is unsurprising given that he operated more like a chemical criminal than a poisoner. Dove was charged with killing his wife, and the prosecution worked tirelessly to accumulate evidence that he carefully planned her death. During the trial it was related "that the prisoner and his wife lived unhappily together; that he wished to part from her; that [William] Palmer's case was talked of, and strychnia was suggested as a safe poison; that he thought it was a poison which was not discoverable; . . . that he did poison a cat; [and] that he carefully read *Pereira's Materia Medica*, to ascertain the action of strychnia."[22] Dove's meticulous research on strychnine and his test run on the cat situate him as one of the more thorough chemical criminals of the day, making his defense that he was an imbecile expressly difficult. As the prosecution put it to the jury:

> He gave four or five doses, too small to kill, but sufficient to produce great agony, in order to lull suspicion; and he opposed the *post mortem* examination of her body. . . . "Tell me, is this infirmity of mind! I direct your attention to these facts, and I ask you whether they do not all speak loudly for his sanity, and his capacity to deliberate and contrive, for his ability to conceal, and for his aptitude in bringing forward facts and circumstances to aid him in his scheme and facilitate concealment?"[23]

To counteract the prosecution, Dove's defense also suggested, as in Alnutt's case, that he was morally insane. Dove offered several pieces of evidence to support the claim, some of it shocking, such as the letters he had written to the devil in his own blood and his repeated reliance on a local "wizard" for advice. There was also sound medical testimony that argued Dove had lost "the power of self-control" and had an "uncontrollable desire to take life."[24] According to this theory, Dove was responding to impulses outside of his control that negated his guilt. His repeated poisonings of his wife and desire to remarry immediately after her death, however, stunk of premeditation and his claim of insanity was rejected.[25] The jury did recommend him to mercy on the grounds of a defective intellect.

---

22. Caleb, Observations, cix. *Materia Medica* is one of the first English works on pharmacology.

23. Caleb, *Observations*, cxiii.

24. Caleb, *Observations*, 19; "Report on Psychological Medicine," 272.

25. For more information on the Dove trial, see Owen Davies's *Murder, Magic, Madness*.

These trials show that it is particularly difficult in poisoning cases to circumvent the issue of criminal responsibility, although, as Eigen notes, "the most transparent of intentions—the fact of poisoning—in no way guaranteed a conviction for murder."[26] None of these cases provides a direct pattern for *The Notting Hill Mystery* or *The Moonstone*, but they do show that the idea of unconscious poisoning was circulating in Victorian print culture and that it presented a thorny issue for jurisprudence. Although it was rejected, Dove's defense in particular started a conversation about the possibility that the body might be guilty of the act, but the person could still be innocent (or at least not culpable) of the crime. Unconscious poisoning seems directly opposed to the idea that poison can criminalize even its victims' bodies. Yet poison's ambiguity allows for these contradictory interpretations—a fact that both Collins and Adams put to good effect in their novels. Individually, each presents a tricky situation for forensic investigation, but combined they attack the foundational logic of the detective process.

UNRULY BODIES AND FORENSIC FAILURE IN *THE NOTTING HILL MYSTERY*

The detective process in *The Notting Hill Mystery* involves a series of interconnected questions: Was Mrs. Anderton poisoned? If so, why is there no trace of poison in her body? Is Rosalie her long-lost twin sister, and is her mysterious poisoning death somehow connected to Mrs. Anderton's murder? And, if these bodies are really poisoned, who is the chemical criminal? As these questions indicate, solving the novel's mysteries relies on the ability of forensics to interpret bodies accurately. In *The Notting Hill Mystery*, however, the limitations of forensic authority are revealed by unruly bodies that resist standard interpretation and therefore circumvent the investigative process. The detective-figure Ralph Henderson struggles to explain the apparently weird and abnormal behavior of the two potential victims' bodies, which at every turn defy attempts to forensically analyze their actions into an understandable form of somatic literacy. He is left presenting his readers two unsatisfying alternatives: The first assumes no crime has taken place, but to do so would mean, as he explains, "ignor[ing] a chain of circumstantial evidence so complete and close-fitting in every respect, as it seems almost impossible to disregard."[27] The other leads "to a conclusion so

---

26. Eigen, *Unconscious Crime*, 126.
27. Adams, *Notting Hill Mystery*, VII: 618.

at variance with all the most firmly established laws of nature, as it seems almost equally impossible to accept."[28] Henderson's hesitance to support this second option derives from the two challenges it presents to mainstream science: It requires Henderson to both legitimate mesmerism—a practice he considers a pseudoscience—and also admit to the fallibility of toxicological testing. Henderson's inability to confidently address these issues means that he cannot offer a concrete explanation of the strange events he investigates. Instead of legitimating scientific forensic work, the novel shows that criminal investigation will fail if it does not take stock of its own weaknesses, or if it rigidly adheres to the anatomical paradigm of the standardized body.

Henderson is primarily inhibited by the fact that forensically cataloguing individuals becomes difficult—even impossible—when bodies do not act in accordance with normal scientific expectations. The strange mesmeric sympathy between the two sisters means that their unruly bodies intermingle in dangerous and unexpected ways, and contact with poison only intensifies their somatic instability. In order to make sense of Mrs. Anderton's death, Henderson presents an unusual theory: Mrs. Anderton has been murdered through the mesmeric transmission of poison. This theory, however, is problematic because it relies on a system not accepted by mainstream science—or even by Henderson himself.[29] In his introductory statement, Henderson almost apologizes for his reliance on "what is called Mesmeric Agency" and states, "Those indeed, who are so unfortunate as to be the victims of this delusion, would doubtless find in it a simple, though terrible, solution to the mystery we are endeavouring to solve."[30] He insists "that I would rather admit my own researches to have been baffled by an illusory coincidence, than lay myself open to the imputation of giving the slightest credit to that impudent imposture."[31] Yet only a few sentences after labeling mesmerism "a delusion," Henderson calls it "a true, though most mysterious law of Nature," and he even buttresses his theory with outside evidence.[32] He includes in his report an extract from *The Zoïst* that supposedly inspired the baron to commit mesmeric murder. The article, which is an actual transcription of an 1854 piece by R. A. F. Barrett entitled "Mesmeric cure of a lady who had been twelve years in the horizontal position with extreme suffer-

---

28. Adams, *Notting Hill Mystery*, VII: 618.
29. See Alison Winter's book *Mesmerized* for more information about attitudes toward mesmerism in the nineteenth century.
30. Adams, *Notting Hill Mystery*, VII: 618.
31. Adams, *Notting Hill Mystery*, VII: 618.
32. Adams, *Notting Hill Mystery*, VII: 619.

ing," claims the author "fed" a hypnotized female patient by eating some food himself:

> I kept her asleep for an hour and three quarters; during the time I ate something for her. She said [the woman can see what is happening in her own body], "Before you ate my stomach was contracted, and had a queer sort of moisture in it; now the stomach is its full size, and does not look shrunk, and part of the moisture is gone."
> I: "But you could not get nourishment so."
> A: "Yes, I could get all my system wants."[33]

Henderson suggests that the poison that killed Mrs. Anderton worked in the same manner as the food from this example. One twin (Rosalie) was dosed with the deadly chemical, while the other, weaker sister (Gertrude) slowly died from the effects. In order for this theory to work, he must confirm mesmerism as a valid practice, yet Henderson wavers on this point in the course of his narrative and often questions the legitimacy of hypnotic influence.

The Notting Hill Mystery thus takes an awkward position toward the practice of mesmerism. In the process of exploring the possibility of hypnotic crime, the novel comes to the uneasy conclusion that some bodies—in this case, Rosalie's and Gertrude's—are more susceptible to mesmeric influence than others. The novel therefore constructs an opposition between normal bodies and mesmerically influenced unruly ones. Many nineteenth-century experts in hypnotism asserted that the percentage of the population prone to the trance state was small, and the amount of people predisposed to hypnotic suggestion was even smaller. To assuage public fears, many proponents of mesmerism were "anxious to emphasise" that susceptible people "are rare, instead of representative."[34] A major factor in determining susceptibility was the nervous constitution of the proposed subject; the more sensitive or hysterical the person, the more likely they would be a good subject. Adams frames both Mr. and Mrs. Anderton as "nervous," with a predilection for trying the newest and most fashionable cures their fortune can afford. While taking the water cure at Malvern, "where the science seems particularly in vogue," they first experiment with mesmerism.[35] Mr. Anderton does not feel any benefits, but Mrs. Anderton becomes an enthusiastic endorser of its curative properties:

---

33. Barrett, "Mesmeric Cure of a Lady," 232.
34. Kingsbury, "Hypnotism, Crime, and the Doctors," 147.
35. Adams, *Notting Hill Mystery*, VII: 646.

On Mr. Anderton the only result seems to have been the inducing of such a state of irritation as might not unreasonably have been expected from so nervously excitable a temperament, in presence of the "manipulations" to which the votaries of mesmerism are subjected. In the case of Mrs. Anderton, however, the result was, or was supposed to be, different. Whether from some natural cause that, at the time, escaped attention, or whether solely from that force of imagination from which such surprising results are often found to arise, I cannot of course say; but it is certain that some short time after the mesmeric "séances" had commenced, a decided though slight improvement was perceptible.[36]

The direct contrast of the different experiences of the husband and wife illustrates that Mrs. Anderton alone is sensitive to the manipulations of the mesmerist. Although Henderson is reticent to believe in the legitimacy of her reaction, he also admits that he "cannot of course say" whether or not her improvement was "a force of [her] imagination" alone. Henderson's inability to discount the effects of mesmerism leaves open the possibility that Mrs. Anderton's body lacks discreteness and could be manipulated by an outside force. This susceptibility to mesmerism places her into a unique category and indicates that if investigative processes are to work, each case (and each body) must be regarded as unique and not standardized.

Unfortunately for an investigative framework that wants to rely on the standardization of bodies, the twins are consistently coded as somatically entangled. This most obviously manifests in the strange spiritual sympathy that connects their bodies. It was not unusual for the Victorians to comment upon the supposed sympathy between twins, and cases of twins who, "although at a considerable distance from each other," experienced "the same malady at the same time, and ran precisely the same course" were not unheard of.[37] In *The Notting Hill Mystery*, the "wonderful sympathy" of the twins is "even more physical than mental," indicating that their connection is primarily somatic, rather than psychological or spiritual.[38] Illness particularly demonstrates their sympathetic link, for both girls are "sadly nervous" and "every little ailment that affects the one is immediately felt by the other also."[39] Even after gypsies kidnap Rosalie, the somatic tie between the girls seems to continue. Gertrude is "subject from time to time to fits of illness to which it is often difficult to assign any sufficient cause, and which after a

---

36. Adams, *Notting Hill Mystery*, VII: 646.
37. Tuttle, *Arcana of Nature*, 133.
38. Adams, *Notting Hill Mystery*, VII: 621.
39. Adams, *Notting Hill Mystery*, VII: 621.

while disappear as strangely as they arose," while Rosalie also "sometimes felt ill, and did not know why."[40]

Upon reaching adulthood, the connection between the two sisters most evidently manifests in their mesmeric compatibility. After Mrs. Anderton's relatives object to the impropriety of the baron working directly on her, he brings in Rosalie to act as a conduit for his mesmeric powers. Mrs. Anderton appears to improve even more rapidly after the introduction of Rosalie, and she seems to recognize that there is a strange link that ties her body to that of the baron's assistant:

> Between these very different persons, however, if we are to credit the enclosed letters, such a "sympathy" sprang up as would, on all ordinary hypotheses, be perfectly unaccountable. Mrs. Anderton could feel—or imagined that she felt—the approach of Mademoiselle Rosalie even before she entered the room; the mere touch of her hand seemed to afford immediate benefit, and within a very few weeks she became perfectly convalescent, and stronger than she had ever been before.[41]

Henderson describes this sympathetic link as "perfectly unaccountable" to "ordinary" medical theories—their bodies are not separate, but permeable and connected—making the task of analyzing, cataloging, and interpreting difficult. Henderson's investigative practice wants to operate upon the theory that all bodies are discrete and inherently similar. The twins' bodies, however, challenge the paradigm of anatomical forensics by providing examples of strange bodies that act in radically different ways. The human body's variability shows the weak point of a forensic technique that relies upon its consistency.

If trying to unravel how mesmerism factors into these crimes is not difficult enough, an imperfect system of toxicological testing, a crucial component for determining the presence of chemical crime, compounds the investigative obstructions offered by the unruly body. In *The Notting Hill Mystery*, there are several incidents that could be categorized as chemical crimes, including Mrs. Anderton's death, Rosalie's repeated poisoning by antimony, and finally Rosalie's suicide. None of these potential chemical crimes are easy for Henderson to solve and each resists straightforward forensic legibility. For example, based solely on her symptoms, it seems clear that Gertrude Anderton was a victim of poisoning by antimony (also called

---

40. Adams, *Notting Hill Mystery*, VII: 622, VIII: 49.
41. Adams, *Notting Hill Mystery*, VII: 647.

tartar emetic). When the doctor first arrives, she is vomiting and "her hands and feet were both quite chilly."[42] She continues "retching with unabated violence for more than an hour" and has "violent pains and great swelling of the *epigastrium*."[43] She also "perspire[s] profusely . . . accompanied with great purging [diarrhea] and severe cramps both in the stomach and the extremities."[44] In his report, Henderson mentions the preeminent British toxicologist Alfred Swaine Taylor's famous book on poisons, and Mrs. Anderton's symptoms adhere closely to medical descriptions of antimonial poisoning found in Taylor's book. Taylor writes that among the symptoms of poisoning by tartar emetic, "there is nausea followed by violent vomiting," "pain in the stomach and bowels, followed by purging," "cramps in the arms and legs," and a "coldness to the surface" of the skin with "clammy perspiration."[45] Based on the similarity between Taylor's widely respected text and the doctor's description of Gertrude's symptoms, the question of Mrs. Anderton's poisoning seems like an easy one to resolve. There is, however, a significant problem with confidently declaring her death a murder: There is no trace of poison found in her body. Suspicious that Mrs. Anderton is being poisoned, her doctor makes "the strictest inquiries as to whether there was in the house any preparation containing this or any other irritant poison," but "nothing of the kind could, however, be found."[46] Furthermore, he has her food and "all the matters tested . . . by a scientific chemist," but this is "equally without result," and the autopsy also "entirely failed in showing the very slightest trace of either antimony or arsenic" in the body.[47] Baffled at the lack of forensic evidence, no one can conclude that Mrs. Anderton died from poison. Even with the strong indications of murder, her body is illegible to the forensic tests and the investigation drops. It seems that the forensic testing of Mrs. Anderton's body has been circumvented by a form of chemical crime that science cannot yet test, analyze, and control.

By making the poison that killed Mrs. Anderton invisible to forensic testing, Adams may have been referencing several failures of Victorian toxicology that occurred shortly before he published his novel. Two of the most famous of these are the lack of poison found in the body of one of William Palmer's victims, and the mysterious test tube number 21 from the Thomas Smethurst case. To begin with Palmer, toxicological tests run on

---

42. Adams, Notting Hill Mystery, VII: 676.
43. Adams, Notting Hill Mystery, VII: 676.
44. Adams, Notting Hill Mystery, VII: 676.
45. Taylor, On Poisons, 477.
46. Adams, Notting Hill Mystery, VII: 676.
47. Adams, Notting Hill Mystery, VII: 676, VIII: 33.

the remains of John Parsons Cook by the aforementioned Taylor only found small amounts of antimony, deemed too miniscule to cause death. Taylor thought that strychnine was actually responsible for Cook's death but discovered no tangible chemical traces of the poison. Ian Burney recounts in *Poison, Detection, and the Victorian Imagination* the scientific showdown that developed at Palmer's trial and "the searching questions about the standing of toxicology as a reliable bulwark against the modern poisoner" raised by the case.[48] On the prosecution's side, Taylor stated that Cook could have been poisoned with strychnine despite the lack of physical evidence, while the equally respected scientist William Herapath argued that strychnine was easily discoverable in forensic tests and declared for the defense that Cook had died from natural causes. Tests done on the exhumed body of Palmer's wife, who had also mysteriously died, were more conclusive: The presence of antimony clearly appeared in the chemical tests.

The Palmer trial at once showed the strengths and weaknesses of midcentury toxicology. In some cases, as with antimony, it could be implicitly relied upon and the chemical traces physically shown to the jury. The *Examiner's* commentary on the trial declared that forensics allowed the dead "to testify" the truth of their death:

> The dead woman has spoken, and science has presented itself as interpreter between her and the judges of the crime attributed to her husband. Not only is the tale of poison told with wonderful precision, but the poison itself is produced in court. The antimony in this bottle, says what remains of the murdered woman, was given me days before I died.[49]

This article sees toxicology as a way to level the field between perpetrator and victim. Bodies can communicate the truth through the voice of science, long after they have been in the grave. As Burney notes, "*The Examiner* thus insisted that bodies, through the offices of toxicological expertise, could be made to testify not as a matter of superstition but as a matter of science."[50] Nevertheless, the absence of strychnine in Cook's body revealed several problems with the state of Victorian toxicology.

Mrs. Palmer's speaking body was able to disclose its truths because her body acted in accordance with medical expectations and seemingly confirmed the reliability of tests for arsenic and antimony. Yet the dependability of these tests was to come under scrutiny with the trial of Thomas

---

48. Burney, *Poison, Detection, and the Victorian Imagination*, 158.
49. "Science in the Witness Box," 35.
50. Burney, *Poison, Detection, and the Victorian Imagination*, 132.

Smethurst, who was accused of poisoning his mistress. At the initial inquest for Isabella Bankes's death, Taylor testified that he found arsenic in only one of the many bottles sent to him for testing. Much to his embarrassment, Taylor was to discover that this was a case of bad chemistry, not chemical crime. Taylor used the Reinsch procedure, which uses copper as a reagent, to test the evidence. The notorious "Bottle 21" containing potassium chlorate kept dissolving the copper gauze needed for the test, so he added more until the solution was saturated. Only then did a deposit of arsenic appear. At the subsequent trial, Taylor admitted that his copper gauze had been impure, and that he had, in fact, found no trace of poison in any of the samples sent for his analysis. Taylor's revelation that his apparatus was unreliable caused a furor in the medical community. Defenders of toxicology insisted upon the legitimacy of its tests, while many others, like the *British Medical Journal*, concluded, "we are very far from having reduced Chemistry to an exact science."[51] The Smethurst case demonstrates the fallibility of toxicology and raises questions about the testimonial body. What if bodies give false testimony, or do not speak the same dialect as science? What if the testing process can be subverted or is flawed? What happens if poison is expected, but not found?

The Notting Hill Mystery takes up these questions, first with Mrs. Anderton's death, and later with Rosalie's repeated illnesses. Only once, in the case of Rosalie's initial attack, does a third party (Dr. Jones) confirm the presence of poison in a victim. Since Rosalie has all the symptoms of poisoning, including vomiting, purging, cold perspiration, and cramping, Jones believes that she has consumed an irritant chemical. When Jones (significantly, with the help of the baron) "applied the usual tests viz., nitric acid, ferrocyanide of potassium, and hydrosulphuret of ammonia" to the "portions of the vomited and excreted matter, and also a portion of the arrow-root in which the tartarised antimony was supposed to have been administered," he "succeeded in ascertaining beyond doubt the presence of antimony in all three."[52] That Rosalie was poisoned seems assured, but it still is an unusual case because the doctor "cannot account for the violent action of so small a quantity" given to her but admits, "the action of antimony varies greatly with different constitutions."[53] The unexpected forensic results can be read in two ways: First, Rosalie perhaps has a constitution particularly sensitive to antimony (which is supported by the text's framing of her body as unruly), and second, the baron might have rigged the sample to reduce the

---

51. "Trial of Thomas Smethurst," 703.
52. Adams, *Notting Hill Mystery*, VII: 704.
53. Adams, *Notting Hill Mystery*, VII: 704.

amount of poison discovered. The smaller dose of antimony is a critical component in making his story—that the maid gave Rosalie a small amount of emetic as a trick—plausible and allows him to avoid a criminal inquest (the maid later retracts her confession and states that she was blackmailed into making it). Whichever reading one supports, both question the efficacy of forensic toxicology to reveal crime. Rosalie either has a body so sensitive to antimony that she can be poisoned with a dose considered medicinal, thus protecting her poisoner from prosecution, or the baron is able to manipulate the forensic tests and therefore avoid legal inquiries.

Henderson is able to supply more convincing evidence that the baron purposefully manipulates forensic testing when it comes to Rosalie's later illnesses. She experiences the same symptoms—"nausea, vomiting, tendency to diarrhoea, profuse perspiration, and general debility. Pulse low, 100. Spirits depressed. Burning pain in stomach—abdomen tender on pressure. Tongue discoloured"—that she experienced during her confirmed poisoning.[54] Again, her symptoms closely mimic Taylor's account of tartar emetic poisoning, which outlines what sufferers experience, including "a violent burning pain in the epigastric region, followed by nausea, vomiting, profuse diarrhoea and syncope. The pulse is small and rapid, sometimes imperceptible; the skin cold, and covered with a clammy perspiration; and the respiration painful."[55] As with Mrs. Anderton's illness, it should be straightforward, forensically speaking, to confirm that Rosalie is poisoned; yet, as in the case of Mrs. Anderton, there is no trace of poison in her body. The novel strongly suggests that this discrepancy is attributable to the baron's involvement in the forensic process. Unsuspicious of the baron, who presents himself as a concerned husband who also happens to be an "expert practical chemist," Dr. Marsden requests his help in performing the necessary chemical tests.[56] Marsden notes his lack of experience with forensics and states that toxicological testing has "not come within my line of practice" before.[57] The testing is completed in the baron's home laboratory and the results are negative for poison. When Henderson later questions Marsden about this forensic procedure, the doctor admits:[58]

> My own share in [the experiment] was limited to the observation of the results, and their comparison with those pointed out by Professor Taylor. I

---

54. Adams, *Notting Hill Mystery*, VIII: 5.
55. Taylor, *Medical Jurisprudence*, 174.
56. Adams, *Notting Hill Mystery*, VIII: 5.
57. Adams, *Notting Hill Mystery*, VIII: 5.
58. Adams, *Notting Hill Mystery*, VIII: 5.

did not take any special pains to ascertain the purity of the chemical tests employed, or of their being in fact what they were assumed to be. That is to say, when a colourless liquid with all the apparent characteristics of nitric acid was taken from a bottle labelled "Nit. Ac." I took for granted that nitric acid was being employed. Similarly, of course, with the other chemical agents. It never occurred to me to do otherwise. Nor did I take any special precautions to identify the matters examined. Others might certainly have been substituted; but, if so, it must have been one by the Baron himself. It was, perhaps, possible that he might have conducted his investigations, under such supervision as I then exercised, with fictitious tests, and it was quite so to substitute other matters and mislead me by subjecting them to a real analysis.[59]

The baron could have manipulated the tests in any way he chose, since his knowledge of forensic testing exceeded that of the doctor. Despite Dr. Marsden's strong assertion that he "had no ground for any suspicion," the text suggests quite the opposite: The ease with which the baron can change the results indicates that even if forensic tests are accurate, it is still possible to tamper with them.[60] *The Notting Hill Mystery*, then, questions the idea that the body can reliably testify in the face of unruly bodies or forensic loopholes.

CRIMINAL INTENT AND NARRATIVE SILENCE

The climax of *The Notting Hill Mystery* is Rosalie's somnambulistic "midnight journey" into her husband's laboratory, where, according to the Baron R**, her "unconscious hand" puts to her lips a "powerful and burning acid" that kills her instantly.[61] Rosalie's suicide ensures that her part in the baron's poisoning of her sister remains unresolved. Henderson's theory is that Rosalie's body is the conduit for the poison that kills her twin sister; Rosalie's body is, in a sense, participating in the crime. But is she guilty, or the innocent victim of an unconscious crime committed when she was under the influence of an uncontrollable force? Her innocence would be easier to accept if Rosalie, like Allnutt and Dove, did not have much to gain from this crime. The death of her sister insured that she would get a large inheritance that could raise her out of the poverty she had lived in her whole life—a motive that perhaps

---

59. Adams, *Notting Hill Mystery*, VIII: 5.
60. Adams, *Notting Hill Mystery*, VIII: 5.
61. Adams, *Notting Hill Mystery*, VIII: 91.

explains her endurance of the repeated poisonings. To understand Rosalie and her part in the poisoning, then, is a question of character; in order for Henderson to make sense of her involvement in these chemical crimes, he has to first establish her identity and then, through an understanding of her character, try to establish her culpability. But just listing the aliases of the lost twin—Rosalie, Angelina Fitz Eustace, the "Little Wonder," Charlotte Brown, Lotty, Catherine Bolton, and Madame R**—gives a striking visual representation of the confusion that attends both identifying her and interpreting her guilt or innocence. Indeed, the narrative's failure in situating her innocence or guilt is directly related to Henderson's inability to confidently assess the character of this twin. Is she a gypsy child or the lost heir to an English fortune? Is she an earnest and hardworking performer, or a drunk and sexually fallen charlatan? And, most important: Is she a murderess, the willing accessory to the baron's schemes, or, like Mrs. Anderton, is she a victim of his criminal machinations? Contemporary critics displayed discomfort with the fact that these questions of identity were never satisfactorily resolved in the novel. A repeated criticism by the book's contemporaries is that the characters were not well outlined or fully developed; one reviewer wrote, "the magnetic influence of life-like character and a well-considered sequence of events are alike wanting."[62]

Despite the lack of "life-like character," a significant portion of time in the novel is devoted to interpreting Rosalie—both in regard to her personal historical identity and her potential criminal identity. Through documentation and evidence, Henderson confidently declares that Rosalie is the lost daughter of the Bolton family. Rosalie *is* Catherine Bolton, but even with her identity established, the true nature of her character remains a mystery. Ronald Thomas argues that in the nineteenth century, Victorian culture shifted from a focus on character to the modern obsession with scientifically provable, somatically grounded identity; he identifies the detective as "the popular-culture figure most explicitly engaged in negotiating this transaction and monitoring this transformation."[63] Thomas argues this shift coincides with the detective novel's preference for forensic evidence over character-driven first-person testimony. Certainly, Henderson, as the detective figure in the text, admirably performs the task of collecting forensic evidence by assessing Rosalie's familial identity, yet the successful establishment of her criminality or victimhood fails. Henderson's ultimate silence about Rosalie's implication in the crime demonstrates forensic science's inability to determine *mens rea*,

---

62. "Novelettes," 178.
63. Thomas, *Detective Fiction*, 11.

since science can only prove what bodies have *done*, not what the mind has *thought*. Adams's narrative choices highlight the limitations of the testifying body, since Rosalie is the only character who does not have a voice in the novel, and the reader never gets a window into her inner thoughts, feelings, and motivations. *The Notting Hill Mystery* therefore refuses to privilege identity over character in the investigative process, revealing that early detective fiction resisted the shift that Thomas identifies and was more willing to challenge the scientization of criminal investigation than previously thought.

It appears that Adams's novel is responding to a contradiction occurring within the issue of poison and criminal intent after mid-century. On the one hand, the poisoned body could be the guilty body (as was speculated with Bravo's case); on the other, the body could commit the act of poisoning without the knowledge or consent of the conscious mind (as was suggested by Dove's defense). Adams recognized that the emergent genre of detective fiction was a natural site to explore these perplexing questions of guilt or innocence because it shifted the perspective of the novel from the criminal or omniscient narrator to that of the detective figure. This move makes the issue of criminal intent central to the narrative's project of revealing guilt, particularly as it relates to assessing Rosalie's culpability in these crimes. Adams presents a collection of documentary evidence from diaries, letters, personal statements, maps, and medical records, which purports to present an accurate and scientific review of events. When Adams was writing *The Notting Hill Mystery*, the use of this narrative structure was in its infancy.[64] Several reviewers of the novel noted its unusual form, and one critic even went so far as to accuse Adams of an "anxiety to reproduce some of the mannerisms of 'The Woman in White.'"[65] Indeed, as Maurice Richardson notes, "it might conceivably have been written as a pastiche of 'The Woman in White' herself. It follows Wilkie Collins' use of the multi-narrational form, but it imparts a streamlined brevity that is more in keeping with [the twentieth] century than the last."[66] The structure of the novel reflects the general trend of the fiction of the 1860s to use this form of narration, which limited the audience's insight into individual characters and therefore, as Adams recognized, could be used to comment on the ability of forensic investigation to determine intent and thus guilt.

Adams highlights the necessity of testimony by making it difficult to position Rosalie as a victim. Rosalie is repeatedly coded as criminalized,

---

64. The first critically recognized use of the form is Wilkie Collins's 1859 novel *The Woman in White*.

65. The Athenaeum, unsigned review of *The Notting Hill Mystery*, 520.

66. Richardson, *Novels of Mystery*, xiii.

beginning with her childhood association with gypsies, who, as Deborah Epstein Nord points out, "functioned in British cultural symbolism as the perennial 'other.'"[67] A band of gypsies steals the infant Rosalie, ostensibly because "her quick intelligence, and lithe, active figure, [would] make her only too valuable an acquisition to the band."[68] That the gypsies identify with and value the physical aspects of Rosalie's body suggests that she is othered even before her kidnapping. Indeed, Rosalie's "dark, gipsy-like complexion and black eyes and hair" are a "remarkable contrast" to her sister's fairness.[69] Rosalie's association with the gypsies forever codes her as a criminal, particularly because gypsies were linked in the English imagination with "primitive desires, lawlessness, mystery, cunning, sexual excess, godlessness, and savagery."[70] True to these stereotypes, the novel features the gypsies' enslavement of Rosalie and her forced exhibition in circuses. They eventually sell her to another suspect figure—Signor Leopoldo—for five pounds.

Although Rosalie can be perceived as an innocent victim of kidnapping and enforced slavery, the continuance of her stage work after parting with the gypsy band challenges the recuperation of her character and reveals how gender stereotypes further hinder this process. Rosalie first performs in a traveling circus as the "Little Wonder," titillating audiences with her tightrope act. Any form of stage work would have brought with it the taint of exposure and prostitution. Rosalie seems to have been a particularly valuable performer because of her "beautiful figure," which, one can assume, was displayed by skimpy costumes during her act. Along with her potentially scandalous performances, Rosalie also partakes in another vice associated with the theatre: alcohol. The statement of her friend, the dancing girl Julie, first exposes Rosalie's dependence on alcohol. Julie admits that Rosalie drank brandy, but protests that she did it only for medicinal purposes:

> She had bad headaches. When she was in that way, physic was no good, only brandy. Brandy took away the headaches. She used to drink brandy sometimes, but not like our ladies. I never saw her the worse for liquor. Her headaches were not from drinking. Certainly not.[71]

Although Julie claims to defend Rosalie's use of alcohol, her emphasis on Rosalie's consumption of brandy acts as a form of apophasis—Julie seems

---

67. Nord, *Gypsies*, 3.
68. Adams, *Notting Hill Mystery*, VII: 622.
69. Adams, *Notting Hill Mystery*, VII: 622.
70. Nord, *Gypsies*, 3.
71. Adams, *Notting Hill Mystery*, VII: 649.

only to confirm Rosalie's dependence on drinking by denying that she is a drunk. Due to injuries from a bad fall (which Julie proclaims were not due to her drinking), Rosalie transitions away from the tightrope into working at a music hall as part of a variety show that includes dancing, singing, and comedic acts. Significantly, her main contribution to the show is to act as a subject for a staged mesmeric demonstration. Not only do Rosalie's performances at the music hall associate her with the suspect arena of the theater and public spectacle, but they also call into question whether or not she is legitimately mesmerized by the baron. Rosalie claims to Julie that the baron's powers are real, yet Rosalie keeps performing even after beginning to work with him. For example, she is willing to act the part of the baron's mysterious foreign assistant by lying about her ability to speak English when she is actually fluent in the language. Even if Rosalie is legitimately mesmerized, it still does not clear her of suspicion. In 1851, *Blackwood's* called the ability to be mesmerized "disgusting" and chalked it up to the weakness and imbecility (or, one can assume, femininity) of the subject.[72] With all these marks against her, it is an uphill battle to read Rosalie as innocent.

The Notting Hill Mystery's incorporation of this narrative structure purposefully obstructs the investigative process. In the novel, every major character, save Rosalie, is allowed to speak through these various mediums of narration—yet Rosalie's voice is excluded from all these documents and neither her voice nor her inner thoughts are made privy to the reader. Therefore, without the crucial component of Rosalie's experience of the events, her implication in the chemical crimes can never be satisfactorily resolved. Henderson's difficulty in constructing a logical story of the crime is due both to the lack of forensic evidence as well as the narrative structure that silences Rosalie. Some critics attribute this latter failure to Adams's lack of mastery; for example, the reviewer for *The Athenaeum* wrote that in his eagerness to employ Wilkie Collins's narrative strategy, "Mr. Felix has lost sight of his master's finer artistic qualities." This critic added that

> a lawyer, accustomed to the labour of building up a story from statements and admissions hidden in a mass of ill-arranged and incongruous papers, may find in the author's pages the vague outline of a story that artistic manipulation might convert into a readable novel; but to less acute and less laborious readers, 'The Notting Hill Mystery' will prove an inexplicable tangle of words, and nothing more.[73]

---

72. "What Is Mesmerism?," 85.
73. *The Athenaeum*, unsigned review of *The Notting Hill Mystery*, 520.

While this reviewer certainly has some valid criticisms, I suggest that the narrative "failure" in *The Notting Hill Mystery* is not a failure at all. Instead, by silencing Rosalie, the novel draws attention to her importance in solving the crime and starkly demonstrates the value of first-person testimony; Rosalie's silence does not result in her erasure from the text, but rather serves to highlight her absence. Perhaps these absences and silences are what caused another critic to rave about the realism of the story; after all, real life rarely affords the coincidences, beyond-the-grave revelations, abundance of forensic evidence, and tidy crime scenes that characterize more successful detective novels.[74] Through this narrative silence and the novel's reliance on unruly, unreadable bodies, *The Notting Hill Mystery* demonstrates the shortcomings of a forensic methodology that attempts to parse out questions of criminal intent.

HOCUS-POCUS

Instead of resolving guilt like most later detective fiction, *The Notting Hill Mystery* uses the chemical criminal to demonstrate the weakness of forensics and reflect anxieties about the permeability of bodies to outside influences. *The Moonstone*'s interpretation of poison's destabilizing power is slightly different. While *The Moonstone* has a chemical criminal in the form of Dr. Candy, Blake does not become a suspected poisoner like Rosalie. He is, however, criminalized through his unconscious theft of the diamond. Collins's novel also focuses on how the chemical criminal can in turn criminalize other bodies, implicating them in guilt against their will. Blake's chemical criminalization is indicative of a change in the way the Victorians perceived poisons and the poisoner in the 1860s and 1870s. As we have seen with *The Notting Hill Mystery*, once Rosalie's suspect and unruly body ingests poison, it becomes implicated in the baron's chemical crimes. In a similar move to *The Notting Hill Mystery*'s intense focus on Rosalie's chemicalized body, *The Moonstone* spends much of its narrative energy interpreting Blake's body. It is significant that while his body is coded as unruly, it only becomes criminal once he imbibes the laudanum. The connection between the ingestion of poison and crime reveals the frightening power of chemicals to both permeate and radically change bodies. In these early pieces of detective fiction, poison has the ability to break down the binaries between guilt/innocence as well as criminal/victim, frustrating the project of detection. While in *The Notting*

---

74. *The Standard*, unsigned review of *The Notting Hill Mystery*, 3.

Hill Mystery forensic science fails because it cannot interpret Rosalie's intent, *The Moonstone* takes a more generous stance toward forensics. Revealing Franklin's intent when he stole the diamond is the whole point of Jennings's experiment, and it is successful in proving Blake's innocence. Yet, Blake's unruly body refuses to reveal all its secrets, and the experiment does not reveal the location of the missing gem; like the earlier novel, *The Moonstone* affirms the limitations of forensics and necessity for personal testimony.

This reading of the novel presupposes that Blake is both a criminal and a victim—something that few scholars have considered. Most, like Sergeant Cuff, consider the surreptitious opium dose in *The Moonstone* to be "a practical joke."[75] But make no mistake about it: Franklin Blake is the victim of a chemical crime. The Offenses Against the Persons Act of 1861 specifically criminalizes nonlethal poisonings, stating that "whosoever shall unlawfully and maliciously administer to or cause to be administered to or taken by any other person any poison or other destructive or noxious thing, with intent to injure, aggrieve, or annoy such person, shall be guilty of a misdemeanor."[76] The act references drugging someone without their knowledge, a practice commonly known as "hocussing" in the nineteenth century. The term "hocussing" derives from the victim feeling that they had been hocus-pocused or magicked into a state of utter bewilderment. The purpose of this practice was primarily for theft (although it could also be used for rape), and the typical hocussing scenario involves convincing the victim to consume a laudanum- or chloroform-laced drink (gin was usual for the lower class; brandy and water for the well-to-do) and rob them once they are debilitated. The cheapness and ubiquity of these drugs at mid-century made this crime economical and offered several advantages to the thief: They could thoroughly search their victim, make a clean getaway, and even reasonably hope that the drugs would cloud their victim's memory. It was cited as an ever-growing problem, particularly in England's cities, where thieves could commit hocussing and then disappear into the urban maze of back alleys and slums.

The Moonstone sensationalizes the traditional hocussing plot by modifying the expected outcome. Instead of *being* robbed after drinking his adulterated brandy and water, Franklin *becomes* the robber and steals Miss Verinder's diamond while in a trance. Franklin's shift from victim to victim-perpetrator reflects an increased suspicion against poisoned bodies. The Victorians no longer took for granted that a poisoned body was a necessarily

---

75. Collins, *Moonstone*, VII: 166.
76. "Offense Against the Persons," 100 24 and 25 Vict.: Sect. 23.

innocent body, and, like the Bravo case, accounts of hocussing can help to explain how poison became a criminalizing agent. The 1853 hocussing of Edward Holl is one such case, as Holl shifts from the victim of theft to a thief within the same relatively short crime report:

> Yesterday morning it was reported at Newport, Monmouthshire, that a great robbery had been committed at a low brothel, in a quarter of the town inhabited principally by prostitutes, and known as Friars'-fields. It was ascertained subsequently that a gentleman who had come to the town on the previous day, professedly to commence business as a coal-merchant, had at night gone into one of the brothels of the Friars'-fields, and, having taken some liquor with the women there, was drugged, became insensible, and in that state was robbed of a large number of 10*l*. Bank of England notes.[77]

Despite Holl being described as a "gentleman," it is already apparent that his character is not unimpeachable. He is hocussed after willingly entering a notorious brothel looking to engage in illegal activity. Most victims of hocussing were men soliciting prostitutes, and Lucy Williams suggests that many of these crimes did not get reported because "married men who had gone home with a strange woman from the pub often chose to 'lose' a watch or a few shillings rather than explain their circumstances to friends and family. Likewise, embarrassed students, doctors, and clerks who were hocussed while visiting bad neighborhoods or brothels chose not to come forward and have their details known in news reports or in court."[78] Hocussing had a particular stigma and signaled that the victim, like Holl, was somehow mixed up in criminal or otherwise inappropriate behavior. Accordingly, the hocussed sometimes found themselves under police scrutiny, as evidenced by the conclusion of Holl's story:

> Throughout the whole of yesterday the effects of the drugging were still visible on the countenance of the victim, as he strolled through the streets, observed by every one. The telegraph, however, by which intelligence of the robbery had been conveyed to other towns, was also made subservient to another purpose—that of informing the Newport police that, if they could secure the party, he was to be locked up on a charge of having absconded with 120*l*. from London. . . . He was at once taken into custody.

---

77. *Times*, October 8, 1853.
78. Williams, *Wayward Women*, 46.

Mr. Holl has made a statement, which, if true, will exonerate him from the charge of robbery. He states that . . . instead of coming dishonestly by the money, the fact was he had quarreled with his wife, drawn a check on the Bank of England . . . and, to avoid further collision with his wife, decamped "on the spree" with the money.[79]

Holl quickly morphs from pitiable victim to potential thief, and finally ends in the dubious position of irresponsible husband. As he is already coded as morally equivocal, it is unsurprising that the police would begin to wonder how Holl came by all those bank notes, but I suggest his poisoning also contributed to the suspicions against him. His body, still marked by the chemical assault, has become a shifting signifier, ambiguous and open to various interpretations—including interpretations of him as a thief. Poison allows guilt to operate along a chain, linking one body (the prostitutes) to their victim (Holl), who then comes under suspicion himself.

Putting Franklin's experience into the context of hocussing can help to explain how his body becomes suspect after its contact with poison, so it is curious why scholars have not discussed this crime in context with the novel before. Most critical discussions of poison in *The Moonstone* focus on the orientalism of opium and its close association with the Indian colonies. The foreignness of opium situates Blake as "othered" and symbolically links him to the three criminalized Indians. These postcolonial readings of the poison in *The Moonstone* certainly have merit, but they have perhaps overshadowed other factors that contribute to Blake's criminalization. And there are strong hints that Collins specifically evokes the crime of hocussing in relation to Franklin's poisoning. The novel does not specifically use the word "hocussing," but it repeatedly conjures its root, "hocus-pocus," such as when Betteredge refers to Jennings's experiment as "this hocus-pocus of yours, sir, with the laudanum and Mr. Franklin Blake."[80] This connection may have escaped observation before because hocussings were specifically committed to disable the victim for criminal purposes and Dr. Candy never intends to rob or rape Franklin. Yet it is still somewhat misleading to label his actions as a joke, since Candy's motivation for the hocussing is a dispute between the two men about the efficacy of the medical profession. Dr. Candy is described as usually "good-humoured," but Blake's attacks on doctoring during Rachel's birthday dinner put him "in a rage."[81] Indeed, Betteredge reports that the doctor was so "hot" at Blake that he "completely

---

79. *Times*, October 8, 1853.
80. Collins, *Moonstone*, VII: 90.
81. Collins, *Moonstone*, VI: 117.

los[t] his self-control, in defense of his profession."[82] Jennings is later able to reveal that in revenge for Blake's comments and to prove that medicine is effective, Dr. Candy secretly colludes with Godfrey Abelwhite to dose Franklin with laudanum. When parsing criminal poisoning from accident or mistake, motive is everything; as Sylvia Pamboukian points out, "it is not poison that creates the poisoner, but the poisoner who, by employing a given chemical in murder, creates the poison."[83] Blake certainly interprets Candy's actions as malicious, stating, "The trick that he played me is not the less an act of treachery for all that. I may forgive, but I shall not forget it."[84] The novel makes little effort to situate him as such, but Candy is a chemical criminal guilty of hocussing. *The Moonstone*, however, is not as interested in exposing the chemical criminal and punishing him (although Candy's illness and memory loss certainly could function as a form of punishment) as it is in exploring how chemicals can criminalize the body of the victim. The novel may not have a distinctly guilty chemical criminal, but it does have a distinctly *chemicalized* criminal. How Blake's chemicalized body makes the investigation difficult, and how Jennings tries to adapt to this strangeness, is Collins's focus.

THE UNRULY BODIES OF *THE MOONSTONE*

As with the crimes in *The Notting Hill Mystery*, the mystery of the moonstone's disappearance is also the story of a body: Franklin Blake's body and its strange reaction to opium. In *The Moonstone*, poison unlocks the strangeness and unpredictability of seemingly "normal" bodies. In her discussion of disability and difference in the works of Wilkie Collins, Kate Flint writes that the author "seems fascinated not so much by the *difference* of the disabled, but their similarity to the able-bodied"; my analysis builds on Flint's observations in order to investigate how Collins is fascinated not only by the similarity of abnormal and normal bodies but also by the inherent strangeness in superficially normal bodies.[85] The strangeness of these bodies makes it difficult to discover truth and reveals some of the limitations of forensic technologies that rely on the stability of the human body. *The Moonstone*, however, does not go as far in its critique of forensic science as does *The Notting Hill Mystery*, in part because Collins's novel makes a more effective

---

82. Collins, *Moonstone*, VI: 118.
83. Pamboukian, *Doctoring the Novel*, 101.
84. Collins, *Moonstone*, VII: 53.
85. Flint, "Difference and Disability," 154.

use of its narrative structure to buttress the scientific evidence discovered by Jennings. Unlike Rosalie, Blake has the chance to narrate his own experience and confirm Jennings's hypothesis.

The Moonstone develops an opposition between visually normal and freakish bodies in part through its detective figures. Although Blake's body eventually becomes the focus of the investigation, initially the novel's visibly freakish bodies are a major distraction for the detectives. Casey Cothran points out, "just as their bodies are disruptive to the narratives of normalcy embraced by Collins's fictional characters and by his living readers, the consequences of disabled characters' actions prove powerfully disruptive to the social spheres in which they move."[86] Rosanna Spearman, who has "one shoulder bigger than the other," quickly becomes a target for Sergeant Cuff's investigation in part because her deformed body readily marks her as "othered" and potentially criminal.[87] It also makes her easy to identify, and Cuff readily links her to the London criminal underworld. Intent on protecting Blake from suspicion, she manipulates their assumptions and allows the detective and the members of the household (and perhaps the socially conditioned reader) to suspect her involvement in the theft. She conceals evidence and prolongs the solution of the crime, but Rosanna nonetheless defies Cuff's interpretation of her as the thief of the moonstone.

In their separate discussions of disability in *The Moonstone*, both Cothran and Mark Mossman situate Franklin Blake's body as "normalized" and use him as a point of comparison for the strange bodies that populate the text.[88] Opposed to more visibly aberrant bodies such as Rosanna Spearman's or Limping Lucy's, Blake's body does seem to represent physical normalcy; after all, his body does not show any outward signs of disability or deformity. Yet Blake's body is linked to the novel's mystery precisely because it does not react to opium in an expected way. Blake's body is not outwardly strange, but even before the novel's denouement the reader is given several hints that its internal strangeness is lying dormant, waiting to erupt in a sensational way. In the opening narrative of the novel, Gabriel Betteredge's initial description of Blake destabilizes his body and situates it as unpredictable:

> While he was speaking, I was looking at him, and trying to see something of the boy I remembered, in the man before me. The man put me out. Look as I might, I could see no more of his boy's rosy cheeks than of his boy's

---

86. Cothran, "Mysterious Bodies," 195.
87. Collins, *Moonstone*, VI: 39.
88. Mossman, "Representations."

trim little jacket.... To make matters worse, he had promised to be tall, and had not kept his promise. He was neat, and slim, and well made; but he wasn't by an inch or two up to the middle height. In short, he baffled me altogether. The years that had passed had left nothing of his old self, except the bright, straightforward look in his eyes.[89]

The unfamiliarity of Blake's adult body and Betteredge's strong reaction to its appearance ("the man put me out") position it as subversive and an object for close examination. The complete absence of the formerly prominent aspects of Blake's physiognomy, such as the disappearance of the rosy cheeks, suggests that his body has defied (and will continue to defy) expectation. Betteredge describes a body that is "average" on point of height and weight, but Blake's radically changed adult appearance confirms that his body is unpredictable and does not conform to the usual rules. There is also something almost deceptive about his body's transformation because, as Betteredge puts it, Blake "had not kept his promise" to be tall. Blake's physical alteration is so abrupt that it partially unsettles and "baffle[s]" Betteredge, who only relaxes once he sees the familiar "straightforward" look in Blake's eyes.

An even more striking instance of his body's latent eccentricity occurs during the first and only meeting between Blake and Limping Lucy. Initially, Lucy, who is named and defined primarily by her disabled body, draws the most visual attention in this scene due to the "horrid drawback" of her leanness and a lame foot.[90] Once face-to-face with Blake, Lucy is able to shift the reader's gaze from her own deformed body to his, which she accomplishes by staring at Blake "as if [he] was an object of mingled interest and horror, which it quite fascinated her to see."[91] He "inspired her with the strongest emptions of abhorrence and disgust," and Blake attempts in vain to "direct Limping Lucy's attention to some less revolting image than [his] face."[92] Being situated as freakish herself seems to give Lucy the ability to see freakishness in others, even when it may be invisible on the surface. Lucy's interpretation of Blake's body as horrifying allows Collins to upset cultural expectations about abled and disabled bodies and hint at the strangeness lurking within Blake's body.

Lucy's delivery of Rosanna's letter leads Blake once more to the Shivering Sand, a geological formation that is the symbolic coalescence of the

---

89. Collins, *Moonstone*, VI: 47–48.
90. Collins, *Moonstone*, VI: 306.
91. Collins, *Moonstone*, VI: 499.
92. Collins, *Moonstone*, VI: 499, VI: 500.

theme of strangeness in the novel since, to use Tamar Heller's words, it is "that site of all that is hidden and buried."[93] The shivering of the sand is a naturally occurring but weird phenomenon that exposes the permeability of the apparently stable sand; underneath the surface lurks a deadly quicksand that draws in anything placed upon its surface. Because Rosanna commits suicide on the sand and uses it to hide her narrative about the crime, critics have often situated it as a symbolic parallel for her own strange and weird body. For example, Heller reads the sand as "an image of the female body" and positions Blake's unearthing of Rosanna's letter as a phallic act of penetration.[94] But Blake's body, too, is implicated in the weirdness of the sand. After all, his retrieval of Rosanna's letter is accompanied by the discovery of his own nightshirt—a piece of evidence that reveals the strangeness underneath the surface of *his*, not Rosanna's, body. Just as the "glittering" and "golden brightness" of the sand "hid[es] the horror of its false brown face under a passing smile," Blake's body also has effectively hidden its secrets underneath an apparently normal surface.[95]

Collins consistently hints that Blake's body is strange throughout *The Moonstone*, and its unruliness is finally revealed through his unusual reaction to opium. Like Rosalie's body in *The Notting Hill Mystery*, Franklin's body has an uncommonly strong response to chemicals. The twenty-five minims of laudanum that Dr. Candy gives Blake is a typical dose for an adult male, but his reaction is anything but typical. Medical experts agreed that sometimes people could have what Alfred Swaine Taylor called a "sensitive organization," or a "peculiar condition of the body, the reverse of habit, in which small medicinal doses of poisons, such as opium . . . seriously affect a person."[96] Taylor, however, attributes these reactions to mitigating causes, such as old age, illness, or infirmity, and it should not happen to a strapping, robust young man like Blake. And yet the laudanum, combined with his sudden cessation of smoking, causes Blake to sleepwalk—an event that is totally at odds with his past history, as Betteredge points out to him: "Walk in your sleep? You never did such a thing in your life!"[97] It is clearly the combination of two chemicals—the cessation of nicotine and the dose of opium—that not only reveals Blake's inherent strangeness but acts as a criminalizing agent when he steals the diamond in a drugged haze.

---

93. Heller, *Dead Secrets*, 151.
94. Heller, *Dead Secrets*, 149.
95. Collins, *Moonstone*, VI: 505.
96. Taylor, *On Poisons*, 101.
97. Collins, *Moonstone*, VI: 547.

Blake's chemical criminalization is troubling, but at least his unusual constitution can account for it. Collins, however, hints that Blake's experience may not be unique. In explaining the effects of laudanum, Jennings admits, "There are probably no two men in existence on whom the drug acts in the exactly same way."[98] If reactions to opiates differ with each individual, then Collins suggests that poison could potentially unlock the strangeness in all bodies. This poses a serious problem for a forensic system based on the idea of the standardized body, which even Jennings, who understands the variability of opium, cannot overcome.

FORENSIC SCIENCE AND THE CHEMICALIZED CRIMINAL: THE EXPERIMENT

The forensic project in *The Moonstone* has to grapple with two problems: It has to prove that Blake's criminalization results from his contact with poison and show that this was a unique and unusual reaction. Proving both is critical for Blake, since situating his innocence is just as important as recovering the diamond. Despite the complex conditions of Blake's trance, Ezra Jennings believes that he can exonerate him if he can faithfully recreate Blake's environmental and psychological conditions on the night of the theft. Jennings's experiment is the most literal way science is applied to the detection of crime in *The Moonstone*, and Thomas argues that the experiment reflects innovative nineteenth-century theories and demonstrates the efficacy of scientific methods in solving crime.[99] In the preface to the first edition of *The Moonstone*, Collins himself explains that he had carefully researched the premise of the experiment; he consulted both "books" and "living authorities" on the matter, and he cites the names of two prominent scientists—William Benjamin Carpenter and John Elliotson—within the pages of the novel.[100] Perhaps Collins felt the need to include this information because he expected that some of his readers would share Betteredge's and Bruff's views that the experiment is "a piece of trickery akin to the trickery of mesmerism, clairvoyance, and the like."[101] Jennings's experiment may be strange, but Thomas is correct that it follows the general rules and ideological foundations of science. Yet the experiment cannot be an unambiguous endorsement of forensic science precisely because it is so strange and out-

---

98. Collins, *Moonstone*, VII: 118.
99. Thomas, *Detective Fiction*, 67.
100. Collins, *Moonstone*, VI: 3.
101. Collins, *Moonstone*, VII: 79.

side mainstream science. It successfully exonerates Blake, but only because it tries to overcome the problem of the unruly body by embracing paradox, rather than standardization.

Jennings goes about setting up the experiment in a manner that is entirely in line with the scientific method. He first follows its dictates by attempting to reproduce the conditions of the original sleepwalking incident, believing that if these conditions can be met, Franklin will replay his somnambulism. His theory was not without scientific foundation, as many emergent branches of forensic science at the time, such as the practice of fingerprinting, assumed that bodies were stable and predictable over time. Accordingly, Jennings is "rigorously scientific" in his attempts to put the house in the exact condition of the previous year. He also is careful to put Blake "into something assimilating to [his] nervous condition on the birthday night,"[102] and he closely monitors Blake's withdrawal symptoms. In this respect, "admitted principles, and recognized authorities" would agree with Jennings; as he says, "Science sanctions my proposal, fanciful as it may seem."[103] By adopting modern scientific method to the unusual behavior of the unruly body, Jennings comes up with a brilliant solution to the novel's mystery—and yet the experiment is only *halfway* successful. Jennings does prove that Blake unconsciously took the diamond while drugged, but Blake falls asleep in the middle of his hypnotic reenactment. While this relieves Blake from any "guilt" in his theft of the diamond, it also means the gem's location is not disclosed.

Franklin's repetition of the night of the theft is the result of Jennings's willingness to adapt his science, and it is significant that the man who comes up with the idea of the strange experiment is strange himself. Coded as othered due to his racial identification (Jennings has a "gypsy complexion") and his nervous, "womanly" temperament ("some men are born with female constitutions—and I am one of them!"), Jennings is already familiar with the idea of the unruly body.[104] This is a man, Collins suggests, who is both outside and within mainstream medicine and who could think beyond the narrow parameters of the standardized body. As Jennings admits, although it follows the dictates of science, the experiment has no basis in real investigative practices and is his own invention. It could only have come from the brain of a man who could combine methodical detection with the variability of the human body. It is effective because it accommodates strange-

---

102. Collins, *Moonstone*, VII: 59.
103. Collins, *Moonstone*, VII: 60.
104. Collins, *Moonstone*, VII: 24, VII: 32.

ness, instead of trying to force conformance to a rigid preestablished set of expectations.

Yet, the failure of the experiment is also due to Jennings's refusal to consider the unruliness of Blake's body in one significant way. Acknowledging that Blake could have had a very strange response to opium is the key to unlocking the diamond's theft, but Jennings's refusal to believe that Franklin was given only twenty-five minims of opium undermines its success. Arguing that such a little amount could not have accounted for his midnight thievery, Jennings theorizes that Candy (who was tipsy the night of the party) was inaccurate while pouring out the dose and increases the amount of opium given to Blake from twenty-five to forty minims. His assumption is wrong, and by rejecting the idea that Franklin's body could react in such a strong way to so little laudanum, the experiment ends abruptly. Indeed, during the course of the experiment, Jennings realizes his mistake:

> A horrible doubt crossed my mind. Was it possible that the sedative action of the opium was making itself felt already? It was not in my experience that it should do this. But what is experience, where opium is concerned? ... Was some new constitutional peculiarity in him, feeling the influence in some new way? Were we to fail, on the very brink of success?[105]

Jennings's question—"What is experience, where opium is concerned?"—practically sums up Collins's point about the fallibility of forensics. When something as unpredictable as poison combines with "constitutional peculiarity," then an inflexible investigative practice will ultimately fail.

The limitation of investigative science is evidenced by the ultimate fate of the diamond. Unlike many detective stories, the novel does not end with the tidy restoration of the stolen object to its owner, and the three Indians prosper in their quest to regain the lost gem. This success is due to their employment, not of science, but of clairvoyance. Collins demonstrates the Indians' use of supernatural techniques early in the novel, when Betteredge's daughter Penelope sees the Indians use an English boy to predict the diamond's future movements:

> The little chap unwillingly held out his hand. Upon that, the Indian took a bottle from his bosom, and poured out of it some black stuff, like ink, into the palm of the boy's hand. The Indian—first touching the boy's head, and making signs over it in the air—then said "Look." The boy became

---

105. Collins, *Moonstone*, VII: 118.

quite stiff, and stood like a statue, looking into the ink in the hollow of his hand.[106]

The strange passes that the Indian makes over the boy, the child's subsequent trance, and his accurate answers about the diamond clearly mark these activities as supernatural. The Indians are not relying on scientific methods for tracking the gem, but rather are evoking the supernatural realm to discover the diamond's whereabouts. Significantly, what causes the trance is the same substance that results in the diamond's loss: opium. The boy stares into some "black stuff" that is like "ink," and after the Indians leave, "a small bottle, containing some sweet-smelling liquor, as black as ink," is found on the ground.[107] Opium is dark in color, thick, with a sticky texture and sweet smell, and it seems apparent this is the drug that puts the boy into the trance. In this scene, Collins presents some interesting doubling with the later experiment. The boy (who, as fair and English, could stand in for a double of Blake) is dosed (we do not know how willingly) with opium in order to find the diamond; Jennings's experiment with Blake does the same thing, with the exception that the Indians get at the truth while the doctor only gets at half. By comparing the two, Collins effects a subtle critique of forensic investigation. Powerful chemicals can provoke unexpected reactions in purportedly normal bodies, and only forms of detection that acknowledge this strangeness can effectively unravel the truth.

Far from establishing forensic science as the most legitimate form of detective inquiry, *The Moonstone* positions it instead as a useful (especially if it can incorporate experimental science), but incomplete, method for detection. Instead, forensic science must be accompanied by other methods, such as first-person testimony, to fully establish the story of the crime and account for the unpredictability of the human body. Unlike *The Notting Hill Mystery*, Collins does assert that certain scientific practices could perhaps assess criminal intent by demonstrating how Jennings's experiment reveals the hidden motivations of Blake's unconscious; however, it is also important to note that the narrative structure of the novel goes a long way to complement the findings of Jennings's experiment. Blake's first-person narratives, as well as the accounts of other characters such as Betteredge, clearly establish him as a reliable narrator and "hero" of the novel, thus making his avowed ignorance of his part in the crime plausible. Furthermore, it is not until Mr. Luker gives his testimony and recounts Ablewhite's story that the mystery of the

---

106. Collins, *Moonstone*, VI: 32.
107. Collins, *Moonstone*, VI: 82.

stone's disappearance is finally solved. Therefore, Sue Lonoff is correct in stating that

> Collins's truth—which in context involves the unravelling of a mystery or crime, accompanied by a full disclosure of the perpetrators' motives and methods—emerges from cumulative voices. The reader is to learn what happened through a series of accounts that gradually enlighten him. If false clues or erring accounts mislead, subsequent voices will correct the record and reveal "one complete series of events."[108]

Forensic detection plays a part in this process, but it does not override the importance of storytelling and narrative creation—the work of human witnesses—to the solution of the crime.

Blake's narrative confirms his innocence, but it is also important in another way: It helps reestablish his masculinity. Being drugged and having his bodily autonomy taken away places him into a feminized position, but his ability to speak and control the narrative reasserts his masculinity and is a privilege that *The Notting Hill Mystery*'s Rosalie is denied. Through his narrative, Franklin can be a constant presence in the text and assert his innocence, while Rosalie's absence places her at the mercy of reader interpretation. Franklin's narrative privilege does not keep Collins from highlighting the necessity of combining forensics with science. *The Moonstone* is deeply concerned with maintaining the human element—in the form of personal narratives and first-person testimonies—even in scientifically grounded forensic detection. Especially in the case of chemical crimes, or crimes involving chemicals, personal testimony is critical for establishing intent and therefore guilt. The human element can be admittedly unreliable, but so can forensic science that cannot negotiate the complexities of the human body. Through the unruly bodies, *The Notting Hill Mystery* and *The Moonstone* illustrate the limitations of forensics and demonstrate that early detective fiction challenges the science of detection. The seemingly rational genre that purports to operate through a binary system of scientific ratiocination is actually poisoned with contradiction, unruliness, and ambiguity.

---

108. Lonoff, "Multiple Narratives," 149.

CHAPTER 4

L. T. MEADE'S FEMALE MAD SCIENTISTS

Science Fiction and the Transformation
of the Chemical Criminal in
Fin de Siècle Detective Fiction

THE TEXTS ANALYZED in the previous chapter, Wilkie Collins's *The Moonstone* and Charles Warren Adams's *The Notting Hill Mystery*, situate forensic science as unable to understand, and therefore interpret, the unruly bodies under examination. Ralph Henderson's repeated resistance to his own theory of mesmerically transmitted poison is a good example of how these texts point out the limitations of Victorian forensic methodologies. *The Moonstone* and *The Notting Hill Mystery* insist that formal forensic investigation fails when its methodological framework is unimaginative and rigidly adheres to established scientific fact. By the end of the century and the beginning of the twentieth, detective fiction begins to feature investigative practices that are much more open to including innovative and even unproven science. For instance, Sherlock Holmes, the ultimate representative of *fin de siècle* investigative authority, finds standard detective practices insufficient. When he first appears in *A Study in Scarlet*, he produces a new test for revealing bloodstains and creatively employs a magnifying glass as a tool for detection.

Holmes certainly uses groundbreaking science, but the same cannot be said for his archnemesis. Moriarty, supposedly the "famous scientific criminal," is really not very scientific at all.[1] When Moriarty plots to kill Holmes in "The Final Problem," he comes up with very conventional schemes lack-

---

1. Doyle, *Valley of Fear*, 12.

ing in scientific sophistication. These attempts include running over Holmes with a cab, bashing his head with a brick, hiring a thug to beat him to death, and finally wrestling him over the side of a cliff. Moriarty does not consider using innovative science, like X-rays or biological weapons, in his plans to murder Holmes. Some of Doyle's contemporaries, however, created criminals who put Moriarty to shame and truly earn the epithet of scientific criminals. This is the case with Elizabeth Thomasina (L. T.) Meade's two series of detective short stories, *The Brotherhood of the Seven Kings* (1898) and *The Sorceress of the Strand* (1902–3), both published in *The Strand*. While these series depict science as highly adaptable and feature detectives who use scientific methodology for forensic purposes, they more often show their criminals using science in imaginative ways. The primary criminal figures in both series—Madame Katherine Koluchy in *The Brotherhood of the Seven Kings* and Madame Sara in *The Sorceress of the Strand*—are adept scientists whose employment of science is highly advanced, signaling that in Meade's works, the criminals are the ones using cutting-edge science.

The sophisticated scientific crime in Meade's short stories differentiates her writing from much late-century detective fiction that focuses on the genius of the detective-scientist, and illuminates her contribution to the continued development of Victorian crime fiction. This chapter argues that Meade's representation of futuristic science links her works to the developing genre of scientific romance or, as it is commonly known today, science fiction. The influence of science fiction on these texts can be traced both in the forms of science employed and in the type of criminal featured. The feminist possibilities offered by New Women meant that in the 1890s the female chemical criminal was poised to evolve into a villain that was much more sophisticated, and much more dangerous, than her predecessors. As Meade realized, it would take only the inclusion of advanced science to make her seemingly invincible, and she turned to the possibilities offered by the emergent genre of science fiction for inspiration. Mesdames Katherine Koluchy and Sara are undoubtedly chemical criminals, as within each of their criminal oeuvres is the frequent use of scientific knowledge to poison victims. Their mastery of science, however, eclipses that of their predecessors and indicates that they represent a new permutation of the chemical criminal influenced by science fiction. Indeed, their scientific prowess and employment of new technology is so pronounced that this chapter argues we need to read these women within the tradition of the "mad scientist" and explore the crossovers between early science and detective fictions.

Not much scholarly work examines the conjunction of science and detective fiction in the Victorian period. Instead, scholars seem to have shared the viewpoint of the twentieth-century science fiction editor John W. Campbell, who felt that the genres of science fiction and mystery were incompatible—at least until the publication of Isaac Asimov's works in the 1950s.[2] It only becomes more perplexing why literary critics have ignored pre-twentieth-century crosses between detective and science fictions when considering the number of texts that combine elements of both. Mary Shelley's *Frankenstein*—long considered the first science fiction novel—also features murders, investigations, and manhunts. Similarly, the early science fiction works of H. G. Wells, such as *The Time Machine* or *The Island of Dr. Moreau*, are structured by the mysteries solved by the protagonist. There is also very little in the definition of science fiction that would necessarily preclude some detective fiction from being considered a part of the genre. For example, here is Paul Fayter's parameters of late-century science fiction:

> While it cannot be limited to secular or future fiction, science fiction can be most simply described as the literature of social change as initiated or mediated by technology and science. . . . Science fiction not only reflected contemporary trends, but in suggesting new scientific and technical possibilities and applications, it helped create the expectation of change.[3]

Fayter argues that science fiction can be defined through its use of science and technology as an agent of change, or as an agent that reveals the need for change: "Science fiction both defamiliarizes (or makes strange) the world of quotidian life and encourages critical awareness (or cognition) of the world's underlying values, beliefs and assumptions."[4] Informed by Darko Suvin's influential definition of science fiction as the genre of "cognitive estrangement," Fayter positions late Victorian science fiction as texts that use speculative science to make the world seem strange, drawing attention to "the ambivalence of attitudes toward science, invention, women, scientists, and social change."[5]

Much in Fayter's generous parameters of science fiction is also applicable to detective fiction: Both genres feature new scientific technology, both defamiliarize the world, both explore social change. Why, then, do critics like Darko Suvin specifically exclude *The Brotherhood of the Seven Kings* from lists of nineteenth-century science fiction when the "cognitive estrangement" of stories results from their inclusion of speculative science and technology?[6] I argue that literary critics have, to borrow Caroline Reitz's phrase, created an

---

2. Campbell, "In Times to Come," 87.
3. Fayter, "Strange New Worlds," 258.
4. Fayter, "Strange New Worlds," 258.
5. Fayter, "Strange New Worlds," 257.
6. Suvin, *Victorian Science Fiction*, 114.

artificial "generic partition" between early science and detective fictions that is based on their supposedly different approaches to science.[7] The speculative, innovative science of science fiction seems to hold little kinship with the rational, disciplinary science of detective fiction. Yet, as the previous chapter has shown, science in detective fiction often diverges from the rational. This is another example of how a reliance on the rational-disciplinary-detective-scientist to define crime genres limits our understanding of how these genres develop.

There is, however, one glaring difference between Katherine and Sara and the likes of a Victor Frankenstein or Henry Jekyll: their gender. While it is arguable whether Meade's works feature the first mad scientist to appear in detective fiction, her stories undoubtedly feature the first who are women.[8] The Mesdames' femaleness means that they differ in crucial ways from their male peers, in part because their characterization is also indebted to earlier depictions of female chemical criminals, especially those found in sensation fiction. Meade's female mad scientists draw from the feminist possibilities of the sensational poisoner, such as her beauty, social sophistication, and business acumen, and combine it with the profound scientific erudition of the mad scientist. The blending of the female chemical criminal with the mad scientist completely collapses the boundary that was supposed to divide women from science, and Koluchy and Sara refuse to conform to conventional expectations about women, scientists, or criminals. This is highly disruptive to the project of detection because it makes the Mesdames notoriously difficult for the men tracking them to read. Repeatedly, the male detectives in Meade's series seem unable to grasp their motivations or unravel their criminal plots. Incorporating elements more traditionally associated with science fiction into her detective fiction allows Meade to continue to question the ability of the forensic sciences to effectively combat (and punish) crime. She creates female villains who, in the words of Ellery Queen, make their contemporary male counterparts "look like sissies" and can give any Sherlock a run for his money.[9]

Just as the female mad scientist reveals artificial generic boundaries, she also collapses the synthetic boundaries between the male realm of profes-

---

7. Reitz, *Detecting the Nation*, 68.

8. In her dissertation, *"Testing Reality's Limits: 'Mad' Scientists, Realism, and the Supernatural in Late Victorian Popular Fiction,"* Jennifer Sopchockchai Bankard argues that we should read Sherlock Holmes as a mad scientist. Her argument has merit, but it is also significant that Meade's characters use much more advanced and futuristic science than Doyle's Sherlock.

9. Queen, *Queen's Quorum*, 44.

sional science and the feminine sphere of domestic life. We have seen authors explore the breakdown of this binary before; chapter 2 examines early crime fiction's pessimistic view that tragedy awaits the scientific woman, while chapter 3 outlines Ellen Wood's worries about the creeping influence of male medical professionals over women's authority in the home. Reacting to the growing presence of science in everyday life, Meade's response is different. By showing how far Madame Sara and Madame Koluchy's poisons can infiltrate the heart of British domesticity, (or, rather, by illuminating how much poison was already there), Meade demonstrates the ubiquity of science in all parts of life—including and especially the home. The distinctions between professional science and domestic life break down when science touches almost all bodies in her stories, whether they are male or female, young or old, healthy or ill.

At the same time Meade shows the depth of science's permeation into daily life, the science she features within her pages appears mysterious to the layperson and is decipherable by only a select number of highly educated specialists. Meade proposes that science is everywhere, but, ironically, an understanding of its discoveries and operations is becoming less accessible to the public. During the nineteenth century, science had expanded and proliferated at an unprecedented rate. As J. A. V. Chappel notes, there was a "tidal wave of fresh observational and experimental knowledge" that demanded the creation of new branches of science, such as seismology and embryology.[10] As the sciences became more specialized, they also became less accessible and foreign to a general audience. At the beginning of the century, most educated laypeople could expect to understand the concepts of even the most cutting-edge science.[11] But by the second half of the century, this was changing, in large part because of the increased professionalization of science. Science soon became the province of specialized experts, who, trading their heavily jargoned findings in specialty journals, created a tight-knit community of fellow professionals.[12]

The mystification of science had a profound effect on the public's perception of the scientist and his experiments. When developing their criminal characters, crime writers were responding to these changing perceptions of scientific fields. In the beginning of the century, laypeople, albeit with strong scientific understanding, are more likely to appear as fictional poisoners. As the century progressed and science became more specialized, criminals became expert scientific professionals who move away from straightforward

---

10. Chappel, *Science and Literature*, 3.
11. Chappel, *Science and Literature*, 7.
12. Martin Willis, *Mesmerists*, 8.

poisoning into even more sophisticated realms of chemical manipulation; thus, this chapter shows the general tendency for fictional poisoners to progress from scientific criminals to criminal scientists. While the former figure embodies fears about the spread of scientific knowledge and the potential employment of science in the commission of everyday crime, the latter represents the perceived corruption and growing power of scientists.

Roslynn Haynes notes, "the master narrative concerning science and scientists" in the nineteenth century "is about fear—fear of a specialized knowledge and the power that knowledge confers on the few, leaving the majority of the population ignorant and therefore impotent."[13] At the end of the century, this gap seemed wider than ever. If the by-products of science are already everywhere, then Meade suggests that this trend of exclusion needs to be reversed and that the study and practice of science should be open to a greater number of people. Noting the inroads New Women were making in science and medicine, Meade explicitly includes women within this group by showing how a science dispensed and controlled by men is ill equipped to deal with the complexities of women's lives. In her works, traditional science often fails women, who then turn to the alternative offered by Meade's villains. The Mesdames bring a uniquely feminine perspective to their science that incorporates realms traditionally associated with women, like cosmetics, into their scientific practice. Meade sets the work of Koluchy and Sara in opposition to male-dominated mainstream science; the female-informed science of Katherine and Sara is practical, resourceful, and unfettered by the responsibilities of male science. Even though Sara's and Katherine's science is used for primarily criminal ends, its brilliance and forward thinking demonstrate that a female-informed science may have much good to offer society, if properly applied. Meade therefore breaks down the artificial opposition between scientific men and domestic women in order to show the small-mindedness of a conventional science that rejects female participation and suggests a radical revision to the practice moving into the new century. By doing so, she offers an important intervention for both detective and science fictions, showing, even more comprehensively than a novel like *Frankenstein* can, how current science fails women on multiple levels.

SENSATIONAL FEMALE CHEMICAL CRIMINALS

When Meade revised the female chemical criminal in the 1890s, she was not resuscitating a lost trope. Developing out of L. E. L.'s Countess March-

---

13. Haynes, "The Alchemist in Fiction," 8.

mont and Bulwer's Lucretia, the sensational female chemical criminal offered authors the opportunity to weave subversive feminism into their works. This iteration of the chemical criminal has the ability to explore how the restrictions of the domestic sphere, as well as women's lack of equal social and legal power, can provide a motive for murder. The stereotypical sensational female chemical criminal joins beauty to resourcefulness and cloaks her methodical crime under an attractive façade—demonstrating at once women's inferior cultural-legal status and the potentially dark implications of this inequality. Characters like George Eliot's Bertha in *The Lifted Veil* (1859) or Valerie de Cevennes in M. E. Braddon's *The Trail of the Serpent* (1861) are personally charismatic yet coldly scientific in the planning and execution of their crimes, using their beauty as a shield to disarm victims or pursuers. Building upon Letitia Landon's and Edward Bulwer's earlier chemical criminals, these sensational poisoners move science out of the laboratory and into the home. While the crimes of a Henrietta Marchmont are reactionary, poisonings in sensational texts are proactive and always premeditated. The sensational chemical criminal's use of science is not nearly as sophisticated as the female mad scientist's, but their beauty, criminal-mindedness, and social sophistication do provide an important pattern for their later counterparts.

Both Elizabeth Carolyn Miller and Janis Dawson identify Wilkie Collins's 1864 sensation novel *Armadale* as influential on Meade's fiction. Miller states that *Armadale*'s "correlation of makeup, commerce, and female criminality ... anticipates" Meade's Madame Sara's plots, while Dawson remarks that Meade's "characters are modelled after" sensational villains like Lydia Gwilt.[14] Gwilt, who is capable of "measuring the doses" of laudanum by eye "and calculating how many of them would be enough to take a living creature over the border-land between sleep and death," is indeed a good example of the sensational chemical criminal who combines charisma with scientific aptitude.[15] Her first foray into chemical crime, the murder of her husband, leaves "no evidence to connect her with the possession of poison," and while the examining doctors "positively declar[ed] that her husband had died by poison," they "differed in their conclusions as to the particular drug that had killed him."[16] Later in the novel, she is perfectly proficient at picking up the scientific breadcrumbs Dr. Downward leaves for her during a group tour of his asylum. After showing her a fumigation apparatus and expounding on the murderous potential of the chemical he labels his "Stout

---

14. Miller, *Framed*, 76; Dawson, introduction to *The Sorceress of the Strand*, 27.
15. Collins, *Armadale*, 359.
16. Collins, *Armadale*, 328.

Friend," Gwilt "knew, as well as if he had confessed it, that he was craftily putting the necessary temptation in her way" to combine two easily accessible drugs in order to gas her victim to death.[17] This gassing involves a careful incorporation of six doses of "Stout Friend" with "a certain common mineral Substance" at proscribed intervals.[18] When Gwilt's plan fails, it is not because her science is bad, but rather that she chooses to commit suicide after she learns she has been gassing Midwinter instead of Armadale.

Gwilt is free to grow as a chemical criminal because her personal magnetism allows her to avoid severe punishment for her crimes. In other words, as the private inquiry agent Bashwood states, "the Law has said her in the plainest possible English, 'My charming friend, I have no terrors for *you!*'"[19] Jennifer Hedgecock notes that she "uses her sexuality to disrupt binary oppositions between dominant and subordinate groups," and I would add that she collapses deviance and domesticity by bringing together the seemingly disparate worlds of science and beauty.[20] The result of these binary breakdowns is a questioning of women's place in Victorian society, particularly, as Hedgecock argues, the "hypocrisy of cultural ideals constructed by conservative ideologues."[21] While Gwilt's crimes are abhorrent, they are attributable to domestic abuse as well as women's lack of legal and financial independence. The motive for her first foray into chemical crime, the murder of her husband, Mr. Waldron, is the physical abuse she faced within a marriage that was practically forced upon her. Gwilt has few options other than to remain a virtual prisoner inside Waldron's lonely Yorkshire mansion when he "strik[es] her across the face with his riding-whip."[22] Knowing that obtaining a divorce, even when there is evidence of abuse, was difficult for women, many readers might have agreed with Bashwood's assessment that Waldron "deserved it" when he died of poisoning.[23] Gwilt's subsequent chemical crimes evoke less sympathy, but still highlight Victorian women's victimization by men. After her release from prison she is penniless, and, desperate to survive, she begins plotting against the family that originally abandoned her. Collins wants his readers to see that Gwilt is also a victim, both of the men who incite her to murder (Manuel, Downward) and of the men who abuse or abandon her (Waldron, Armadale).

---

17. Collins, *Armadale*, 517, 514.
18. Collins, *Armadale*, 517.
19. Collins, *Armadale*, 329.
20. Hedgecock, *Femme Fatale*, 142.
21. Hedgecock, *Femme Fatale*, 143.
22. Collins, *Armadale*, 324.
23. Collins, *Armadale*, 325.

It is an interesting question to consider why Meade, writing in the 1890s, goes back to the female chemical criminal of the 1860s for inspiration. It might be because a sensationalized real-life poisoning case in 1889 resurrected the same issues of adultery, abuse, cosmetics, and chemical crime found within the pages of *Armadale*. Florence Maybrick's trial for murdering her husband, James, with arsenic seems like another moment of life imitating art.[24] As a beautiful nineteen-year-old, the American-born Florence Chandler married the much-older James Maybrick after meeting him aboard a ship. The marriage produced two children but was not a happy one. James's business was failing and he had a number of mistresses, one of whom bore him five illegitimate children.[25] Frustrated, Florence began her own extramarital affair with a man named Alfred Brierley, a business associate of her husband's. After hearing reports of his wife's behavior, James violently confronted Florence, knocking her down and giving her a black eye. The couple meditated divorce but eventually reconciled. A month later, James started suffering from a gastrointestinal illness and died shortly thereafter.

During his brief illness, James's brothers became suspicious of Florence, particularly after reading a stolen letter she wrote Brierley. The brothers alerted the attending doctors, who speculated that James might be suffering from poison. Tests on his body fluids while alive revealed no poison; after death the autopsy discovered only a trace of arsenic, not nearly enough to be lethal. James's own actions could account for this residual poison, as he was a noted hypochondriac who dosed himself daily with a variety of drugs—including special aphrodisiac tonics made primarily of arsenic. Florence had also bought arsenic in the form of flypapers, ostensibly for the harmless purpose of using the arsenic as a cosmetic face wash. Nevertheless, making her own chemical preparations, which required knowledge of how to soak the papers in water to extract the arsenic, may have seemed a bit too skilled—a bit too scientific—and she was indicted for trial. The pieces of evidence presented against her, particularly the scientific and medical, were not on their own convincing, but the presiding judge made much of the circumstantial facts. Sir James Fitzjames Stephen greatly emphasized her affair, and instructed the jury to deliberate primarily on the "horrible and incredible thought, that a woman should be plotting the death of her husband in order that she might be left at liberty to follow her own degraded

---

24. The following account of the case is taken from Alexander Macdougall's *The Maybrick Case*, unless noted.

25. Robb, "Out of the Doll's House," 29.

vices."[26] Helen Densmore later wrote that the judge's actions in effect put "this unfortunate woman . . . on trial for adultery instead of murder," and despite strong expectation of her acquittal, the jury found her guilty.[27] There was an immediate public outcry against the verdict and petitions flooded the home secretary from both sides of the Atlantic. Florence's conviction was commuted from death to a life sentence and she would serve fifteen years in Woking prison.

Florence's case shares many details with Lydia Gwilt's fictional murder trial: an abusive husband, a lover waiting in the wings, a guilty verdict, a converted death sentence, and time spent in prison. There is one big difference, however, between how Gwilt and Maybrick escaped capital punishment. In Collins's novel, the "young buccaneers of literature" whip up the sentiments of "the British Public," who "rose to protest as one *man* against the working of its own machinery."[28] Collins suggests that men put the cogs in motion to free Gwilt, but in Maybrick's case, it was primarily women, many of whom were dedicated to the cause of the New Woman, who agitated tirelessly for her release and kept her name in circulation long after the trial ended. Disgusted by the sexual double standard the trial exposed, New Women saw an opportunity to get public sympathy for their cause. According to George Robb, "Maybrick's supporters articulated a new, more outspoken feminist consciousness" in response to the case.[29] The female chemical criminal's predilection for poisoning men had long associated her with dangerous feminist sentiment, but for the first time she was made a poster woman for British feminism. Unsurprisingly, there was backlash. Robb discusses the dark side of associating a convicted chemical criminal with the cause, noting "to imagine Maybrick as an active woman" was also "to imagine an entity to be feared—The New Woman as virago."[30] Imagining the New Woman as a criminal virago is exactly what Meade does with Mesdames Koluchy and Sara, and she makes full use of "the dark possibilities of female rage against men" that the Maybrick case inspired.[31] At the same time, Meade is also sensitive to the issues the New Women raise, particularly inequality and domestic abuse and, as we shall see, levels her feminist critique directly at Victorian science's contribution to these inequities.

---

26. Macdougall, *Maybrick Case*, 549.
27. Densmore, *Maybrick Case*, 25.
28. Collins, *Armadale*, 330–31.
29. Robb, "Out of the Doll's House," 29.
30. Robb, "Out of the Doll's House," 32.
31. Robb, "Out of the Doll's House," 32.

BIRTH OF THE FEMALE MAD SCIENTIST

Meade, who, as Janis Dawson notes, was "particularly adept at following literary trends," had no problem blending the sensational chemical criminal with the representative villain of science fiction.[32] In birthing the female mad scientist, Meade radically revised the ultimate symbol of science fiction's gender problem. Beginning with *Frankenstein*'s depiction of Victor's arrogant and obsessive probing of Nature's secrets and his fall at the hands of his creation, the distinguishing traits of the mad scientist have been a specifically masculine pursuit of forbidden knowledge.[33] Victor's literary descendants, from Robert Louis Stevenson's Dr. Jekyll to H. G. Wells's Invisible Man, have also been overwhelmingly male and repeat Shelley's formula of an isolated, brilliant male scientist who trespasses into the realms of forbidden knowledge and whose obsession with the pursuit of arcane knowledge ultimately enslaves them to the science that they sought to control. These texts do not unambiguously romanticize the lone male hero-scientist, and Brantlinger notes that the "nightmarish plot of the mad scientist often illustrates the dangers of scientific overreaching"; what Brantlinger leaves unsaid, however, is how peculiarly male these dangers are.[34] Whether their motivations stem, like Victor Frankenstein's, from a presumptuous yearning to pursue new knowledge, or if the mad scientist is like Dr. Jekyll in his quest to gratify illicit desires, the work of the male mad scientist is driven by an inherently masculine ego. The mad scientist usually attempts to frame his work as ultimately beneficial to society, and excuses his trespasses into Nature's secrets as a necessary step in the furtherance of knowledge, but as Anne Dewitt points out, these characters have a "dangerous tendency to withdraw from society and pursue questions that have no relevance to ordinary human life."[35]

Any critique of women's issues that these works make is from a standpoint of women's absence from, or victimization by, the scientific realm. The female mad scientist, who began spontaneously appearing in the fiction of the 1890s, incorporates aspects of the sensational villainess to revise this trend. She is born during a time when the New Woman and a handful of college-educated women scientists enabled Victorian readers to imagine

---

32. Dawson, introduction to *Sorceress of the Strand*, 15.
33. This is not to say that Shelley ignores nineteenth-century science's problematic relationship to women; her depiction of Frankenstein as a male scientist working to usurp the female realm of human generation clearly critiques a masculine science.
34. Brantlinger, "Victorian Science Fiction," 373.
35. Dewitt, *Moral Authority*, 167.

their villains as both scientific and female. Appearing in print a few years before the arrival of Meade's criminal women, the very first female mad scientist is the titular *Olga Romanoff* of George Griffith's 1893 science fiction novel, and she marked a significant step in the development of the mad scientist.[36] *Olga Romanoff* is set in a futuristic society that has been ruled for over a hundred years by the Aerians—a master race that has kept the world at peace through their monopolization of flying machines and advanced weaponry. Olga is a descendant of the Russian Romanoffs, whose ancestors unsuccessfully fought against the Aerians, and she is determined to resuscitate her family's lost monarchy. Using secret scientific technology, Olga leads a group of anarchists in her attempt to overthrow the Aerians. As a mad scientist, Olga differs in several significant ways from her male peers. While she brilliantly applies new scientific technology, Olga is not the inventor of this technology; instead, she works with information passed down to her from her father, Vladimir, who "had devoted his life . . . to the task of discovering the secret of the motive power of the Terrorists' air-ships."[37] Vladimir's devotion to his scientific experimentation, which he conducts in "the utmost secrecy in a lonely hut buried in the forests of Norway," aligns him more closely than Olga with earlier mad scientist figures like Frankenstein.[38] Like many mad scientists before him, Vladimir's withdrawal from society and narrow focus on his work lead to his demise because he is unable to recognize the betrayal of one of his workers and is subsequently vaporized by the Aerians.

Olga is able to circumvent the fate of her father, in part, because all the work of invention is already done for her. Her strength lies not in experimentation, but in the practical application of cutting-edge technology. In that respect, she differs from male mad scientists whose desire for world domination (if they have such a desire) is a secondary consideration to the primacy of their experimentation. For example, Griffin in H. G. Wells's *The Invisible Man* does not create invisibility in order to go on a crime spree; rather, he feels his "Reign of Terror" is necessitated by his self-imposed deformity. Olga's desire for world domination, on the other hand, is not a result of her scientific practice, but a reason for her to engage in this practice.

Olga's scientific practicality is responsible for her military successes, and a sign that she does not purely derive from the tradition of the mad scientist. While she realizes that she alone must lead the rebellion, Olga also

---

36. Sian MacArthur also identifies Olga as the first female mad scientist in *Gothic Science Fiction: 1818 to the Present*.

37. Griffith, *Olga Romanoff*, 22.

38. Griffith, *Olga Romanoff*, 22.

understands she requires help from other people to be successful. Therefore, instead of isolating herself in the Norwegian forest, Olga's first move is to distill a powerful poison and a mind-control drug that will allow her to steal an airship and jump-start her rebellion. The distillation of this poison illustrates Olga's generic hybridity, as it simultaneously highlights her vast scientific training while also linking her to a tradition of the female chemical criminal. After making "a series of calculations" not once but "three times over," Olga goes about her work "with all the care and deliberation of a chemical analyst performing a delicate and important experiment" as "she proceeded to weigh out tiny quantities of the powders, and to mix them very carefully in the little glass mortar."[39] Highlighting Olga's mastery of chemistry and mathematics, the text demonstrates her scientific legitimacy and links her to the mad scientist tradition that her father represents. At the same time, Olga muses upon the cultural implications of her actions, declaring, "If anyone could see me just now, I fancy they would take me rather for a witch or a poisoner of the fifteenth century than for a girl of the twenty-first," and she later notes that "in the light of that horrible flame I might have sat for the portrait of the lost soul of Lucrezia Boghia [sic]."[40] These latter passages markedly link Olga to previous narratives of the female poisoner, and as the scene continues, the narrative stylistically mimics earlier works of crime fiction in the way that it presents its female subject:

> The weird, unearthly light of the flame changed the clear, pale olive of her skin into a sallow red, and cast what looked like a mist of vapour tinged with blood across the dark lustre of her dusky eyes. It seemed as though the light that she had called forth from the darkness had melted the beautiful mask which hid her inner self from the eyes of men, and revealed her naked soul incarnate in the evil shape that should have belonged to it.[41]

In this passage's gothicized vision of Olga, exemplified in the red cast to her skin, her dusky eyes, and the evilness of her exposed soul, the connection between this female mad scientist and the female chemical criminals of earlier literature is clearly delineated. This passage in particular hearkens back to the description of *Ethel Churchill*'s Henrietta Marchmont discussed in the second chapter. As Henrietta creates the poison in her uncle's laboratory, she too is described as evil and unearthly and has a "supernatural appearance"

---

39. Griffith, *Olga Romanoff*, 54.
40. Griffith, *Olga Romanoff*, 56.
41. Griffith, *Olga Romanoff*, 55.

as she completes her chemical work.[42] Like Marchmont, Olga also hangs her poison vials upon a necklace, at once drawing attention to her femininity while also challenging the idealization of the Victorian woman. Olga uses chemical drugs, along with her personal attractions, to manipulate the men around her—a tactic that ensures her success but also demonstrates her departure from the male mad scientist. Olga does not spend the course of the narrative pent up in her laboratory, where she shuns human society to conduct her experiments. Instead, she leaves the laboratory behind and goes out into the world, using both her scientific skills and her physical attractiveness to further the cause of her rebellion.

Whether or not Meade was familiar with Griffith's *Olga Romanoff*, it is undeniable that there are striking similarities among Olga, Katherine, and Sara, demonstrating, at the very least, that Meade also found this combination of the sensational chemical criminal and the mad scientist powerful—especially for the creation of a master criminal. But the move from science fiction to the world of the realistic detective story means that Koluchy and Sara do not live in an alternate universe or far into the future. Meade takes the female mad scientist and evolves her to meet the demands of late-century reality. The Mesdames' warfare is not that of the battlefield, but the drawing room, and their everyday concerns revolve around developing their criminal schemes and avoiding detection. To that end, Koluchy and Sara make full use of their beauty as a means to manipulate others. Madame Koluchy, with whom the narrator, Norman Head, was once in love, has a face "marked by intelligence and power" and has "a beauty beyond that of ordinary mortals."[43] Madame Sara's beauty is even more pronounced. Sara is blonde and blue-eyed, and "her complexion was almost dazzlingly fair."[44] Her "face [is] refined in expression, her eyes penetrating, clever, and yet with the innocent, frank gaze of a child. Her dress was very simple; she looked altogether like a young, fresh, and natural girl."[45] Sara is not only attractive, but she has a "childlike" quality that argues for her innocence. Like Lydia Gwilt, who passes as younger than her actual age, Sara too appears twenty-five, although the text hints she is at least twice that age. One character (herself twenty years old) declares that while "no one knows her age," Sara "was bridesmaid at my mother's wedding thirty years ago."[46] Throughout the two detective series, Koluchy's and Sara's victims are beguiled by their beauty,

---

42. Landon, *Ethel Churchill*, II:326.
43. Meade, "At the Edge of the Crater," 86.
44. Meade, "Madame Sara," 389.
45. Meade, "Madame Sara," 389.
46. Meade, "Madame Sara," 390.

which effectively hides their criminality and even causes their victims to defend their honor and innocence. One of Madame Sara's male victims, for instance, proclaims that she is "the reverse of dangerous; she would help a fellow at a pinch. She is as good as she is beautiful."[47] When faced with criminal charges, Sara's physical attractiveness saves her: "She appeared before the magistrates, looking innocent and beautiful, and managed during her evidence to baffle that acute individual."[48] Although Sara's wit certainly had a hand in baffling the magistrate, like Gwilt, her almost childlike beauty acts as a shield to save her from prosecution.

Their beauty is just one tool in the expansive kits of Katherine and Sara, and one that usually complements their social skills. Both series highlight the importance of social relationships and networking in the commission of crime, and the two Mesdames display a Machiavellian understanding of social politics. Their engagement with advanced science does not make them disillusioned social outcasts, but rather strengthens their well-connected criminal enterprises. In a steep departure from the tradition of the lone and isolated male mad scientist, Koluchy and Sara interact with complex criminal networks. They are both highly courted by society and their criminal enterprises rely heavily on social interaction and having entrée into the upper classes of British society. Katherine is the "chief and queen" of a "secret society based upon the lines of similar institutions so notorious on the Continent during the last century."[49] The series follows the exploits of this secret society, which is far-reaching—Madame Koluchy has agents not only in England but also across Europe—and commits a wide variety of crimes, including theft, murder, and kidnapping. The success of the Brotherhood of the Seven Kings, as the organization is known, rests not only with "the fascinations and influence of one woman" but also with "the wide extent of its scientific resources, and the impregnable secrecy of its organization."[50] The strength of this network is apparent in "The Iron Circlet," the leading story for *The Strand*'s August 1898 edition. Madame Koluchy plays a sophisticated cat-and-mouse game with Norman Head, using her vast criminal organization to isolate Head and then attempt his murder. Knowing that Head and the lawyer Drufrayer are watching her every move, Koluchy places an open advertisement in the *Times* for a "first-rate Bacteriologist," which is answered by the celebrated scientist James Lockhart.[51] Fearing that Lock-

---

47. Meade, "Talk of the Town," 69.
48. Meade, "Madame Sara," 401.
49. Meade, "At the Edge of the Crater," 86.
50. Meade, "At the Edge of the Crater," 86.
51. Meade, "Iron Circlet," 3.

hart's research in bacilli—a family of bacteria that includes anthrax—will be used to create a biological weapon, Head warns him against Madame and follows him to the coast. In reality, the "bluff and hearty" Lockhart's "merry smile" belies the fact that he is really one of Madame's agents, and he carefully draws Head into a trap.[52] As Head lies helpless, surrounded by Koluchy and four of her agents, he miserably reflects on his gullibility in trusting Lockhart:

> But Lockhart—Lockhart, whom I had trusted! His name was well known in the scientific world. All men sang his praises, for was he not by his recent discoveries one of the benefactors of the race; and yet—and yet—my dizzy brain almost turned at the thought—he was in reality one of Madame's own satellites, a member of the Brotherhood of the Seven Kings.[53]

Hiding behind a mask of humanitarianism and respectability, Lockhart represents the extent of the Brotherhood's network, which has spread to even the "highest and most influential circles" of Victorian society.[54] Koluchy's social astuteness is apparent in the fact that she employs seemingly respectable agents, like Lockhart, instead of only the stereotyped lower-class criminal. In addition, Koluchy's organization is as effective as (and maybe even more so than) her male-counterpart Moriarty's because she is an active participant in her schemes, while Moriarty "does little himself" other than sitting "motionless, like a spider in the centre of its web."[55] Bringing her scientific expertise to bear upon the wider world is a central component of Koluchy's success.

The Mesdames' social manipulations demonstrate their intelligence, which, influenced by the New Woman, Meade expands to include scientific aptitude. Madame Koluchy is "a scientist of no mean attainments" who "has science at her fingers' ends."[56] Across the nine stories in which she appears, she displays familiarity with chemistry, anatomy, biology, and physics along with other branches of science. As for Madame Sara, her "scientific attainments were marvelous" and she "knows a little bit of everything, and has wonderful recipes with regard to medicines, surgery, and dentistry."[57] Like proper mad scientists, both women have elaborate labora-

---

52. Meade, "Iron Circlet," 6.
53. Meade, "Iron Circlet," 13.
54. Meade, "Bloodhound," 304.
55. Doyle, "Final Problem," 303.
56. Meade, "At the Edge of the Crater," 86; "Winged Assassin," 146.
57. Meade, "Talk of the Town," 68; Meade, "Madame Sara," 388.

tories. Madame Koluchy has "two laboratories, an inner and outer," which Head describes as "fitted up with every modern device, and excited my curiosity as well as envy."[58] Katherine's "magnificent laboratories," which are equipped with cutting-edge technology like electric lights and powerful magnets, are an appropriate location for her to dream up her scientific crimes. Meade expends even more lines describing Sara's laboratory, which is nestled within her home:

> There stood a polished oak square table, on which lay an array of extraordinary-looking articles and implements—stoppered bottles full of strange medicaments, mirrors, plane and concave, brushes, sprays, sponges, delicate needle-pointed instruments of bright steel, tiny lancets, and forceps. Facing this table was a chair, like those used by dentists. Above the chair hung electric lights in powerful reflectors, and lenses like bull's-eye lanterns. Another chair, supported on a glass pedestal, was kept there, Madame Sara informed me, for administering static electricity. There were dry-cell batteries for the continuous currents and induction coils for Faradic currents.[59]

The amount of detail Meade includes is unusual, as previous mad scientists' laboratories are only described briefly. Matthew Hadley points out that Frankenstein's lab "figures so sparingly that a reader may easily read over the several brief references to where Victor actually worked."[60] In contrast, Meade's rich description of static electricity, batteries, and Faradic currents legitimates Sara as not only a scientist, but a highly advanced one. At the same time, situating Katherine's and Sara's scientific spaces within the home indicates that their knowledge of the domestic plays a large part in their practice.

Sara and Katherine draw from a wide range of scientific fields for their schemes, but they particularly excel in medicine and chemistry, revealing the debt Meade's female mad scientists owe to the chemical criminal. Koluchy is "a doctor to have confidence in," whose "cures are so marvelous" that "the men of the profession are mad with jealousy."[61] Indeed, Katherine is presented as having access to medical knowledge that far surpasses the scope of late-century British medicine, and she can cure patients "where the medical

---

58. Meade, "Bloodhound," 307.
59. Meade, "Madame Sara," 392.
60. Hadley, "Mary Shelley's Literary Laboratory," 84.
61. Meade, "Winged Assassin," 139.

profession gave little hope."[62] Sara, too, offers medical services to her clients and "does what is necessary for them. It is a fact that she occasionally performs small surgical operations, and there is not a dentist in London who can vie with her."[63] They put this knowledge to use in their criminal plots, which often put a twist on chemical crime by combining it with state-of-the-art science. For example, in the first story in *The Brotherhood of the Seven Kings* series, Madame Koluchy schemes to murder an adolescent boy so his dissolute cousin can inherit the boy's money and title. The boy, Cecil Doncaster, has a weak constitution, and his mother consults Katherine for a program of treatment that will improve his health. Koluchy recommends a sea voyage under the guidance of one of her doctors, a foreigner by the name of Dr. Fietta. Head surreptitiously takes a passage on the same boat as Cecil and Dr. Fietta and during an examination of their berth discovers hypodermic needles containing "half-liquefied gelatin such as I knew so well as the medium for the cultivation of microorganisms."[64] After more investigation, Head finds out that the "infernal culture" in the needles is the bio-organism responsible for Mediterranean fever, which Madame Koluchy has found a way to make unfailingly lethal.[65] While not a traditional poison, the culture of Mediterranean fever offers a clever way for Koluchy to commit an almost perfect crime: It is just as deadly as arsenic or strychnine, and since it is endemic to the area of the world in which the boy is traveling, there is little reason to suspect that he did not come by his illness naturally. The relative newness of the technology she uses also helps mask her crime. It was not until the late 1880s that gelatin media were created for the culture of microbes, and not many people would have noticed the difference between the "whitish" material in the syringe and the morphine Fietta claims he is giving Doncaster. It is only because Head is already familiar with this new technology that he recognizes the "half-liquefied gelatin" and is able to foil her plans.

Similarly, in "The Talk of the Town," Sara attempts to poison Professor Piozzi, "the greatest and youngest scientist of the day," with a unique contraption of her own design.[66] Piozzi has made an important scientific discovery, although he does not realize the commercial potential of his work.

---

62. Meade, "At the Edge of the Crater," 87
63. Meade, "Madame Sara," 388. As Elizabeth Carolyn Miller has noted, the reference to Sara's willingness "to do what is necessary for her clients" suggests that she may offer illegal services, such as abortions. See Miller's *Framed*.
64. Meade, "At the Edge of the Crater," 91.
65. Meade, "At the Edge of the Crater," 91.
66. Meade, "Talk of the Town," 67.

Before he makes his new innovation public, Sara manages to gain access to his notes and "at a glance saw what [several men] have not grasped at all": that Piozzi has unconsciously found "a means of manufacturing artificial foods in a manner which has long been sought by scientific men but which has so far eluded their researches."[67] Piozzi's discovery of the "chemical synthesis of albuminoids" is at the absolute cutting edge of early twentieth-century science, but only Sara's female perspective can instantly apprehend the domestic application of the discovery. Sara needs to dispose of Piozzi so she can profit off his invention and attempts to poison him twice. First, she tries to kill Piozzi with a cocaine-like poison, which she mixes with his milk. The adulteration of a domestic liquid, and specifically a liquid linked to women, certainly evokes the trope of the sensational female chemical criminal who took advantage of her position as the caregiver of the family to slip her victim poison. Sara is foiled in this more traditional poison plot, however, and turns instead to a more creative form of chemical crime. She places a fake palm tree on the professor's lecture platform that has hollow branches in order to shower him with carbon monoxide gas. Like Koluchy's plan to poison with biological agents, Sara's noxious palm blends poison with science fiction. Here, as Miller notes, "Meade reclaims the popular, misogynist 'poison panic' for feminist purposes: in representing Sara's expert use of chemical poisons, she invariably emphasizes Sara's 'scientific genius.'"[68] Sara's use of a nontraditional poison means that she has evolved from a domestic poisoner to one who is much more worldly.

Meade repeatedly collaborated with the doctor Robert Eustace Barton to ensure that Sara and Koluchy were legitimate scientific geniuses. Yet some scholars have been dismissive of the validity of science in Meade's works. For example, in his survey of Golden Age detective fiction, LeRoy Panek takes an indifferent tone toward Koluchy's scientific aptitude. In his discussion of *The Brotherhood of the Seven Kings*, he posits that there are only "bits of science" that are "tossed in at the denouement to wrap up the narratives"; later, he writes that *The Sorceress of the Strand* stories "didn't contain very precise science."[69] I disagree with Panek that the science is just "tossed in" at the end, and interpret the science as more fully integrated into the story than he suggests. Panek's argument that the stories do not contain "very precise science" may derive from the influence of science fiction on Meade's works. Meade's science may not seem specific when she discusses the weaponization of X-rays or microorganisms because these were speculative enterprises

67. Meade, "Talk of the Town," 78.
68. Elizabeth Miller, *Framed*, 97.
69. Panek, *After Sherlock Holmes*, 180, 107.

and not yet scientific reality. Trivializing the science in these stories misses the impact that the emergent form of science fiction was having on detective fiction; it particularly masks the impact criminal, rather than forensic, science was having on the development of this genre. Even more troubling, it ignores Meade's vision of an advanced science shaped by the female experience of its practitioners—a science that in many cases exposes a need for the same reforms outlined by the New Women.

OUTSIDE THE MAINSTREAM: FEMALE SCIENCE

Seductive and clever, Meade's two criminal masterminds display the specific mixture of the chemical criminal and mad scientist that the earlier Olga Romanoff represents, but Mmes. Koluchy and Sara are better scientists and are more creative in their application of new technology than Olga. Men do not train Koluchy and Sara, nor is their scientific knowledge derived from men. "I do not hold diplomas," Madame Sara informs Druce, a fact that marks her as outside of the male-dominated professionalized sciences even while her scientific prowess is unambiguously acknowledged. These female criminal masterminds could only have been written at the end of the century, when the Victorian reading public could accept the existence of clever, scientific women. As Chris Willis and Elizabeth Carolyn Miller have argued, the New Woman certainly influences the construction of these female criminals, and Miller notes that Sara "demarcates the boundaries of new territories that turn-of-the-century women were on the verge of penetrating."[70] Along with examining how female science resists forensic legibility, this chapter argues that Meade's criminal women are a feminist creation intended to highlight late-century gender disparity and present women as the intellectual equals of men. Significantly, Koluchy and Sara are not masculinized like so many other fictional New Women; instead, Meade's criminals retain their femininity in relation to both their physical appearance and their scientific practice.

Katherine's and Sara's formidable scientific understanding is perhaps enough to explain their criminal successes, but the ease with which these women circumvent their detective adversaries is also linked to gender and their particularly feminized scientific practice. In contrast to the individualistic, highly regulated, theoretical science that is the realm of masculine science, the female mad scientist's work is collaborative, exploratory, and practical. Katherine and Sara apply their science to issues relating to women.

---

70. Elizabeth Miller, *Framed*, 100; Willis, "Female Moriarty," 57–68.

Through their practice of a specifically feminized science, these female mad scientists are liberated from the parameters of male-dominated science and question the ideals of Victorian womanhood. As Miller argues, Sara's and Koluchy's "principle feminist innovation is their depiction of science" because it "not only proves women can practice science, but also undermines the image of Victorian women as purely domestic."[71] Their refusal to conform to the rules and ethical obligations of both femininity and professional science makes Mmes. Koluchy and Sara better criminals. As the one of *The Sorceress of the Strand*'s detectives notes, "that scientific knowledge which Madame possesses, and which is not a smattering, but a real thing, makes a woman at times—dangerous."[72] Throughout both *The Brotherhood of the Seven Kings* and *The Sorceress of the Strand*, the female mad scientist consistently gets away with her crimes, demonstrating the power of female science to undermine investigative practices and revealing Meade's underlying feminist project.

To position her female mad scientist outside of the mainstream science, Meade compares Koluchy and Sara to her detective figures, whose scientific practice aligns them with the tradition of the male mad scientist. Both Norman Head and Dixon Druce display traits of the male mad scientist, including their social isolation and obsession with theoretical (as opposed to practical) science. After joining and defecting from Madame Koluchy's Brotherhood, for instance, Head "left the bustling world and found [his] solace in the scientist's laboratory and the philosopher's study."[73] Unmarried and isolated, Head "worked at biology and physiology for the pure love of these absorbing sciences."[74] The fact that Head's "researches were unknown to the world" is also suggestive of the mad scientist, whose work—whether through its accidental nature, like Jekyll's potion, or its Frankensteinian self-destruction—ultimately provides no real advancement to the furtherance of scientific knowledge.[75] One character even asks Head jokingly if he is working on "the Elixir of Life or the Philosopher's Stone," highlighting the fruitlessness of his researches.[76] Like the traditional mad scientist, Head is a "recluse," and while he uses his science in an acceptable manner by trying to stop the Brotherhood, his singular obsession with apprehending Kath-

---

71. Elizabeth Miller, *Framed*, 96.
72. Meade, "Talk of the Town," 68.
73. Meade, "At the Edge of the Crater," 86.
74. Meade, "At the Edge of the Crater," 86.
75. Meade, "Swing of the Pendulum," 244.
76. Meade, "Twenty Degrees," 529.

erine rings true to the stereotypical fixation of the mad scientist.[77] Head's counterpart in *The Sorceress of the Strand*, Dixon Druce is not a scientist by trade, but he too has an interest in science and has "the best private laboratory in London," where he "spent all [his] spare time making experiments and trying this chemical combination and the other, living in hopes of doing great things some day."[78] Again, like Head, the single Druce is situated as an isolated, unproductive scientist. Compared to these two men, Koluchy and Sara's science appears fresh, innovative, and intimately connected to *fin-de-siècle* life. Meade's criminal women are not waiting to do great science *someday*; they are always actively hatching new schemes and experimenting with new technology. Head's and Druce's plodding science is reactionary—they use it unravel their adversaries' complex plots, but they cannot achieve the scientific brilliancy of the women they hunt. Working within the rarified and theoretical realm of the male mad scientist—and unable to broach the ethical obligations of professional science—their work repeatedly fails to understand Katherine's and Sara's criminal schemes.

Another barrier to Druce's and Head's successful apprehension of the female mad scientist is that Katherine and Sara often commit their scientific crimes within the realm of specifically feminine concerns. As Willis points out, "Sara's closest associates are women," and "many of her victims are young women," most of whom feel they cannot trust their problems to men.[79] In "The Mystery of the Strong Room," Madame Koluchy successfully blackmails Mrs. Carlton by pretending that the remarried widow's former husband is still alive. As Mrs. Carlton states, "My trouble is of such a nature that my [current] husband is the very last person in the world to whom I can confide it" because it would mean the dissolution of her marriage and the disinheritance of her son.[80] Koluchy manipulates Mrs. Carlton into abetting the theft of a priceless diamond based on the threat of a forced reunion with her former husband, who had "subjected [her] to almost every cruelty."[81] Although Mrs. Carlton wished to resist the plot, she admits that Katherine "piled on the agony, showing me only too plainly what my position would be did I not accede to her wishes. She traded on my weakness; on my passionate love for the child and for his father."[82] Here, Meade highlights the problem with strict Victorian family laws, which offered women

---

77. Meade, "Twenty Degrees," 529.
78. Meade, "Madame Sara," 390.
79. Willis, "Female Moriarty," 57–68.
80. Meade, "Mystery of the Strong Room," 129.
81. Meade, "Mystery of the Strong Room," 130.
82. Meade, "Mystery of the Strong Room," 131.

in Mrs. Carlton's position little recourse. Had her husband really been alive, Mrs. Carlton would have been forced back into an abusive marriage that she could not legally dissolve and her son would become a bastard in the eyes of English law. When Head offers to help her, Mrs. Carlton tells him to "think of the wreck of my complete life, think of the dishonor to my child. Mr. Head, I know you are kind, and I know your advice is really wise, but I cannot act on it."[83] Head remains baffled by Mrs. Carlton's unwillingness to turn to the help of the law because he cannot fully grasp the horrible reality of women's inequality within the legal system. To Head, following the law trumps personal considerations and the solution is as simple as revealing the secret to Mr. Carlton; to Mrs. Carlton, legal intervention could mean her complete ruin. At the crux of the opposition between women's problems and masculine law is where the female mad scientist operates. As Miller notes of Madame Sara, her "genius lies in how she manages to criminalize or corrupt her female clients at the same time that she victimizes them."[84] Miller's astute reading of Sara can equally be applied to the way that Katherine manipulates social customs and the law to control her female victims like Mrs. Carlton. Significantly, the ambiguous ending of the story—Koluchy scientifically manufactures a special key to steal the diamond and reveals that Mrs. Carlton's first husband is actually dead—suggests that Mrs. Carlton was perhaps right to deal with her issue privately. The ending is unclear if Mrs. Carlton will face any legal consequences for her part in the theft; more important to her, the validity of her current marriage and her son's right to his inheritance is secure. Head's failure to catch Koluchy results from his inability to see beyond the law for a solution and his insistence that Mrs. Carlton play by rules that benefit men but not women.

Another tale from *The Brotherhood of the Seven Kings* series, "The Star-Shaped Marks," actively suggests that masculine science cannot adequately solve women's problems. In this story, Loftus Durham's child is missing and Head believes that Madame Koluchy has helped Lady Faulkner kidnap the boy. When Lady Faulkner is forced to show the contested child to Durham, he suddenly and without explanation falls deathly ill. His doctor notes that Durham's illness "is a mystery" and "unlike anything I have seen before"; the skin of the sick man "had a very strange appearance. It was inflamed and much reddened."[85] Upon Head's closer examination, he finds "star-shaped" marks upon the skin that "radiated from various centres."[86] This

---

83. Meade, "Mystery of the Strong Room," 132.
84. Elizabeth Miller, *Framed*, 86.
85. Meade, "Star-Shaped Marks," 662.
86. Meade, "Star-Shaped Marks," 662.

"weird situation" has Durham's doctors and Head stumped, with the latter declaring that Madame Koluchy "is poisoning him—we have got to discover how."[87] Head, recalling some experiments he witnessed, is suspicious that Durham is being poisoned with a "powerful cathode and X-rays."[88] He breaks into the adjoining house and finds "within a few feet of where the sick man's bed had been, was an enormous focus tube, the platinum electrode turned so as to direct the rays through the wall."[89] Once the machine is disabled, Durham recovers—although both Madame Koluchy and Lady Faulkner have disappeared and avoid facing justice for their crimes.

"The Star-Shaped Marks" certainly raises questions about experimental science and its potential weaponization, but, like science fiction, it also uses science to addresses some "underlying assumptions" of Victorian culture, particularly in relation to women. For instance, although Lady Faulkner kidnaps Robin Durham and is complicit in the attempted murder of his father, she is treated very sympathetically in the story. Orphaned as a child, Lady Faulkner is raised by an aunt who does not care for her and wants to marry her off as quickly as possible. Lady Faulkner is ecstatic when her future husband proposes, but when she tells her family doctor about her marriage prospects, he sternly tells her that she is "wrong to marry."[90] Lady Faulkner tearfully relates the secret Dr. Macpherson reveals to her:

> There is a terrible disease in your family, he said, you have no right to marry. He then told me an extraordinary and terrible thing. He said that in my family on the mother's side was a disease which is called pseudo-hypertrophic muscular paralysis. This strange disease is hereditary, but only attacks the male members of a house, the females absolutely escaping.[91]

He hands down to her a terrible edict and forbids her to wed; yet, she is anxious to leave her present unhappy circumstances and marries anyway. To her horror, she discovers that her husband's "chief reason for marrying" her was not love, but rather "to have a healthy heir for his house," and she feels trapped and unable to reveal her secret to him.[92] She has a son three years into the marriage, but Dr. Macpherson's prediction is correct and the child withers away and dies while her husband is abroad. Noticing that Robin

---

87. Meade, "Star-Shaped Marks," 662.
88. Meade, "Star-Shaped Marks," 663.
89. Meade, "Star-Shaped Marks," 664.
90. Meade, "Star-Shaped Marks," 660.
91. Meade, "Star-Shaped Marks," 660.
92. Meade, "Star-Shaped Marks," 660–61.

Durham looks remarkably like her lost son, she plots with Madame Koluchy to kidnap him and pass him off as the deceased Keith Faulkner.

Her motivation for the crime—to save her marriage, ensure an heir for her husband, and heal her broken heart—is a perversion of her female role and does not justify the child's kidnapping and the attempted murder of his father, but it does lend significant sympathy to her situation because medicine has failed her. At the root of Lady Faulkner's tragedy is the inability of medical science to help her save her son or give birth to healthy children. While the text suggests that Lady Faulkner is wrong to hide her genetic secret from her future husband, its revelation would have doomed her to a miserable life. The stern Dr. Macpherson, who as the family doctor metaphorically stands in for patriarchal authority, can only condemn her to a loveless and miserable single life—he cannot remedy her genetic problem. Medical science in "The Star-Shaped Marks" is almost a gothic bogeyman, serving only to pass moral judgment on Lady Faulkner and reveal that her seemingly healthy body is as monstrous within as Loftus Durham's radiated skin is without.

Realizing that legitimate scientific solutions to their problem are nonexistent, women across the two series resort to alternative, female networks to solve their problems. Meade makes it very apparent why these women would risk criminal entanglements to do so, but her male detectives are stubbornly naïve about the realities of women's lives. Vandeleur—a trained medical doctor—cannot comprehend why a young, wealthy wife could feel stressed or depressed, exclaiming: "*I don't understand* a healthy English girl being shattered by nerves."[93] His friend Druce, an unmarried man, also "*cannot understand* any circumstances in which a wife could rightly have a trouble apart from her husband."[94] Both Vandeleur and Druce seem unable to see past the gloss of polite society and idealized gender roles. Through the detective's refusal to understand the complexities of women's lives, Meade reveals the blinders limiting early twentieth-century investigative practices.

FEMALE SCIENCE DISRUPTING DETECTION

Meade's imaginative portrayal of female criminal science disrupts the project of detection operating within the text because, while is always clear *who* commits the crime, *how* she commits it often leaves the detective baffled.

---

93. Meade, "Bloodstone," 199. Emphasis mine.
94. Meade, "Bloodstone," 201. Emphasis mine.

The detectives of both series often voice this frustration by linking Koluchy and Sara to the occult—a move that allows them to attribute the women's criminal success to supernatural powers rather than their scientific prowess. This enables the male detective to maintain the aura that his scientific and investigative methods are superior even when faced with mystery. Both of the detective figures in *The Sorceress of the Strand*, Dixon Druce and Eric Vandeleur, for instance, feel "haunted by [the] idea of Madame Sara, and find themselves thinking obsessively about her."[95] In the story "Twenty Degrees," a young man named John North falls under Madame Koluchy's influence. His fiancée (who has apparently been forgotten by her lover) tells Head, "I know there is a spell over him."[96] Despite the fact that a jealous fiancée is certainly not the most reliable source of information, Head unquestioningly accepts her assertion of Madame Koluchy's preternatural powers. This mind-set leads the detectives to persistently underestimate Sara's and Katherine's science. For example, in *The Brotherhood of the Seven Kings* Head situates the source of Koluchy's medical science as ambiguous, hinting that it could have a supernatural origin:

> What she did and how she did it remained more than ever a secret. She dispensed her own prescriptions, but although some of her medicines were analyzed by experts, nothing in the least extraordinary could be discovered in their composition. The cure did not therefore lie in drugs. In what did it consist? Doctors asked this question one of another, and could find no satisfactory answer.[97]

It may be tempting to side with the detective-narrators of these stories and interpret Madame Koluchy and Sara as quasi-supernatural figures, but I agree with Jennifer Halloran that this would be a misreading of the text. In her article on *The Sorceress of the Strand*, Halloran notes that the two detective figures often endow Sara with "supernatural characteristics" to explain their inability to stop her, but in reality their failure results from "her ability to out-think her pursuers."[98] The mystery surrounding the female mad scientist's work does not necessarily mean that it is occult. Rather, it suggests that this work is so advanced it seems possible only through supernatural means. As another character from *The Brotherhood of the Seven Kings* states: "I have heard much about Mme. Koluchy's marvelous occult powers . . . the

---

95. Meade, "Talk of the Town," 67.
96. Meade, "Twenty Degrees," 535.
97. Meade, "Luck of Pitsey Hall," 379.
98. Halloran, "Ideology behind *The Sorceress of the Strand*," 181.

profession, of course, pooh-pooh her, I know, but if one may credit all one hears, she possesses remedies undreamt of in their philosophy."[99] Evoking the famous line from Shakespeare, this character suggests that while mainstream medicine science would like to discount Katherine's work, she in truth has advanced beyond their capabilities; in keeping with this idea, a foreign doctor tells Head: "As a medical man myself, I can vouch for her capacity, and unfettered by English professional scrupulousness, I appreciate it."[100] It is Head's position within the world of professionalized, British science that limits his understanding of Katherine's abilities. Bordering on the edge of science fiction, the Mesdames' work might seem otherworldly, but Meade makes it clear that these women are very good scientists, not witches.

Katherine and Sara are not endowed with magical capabilities, yet they nonetheless regularly manipulate their occult status. They are perfectly aware that these men associate them with the supernatural: For instance, Madame Sara teases Druce when he displays shock at her surprise appearance at a house party, wryly saying to him: "You have no cause to be alarmed . . . I am not a ghost."[101] Indeed, Meade plays with long-held cultural stereotypes of women that connected female power to witchcraft and opposed it to the male realm of logic and science. Meade reveals these cultural assumptions by having Mmes. Sara and Koluchy deftly manipulate these assumptions in the planning of their criminal schemes, which hides their scientific crime under a veil of supernatural mystery. The best example of this is Katherine Koluchy's murder of her adversary Drufrayer in "The Doom." In the story, Head and Drufrayer are staying at a country house that has a ghostly legend attached to it, about a gypsy woman who murders the man that seduced her daughter. The haunted room—which is assigned to Drufrayer's use—supposedly has a secret passage linked to it that allowed the murderess to slip in and kill her daughter's seducer. Madame Koluchy integrates the mystery of the ghostly herb-woman into her plot, repeating her supernatural predecessor's actions by using the secret passage and sneaking into Drufrayer's room. She further heightens the atmosphere of mystery by posing as a fortune-teller and predicting the detectives' deaths—a move so distracting to Head that, despite knowing the location of the secret passage, he once again fails to figure out the danger his friend is in. After successfully poisoning Drufrayer in his sleep, Koluchy is accidently seen by the daughter of the house, Rosaly Sherwood:

99. Meade, "At the Edge of the Crater," 90.
100. Meade, "At the Edge of the Crater," 90.
101. Meade, "Bloodstone," 204.

"The herb-woman," she sobbed, "the ghost of the herb-woman. I heard a noise and ran on to the landing. I met her—she was coming from Mr. Drufrayer's room—she was making straight for yours, Mr. Head. Suddenly she saw me, uttered a cry, and fled downstairs. Oh, catch her, the ghost! the ghost!"[102]

Rosaly's superstitious fear and her paralysis at seeing the "ghost" gives Madame Koluchy enough time to escape back down the passage. She leaves behind the body of her victim, Drufrayer, whom she injected with a mysterious "whitish-grey substance."[103] Here, the whitish-gray poison, which turns out to be "nitro-glycerine in strong solution," takes on the ambiguous, ghostly appearance of the retreating figure.[104] Like Koluchy herself, the poison is both spectral and scientific, demonstrating the effectiveness of Katherine cloaking her scientific crimes within the supernatural.

Cosmetics are another realm that combines the uncanny ability to alter bodies with scientific reality. Madame Koluchy is said to be "able to restore youth and beauty by her arts," while Sara is "a professional beautifier" who "claims the privilege of restoring youth to those who consult her. She also declares that she can make quite ugly people handsome."[105] The mysterious art of "beautifying" is a large part of both Katherine's and Sara's criminal schemes, and it has a sophisticated scientific basis. When Druce tours Sara's laboratory, he sees several scientific instruments used for cosmetic purposes, like "platinum needles for burning out the roots of hairs."[106] A second room that he tours contains "a still more formidable array of instruments" that includes "a wooden operating table and chloroform and ether apparatus."[107] Sara's hybrid beauty parlor–laboratory reveals that her cosmetics go beyond puffs and powders and instead are based on advanced medical techniques and science; Sara has a specifically scientized cosmetic practice and very well may be the first plastic surgeon represented in print. The text therefore hybridizes Katherine's and Sara's cosmetic practice, linking it as much to science as to art.

When it comes to the project of detection, both Sara's and Katherine's association with cosmetics helps them avoid capture and the two series repeatedly connect Koluchy's and Sara's bodies with forensic illegibility. For

---

102. Meade, "Doom," 426.
103. Meade, "Doom," 426.
104. Meade, "Doom," 426.
105. Meade, "At the Edge of the Crater," 86–87; Meade, "Madame Sara," 388.
106. Meade, "Madame Sara," 392.
107. Meade, "Madame Sara," 392.

example, in the two last entries in the *Brotherhood of the Seven Kings* series, "The Bloodhound" and "The Doom," Madame Koluchy uses her cosmetic arts to disguise herself. She appears to Head and the other detectives as "a tall old woman" with "piercing eyes . . . under shaggy brows" who wore "a sort of night-cap with a deep frill."[108] At no point does Head question the identity of this woman, whom he allows to sneak away while he searches Madame Koluchy's home. The female detective on the case, Miss Beringer, however, is able to see through Koluchy's disguise by paying close attention to the old woman's body language. When she discovers that the men have let Katherine slip away, she upbraids their ignorance: "Fools! all of you! How was it she escaped? Did you not recognise her?"[109] Similarly, in "The Bloodstone," Sara impersonates a woman to set her up for a crime. To that end, she purposefully appears before the woman's husband in disguise. Unable to tell Sara apart from his wife, the husband gets taken in by the trick, believing that his wife has abetted the theft. The Mesdames' fusion of the masculine world of science with the feminine realm of cosmetics effectively blinds the men to their presence.

Detective fiction is usually preoccupied with reestablishing comforting order after a crime has been committed, as evidenced by the tidy endings provided by most detective stories; indeed, many critics attribute detective fiction's popularity to the fact that it provides only a temporary inversion of social rules and returns things to normal by story's end. Meade's stories (as we have seen) rarely have the typical ending of a detective story where the criminal is conveniently identified and consequently punished. I argue that Meade's notoriously unresolved endings are directly related to her feminist project of using the female mad scientist to subvert male detection. As Miller notes, "the female criminal is an unstable element in the scientific system of criminal detection."[110] This is because the detectives of *The Brotherhood of the Seven Kings* and *The Sorceress of the Strand* share a masculine worldview linked to the rhetoric of competition and dominance. Eric Vandeleur likens his adversarial relationship to Madame Sara to big game hunting, proclaiming to Druce that "hunting her as a recreation is as good as hunting a man-eating tiger."[111] He also declares, "I have staked my reputation on bringing this woman to book. She shall not escape."[112] Yet, escape she does, again and again. In the same story where Vandeleur makes this declaration, "The

---

108. Meade, "Bloodhound," 305, 312.
109. Meade, "Bloodhound," 316.
110. Elizabeth Miller, *Framed*, 92.
111. Meade, "Talk of the Town," 67.
112. Meade, "Talk of the Town," 70.

Talk of the Town," Madame Sara almost gasses Professor Piozzi to death but escapes responsibility for the crime. Druce's boast that "Madame was not successful" in killing Piozzi is hardly satisfactory. In fact, "The Talk of the Town" is one of a few instances where Sara or Katherine are not completely successful in their criminal plans. Far more often, the detective is left at the end of the story sadly relating, "once again Madame had escaped. The ingenuity, the genius, of the woman placed her beyond the ordinary consequences of crime."[113] In the world of Meade's stories, the two Mesdames are rarely foiled; usually the precious gems are lost forever and the murders go unavenged. Despite the detective's use of the masculine rhetoric of dominance, he is often impotent to stop Katherine's and Sara's crimes.

THE UBIQUITY OF SCIENCE: OTHERING THE BODY

In "The Doom," Katherine asserts her determination to subvert male control by committing suicide by dropping into a pit of fire, rather than submit to capture. Koluchy's self-immolation is highly reminiscent of H. Rider Haggard's Ayesha, who also dies in a pillar of fire. As Brian Aldiss notes, "from Haggard on, crumbling women, priestesses, or empresses—all symbols of women as Untouchable and Unmakeable—fill the pages of many a scientific romance."[114] But it is not just the woman that is untouchable—the two series also emphasize that science has also become increasingly untouchable, unmakeable, and incomprehensible. Repeatedly Meade's detective figures exclaim, "It is impossible to tell what may happen," or wonder, "What do you suppose Madame is after?"[115] The detectives' frustration at their inability to predict the Mesdames' scientific schemes parallels the public's anxiety about the growing specialization of science that was occurring at the beginning of the twentieth century. As fewer and fewer members of the public could comprehend the intricacies of new discoveries, the public (much like Head and Druce) increasingly felt that they were missing something or being left behind. With *The Brotherhood of the Seven Kings* and *The Sorceress of the Strand*, Meade explores these fears and outlines the abuses that may occur if scientific knowledge devolves only to the minds of a few. The fact that Sara and Katherine operate on the outside of the establishment suggests that Meade saw the need for more oversight and regulation as science became more advanced. At the same time, she realized that the progress of

---

113. Meade, "Luck of Pitsey Hall," 392.
114. Aldiss, *Billion Year Spree*, 139.
115. Meade, "Doom," 428; Meade, "Talk of the Town," 70.

science could not be stopped, and indeed, that science had already saturated modern life.

By the 1890s, the by-products of modern science had filtered so deeply into everyday life that it was easy to overlook just how ubiquitous they had become. One of the most insidious ways humans interact with science on a daily basis is through the chemicals we consume, and the late-century household was awash with a slew of different chemicals, many of them dangerous. Scheele's green, a popular color for fabric, wallpaper, paint, and carpets, contained arsenic, and turned the home, "even for the highest in the land," into "a health threat and a deathtrap."[116] Environmental chemicals, combined with purposefully consumed medicines and drugs, meant that Victorian bodies were in a state of constant chemicalization, with the by-products literally oozing out of their bodies. Meade highlights the ubiquity of this chemicalization in "The Bloodstone," a story in which the forensic scientist Vandeleur is able to clear Lady Bouverie from participation in the theft of a precious stone through her tears:

> "The medicine I have been giving her happens to contain large doses of iodide of potassium. You may not be aware of it, but the drug is eliminated very largely by all the mucous membranes, and the lachrymal gland, which secretes the tears, plays a prominent part in this process. The sobbing female whom you are prepared to swear on oath was Lady Bouverie at the rendezvous by the summer-house dropped a handkerchief—this one." He laid his finger on the first of the two packets. "Now, if that woman was really Lady Bouverie, by analysis of the handkerchief I shall find, by means of a delicate test, distinct traces of iodine on it. If, however, it was not Lady Bouverie, but someone disguised with the utmost skill of an actress to represent her, not only physically, but with all the emotions of a distracted and guilty woman, even to the sobs and tears—then we shall not find iodine on the analysis of this handkerchief."

Lady Bouverie's handkerchief does test positive for iodine, while the one Madame Sara drops does not, saving the former from ignominy. Yet, the iodine seeping out with her tears also exposes the extent to which Lady Bouverie's body has been saturated with chemicals.

Lady Bouverie was purposefully taking a medication that altered the chemical composition of her body, but Meade makes full use of the opportunities offered by chemical crime to suggest that our bodies contain

---

116. Bartrip, "How Green Was My Valence?," 891–92.

more chemicals than we know. For instance, in the first story of the series, "Madame Sara," a woman named Edith Dallas is mysteriously poisoned during breakfast:

> Miss Dallas came down, looking quite in her usual health, and in apparently good spirits. She ate with appetite, and, as it happened, she and my wife were both helped from the same dish. The meal had nearly come to an end when she jumped up from the table, uttered a sharp cry, turned very pale, pressed her hand to her side, and ran out of the room.[117]

The passage indicates that prior to the action of the poison, Edith's body is quite normal, and in its "usual health." The lack of poison traces in her food combined with Edith's good health leads Vandeleur to surmise that the crime must have been committed by "a criminal of the highest order of scientific ability," although he does not know how the poison was administered.[118] Edith's body poses a challenge to the project of detection because, while it reveals that it was poisoned, it hides how the poison entered her system and displays no signs of physical aberration. Eventually, Vandeleur realizes that the poison has been placed into a tooth during a dental operation done by Madame Sara. When Edith chewed her breakfast, the flimsy plug came loose and exposed her to the poison. Edith's sister, Mrs. Selby, has had the same dental work and is also at risk; when he pulls out Mrs. Selby's tooth, he finds evidence of "a powerful poison, unknown to European toxicologists," that has been placed into the cavity of the tooth and stopped up with "gutta-percha."[119] With this form of poisoning, Meade not only points out how saturated our bodies are with chemicals but also shows how Madame Sara essentially uses the women's bodies against them, and the action of mastication becomes the act of poisoning. This chemical crime reveals fears of poisons lurking within that can turn our bodies into weapons.

Similarly, in "The Blood-Red Cross," a young woman named Antonia Ripley, who is recently engaged to the rich George Rowland, goes to Madame Sara in order to have "a disfiguring mole or wart" removed from her neck so she can wear the Rowland family pearls on her wedding day.[120] Although there is nothing physically wrong with her health, Ripley is eager to get rid of the "large, brown, and ugly" mole and will risk surgery to

---

117. Meade, "Madame Sara," 395.
118. Meade, "Madame Sara," 396.
119. Meade, "Madame Sara," 401.
120. Meade, "Blood-Red Cross," 513.

make herself beautiful—suggesting the danger of integrating science into domestic concerns. As Ripley tells Druce, going to Madame Sara is her only option, as the doctors she previously consulted "would not remove it" because they were afraid of cutting into an artery and causing a "very dangerous hæmorrage."[121] Madame's superior surgical skills, however, allow her to safely remove the mole—but she leaves something sinister in its place. After leading Ripley into an operating room lit only by an eerie red light, Madame Sara doses her with chloroform and completes the surgery, but she also writes the following in nitrate of silver upon Antonia's neck: "I AM THE DAUGHTER OF PAOLO GIOLETTI, WHO WAS EXECUTED FOR THE MURDER OF MY MOTHER, JUNE 20TH, 18—."[122] Playing on Victorian fears of criminal inheritance, Sara writes the true family history of the orphaned Ripley on her neck, knowing that her victim will go to great lengths to hide this secret from her future husband. Readers of Wilkie Collins's *Poor Miss Finch* would perhaps be aware that silver nitrate can discolor the skin, and in fact, Madame Sara has tattooed Ripley's neck with an ink that will stay invisible only until she exposes it to the light. As Vandeleur explains, "nitrate of silver eats into the flesh and is permanent. Once exposed to the light the case is hopeless, and the helpless child becomes her own executioner."[123] Here, Madame Sara has once again turned a woman's body into a self-destructive weapon since only Antonia can reveal her own secret. Vandeleur's use of the word "executioner," while perhaps overly dramatic, highlights the fact that Antonia's body is now a living document that has the power to ruin her life. After Vandeleur has Antonia's neck bathed with more poison—in this case, cyanide of potassium—her "neck contains no ghastly secret."[124] The ghastly secret of the story, however, is not Antonia's murderous family history, but rather the anxiety that, like ghosts, chemicals hide in our bodies, waiting only for the proper exposure to become life altering.

The victimization of these young women is a reminder to Meade's readers that the by-products of scientific discovery are not only in their homes but also in their eyes, their teeth, their skin. Meade's series suggest that the increased presence of science in *fin de siècle* life means that all bodies are already poisoned. This poisoning could be literal—as the stories of Edith Dallas and Antonia Ripley suggest—or it could be figurative, becoming symbolic of the hidden dangers of everyday science.

---

121. Meade, "Blood-Red Cross," 509.
122. Meade, "Blood-Red Cross," 514.
123. Meade, "Blood-Red Cross," 514.
124. Meade, "Blood-Red Cross," 517.

THE BODY OF THE POISONED SCIENTIST; OR, WHAT KOLUCHY KNOWS

To conclude this book's reading of science and the chemical criminal, I will examine the same image that began the chapter readings: the dead body of the poisoned woman. In the final story of *The Brotherhood of the Seven Kings* series, "The Bloodhound," Head is tracking Katherine when he stumbles upon her body in her laboratory:

> It was the body of Mme. Koluchy. Yes, there she lay. The well-known face, in all its magnificent beauty, wore now the awful repose of death. Beside her was a small hypodermic syringe, and also an open bottle containing some clear solution. From that open bottle has issued the smell which pervaded the outer and inner laboratory.[125]

This body is evocative of the image I opened the chapter readings of *Chemical Crimes* with: the poisoned body of the writer Letitia Elizabeth Landon, found with the poison bottle still clutched in her hand. As with Landon's body, here the image of a poisoned female body is a warning about the dangerous interaction between women and science. The poison she uses to harm others becomes her destruction, affirming the comforting worldview that the female scientist is the cause of her own undoing.

The poetic justice of Koluchy's death by her own poison might have been a satisfying ending for many of Meade's readers, yet the author is unwilling to let this be Katherine's fate. In a plot twist, Meade reveals the body in the laboratory is not Koluchy's, but rather a perfect double, who was "like [her] in each feature, in height, proportion, even to the expression of the face."[126] Koluchy is still alive, and as she explains to the captive Miss Beringer, she kept her body double frozen in order to trick her pursuers:

> I kept the body at a very low temperature, and when I came to England in my own yacht, brought it with me. Since then it has remained in a frozen chamber beneath the floor of the inner laboratory, thus retaining its likeness. . . . The time has come when I must use my double in order to effect my own escape. . . . I mean to put a hypodermic syringe and a bottle of strong poison near the body of the woman.[127]

---

125. Meade, "Bloodhound," 314.
126. Meade, "Bloodhound," 317.
127. Meade, "Bloodhound," 317.

Instead of the poisoned woman's body representing the self-destructive relationship between women and science, here it once again signifies Koluchy's mastery of criminal science and her ability to outthink her rivals.

The (seemingly) poisoned body—literally a relic of the past frozen in time—becomes symbolic of the ways that the Victorians had previously linked women to poison. Here, the body, like the poison placed next to it, is deceptive; the detectives misread the body when they assume that a woman's engagement with science will ultimately lead to her death. These men are, Meade suggests, stuck in an older way of understanding women and their capacity for science—a way that is more reminiscent of the 1840s than the 1900s. This retrograde thinking enables Katherine's and Sara's success because the men chasing them refuse to see things from a female perspective. Meade's texts, therefore, are not as much about the fear of women's education as they are about the need for women to be integrated into mainstream science. Meade establishes that women are as scientifically capable as men, but by placing both Sara and Koluchy on the fringes of contemporary scientific practice, she suggests the need for their integration. Science can be abused, as Meade's female mad scientists demonstrate, but with the oversight provided by professional organizations that abuse can be mitigated. After all, both women are brilliant scientists who could offer much for the betterment of society.

AFTERWORD

IN THE LAST CHAPTER, I ended with an examination of Madame Koluchy's faked death in the final story in L. T. Meade's *The Brotherhood of the Seven Kings* series. Madame Koluchy does eventually die, but, significantly, not by poison. Finally cornered in her laboratory, Koluchy refuses to submit to the male detectives who have trapped her. Instead, she first disarms them with a powerful magnet, and then commits suicide in a spectacular fashion. In the floor of her laboratory, Madame installed an "8ft. deep and circular pit" fitted with cylinders that can emit jets of fire. Realizing she was about to be captured, "Madame must have released the iron trap and descended through a column of this fearful flame, not only causing instantaneous death, but simultaneously also an absolute annihilation."[1]

Ending where the book began—with another dead female scientist—may suggest that the Victorians' ideas of science, gender, and crime did not evolve much during the century. As this book has shown, one of the boundaries that chemical crime most persistently erodes is that of gender. From the wealthy educated woman to the medical Bluebeard to the feminized unconscious criminal and finally to the female mad scientist, this book has examined the gender implications of chemical crime. It finds that not only is criminal science a significant factor in the generic development of Victorian

---

1. Meade, "Doom," 429.

crime fiction, but so are considerations of gender. With each new generic development, a new form of chemical criminal develops to probe Victorian science's impact on conceptions of gender. The intersection of science and crime was one of many sites the Victorians used to address contradictions in the opposition of male/female.

Therefore, if we compare Koluchy's death to, for instance, *Ethel Churchill*'s Henrietta Marchmont, there are distinct differences. Henrietta ends her life in a way that 1830s fiction found appropriate: Her chemical crimes lead to the loss of her youth, freedom, and rationality. Although doomed to "hopeless," "incurable insanity," her ravings still "revealed the fiery world of that beating and passionate heart."[2] Henrietta's unrealized ambitions and intellect continue to torment her long after her rationality fades. Koluchy, on the other hand, does not have to choose between convention and ambition. She is as much admired in society for her science as Henrietta was for her beauty and there is no threat to her sanity. When *The Brotherhood of the Seven Kings* ends, she gives her persecutors one final demonstration of her exceptional scientific skill and dies on her own terms, without pain, shame, or having her secrets exposed. Even in death, she is always outside the control of men.

But does she die? All the detectives find of her body is "a small heap of smouldering ashes" at the bottom of the pit, and no one witnesses her actual death.[3] Indeed, Madame Sara can be read as Koluchy's literary, if not literal, reincarnation.[4] Madame Sara's phoenix-like rebirth from the ashes of Koluchy is symbolic of the persistent appearance of the chemical criminal throughout the nineteenth century. New problems arising in science brought new iterations of the chemical criminal, and newly developing genres of crime literature offered these poisoners a place to thrive. Nor has the chemical criminal been forgotten today: On the contrary, this figure has become a lasting symbol of Victorian crime, especially for contemporary artists, writers, and musicians who conjure this image as a symbol for the dark side of Victorian life. Case in point are the numerous reincarnations of poisons and chemical criminals in neo-Victorian, steampunk, or neo-gothic art, the most mainstream example of which is Andrew Motion's 2000 neo-Victorian work *Wainewright the Poisoner: The Confession of Thomas Griffiths Wainewright*. Wainewright was an early nineteenth-century writer who was accused of systematically poisoning several family members. In his famous essay "Pen, Pencil and Poison," Oscar Wilde described Waine-

---

2. Landon, *Ethel Churchill*, III: 327.
3. Meade, "Doom," 429.
4. Chris Willis also suggests that Koluchy may have escaped alive. See "Female Moriarty."

wright as "not merely a poet and a painter and an art-critic, an antiquarian, and a writer of prose, an amateur of beautiful things, and a dilettante of things delightful, but also a forger of no mean or ordinary capabilities, and as a subtle and secret poisoner almost without rival in this or any age."[5] Motion, a former poet laureate of the United Kingdom, wrote the work as an "experimental biography." In it, he takes on the voice and persona of the chemical criminal Wainewright, writing the text in a novelistic first-person style, yet carefully footnoting his inexhaustible research into Wainewright's life. As with so many Victorian poison narratives, including earlier works fictionalizing Wainewright's life like Edward Bulwer's *Lucretia* or Charles Dickens's "Hunted Down," Motion uses the chemical criminal as a way to test the limits and possibilities of genre crossing.[6] *Wainewright the Poisoner* is not purely a novel, nor is it exactly a biography; rather, it is a hybrid work that (like earlier Victorian works) uses Wainewright's status as an artist and a poisoner to explore the issues of aesthetics, crime, science, and genre. Like the reactions to earlier innovating crime fiction, Motion's criminal biography inspired mixed criticism. While John Carey, of the *Sunday Times*, described the work as "brilliantly innovative, gripping," and "intricately researched," Jonathan Bate called it a "broken-backed compromise."[7]

Whether or not the work will go down as a success, *Wainewright the Poisoner* demonstrates the hybrid power of the chemical criminal and explains the Victorian fascination with this particular kind of villain. In Motion's hands, Wainewright (like the fictional chemical criminals of the nineteenth century) is intelligent, witty, sensitive, and artistic, as well as intensely selfish, greedy, judgmental, and snobbish. As Motion subtly points out, Wainewright's Janus-like nature is like the two sides of the period: The Victorian age was one that saw great progress and the development of great problems.

Motion's deliberate play with genre brings to mind an interesting chapter on Thomas Hardy by Richard Nemesvari, who explores "the social function of the notion of genre" in Hardy's fiction.[8] Noting that Hardy often mixes generic forms, Nemesvari argues that Hardy "insists on an interdependent play of forms as the only way to adequately represent the complexities of class and gender interaction which dominate his texts." This book makes a similar argument, suggesting that authors mimicked poison's malleability through generic hybridity, and that this hybridity is necessary for exploring

---

5. Wilde, "Pen, Pencil and Poison," 41.
6. For more information on Wainewright and Charles Dickens's "Hunted Down," see my article "Probability and Capital Crime."
7. Moss, review of *Wainewright the Poisoner*.
8. Nemesvari, "'Genres are not to be mixed,'" 103.

the complex intersection of science and crime. In other words, the form of fiction featuring chemical crime mirrors its ambiguous subject matter, highlighting poison's ability to disrupt boundaries and explore paradoxes.

Throughout *Chemical Crimes*, I have asked my reader to consider the ways that Victorian crime fiction poisons and is poisoned—both in relation to this fiction's ambivalence toward science and in how its genres are always already impure. Previous to this work, scholars have ignored this poisoning, largely focusing only on how science helps legitimate the detective, and in turn how this legitimization structures the development of crime fiction. *Chemical Crimes*, however, has demonstrated that this is not the only way that science and crime interact during the nineteenth century. Rather than seeing the detective as the disciplining directing energy of generic development; this book shows that scientific criminals always precede the scientific investigator. Victorian crime fiction is not just dedicated to legitimating science but engages with the very complex realities of science's beneficial *and* harmful impacts on nineteenth-century society. Getting away from a focus on the scientific detective allows us to see how Victorian authors are less interested in disciplining crime than we previously thought, and more interested in the tangled web of social problems that crime illuminates.

BIBLIOGRAPHY

"A Critic's Morality(?)" *The Lancet*, April 2, 1881.

Adams, Charles Warren. *The Notting Hill Mystery*. Vols. 7 and 8 of *Once a Week*. London: Bradbury and Evans: 1862–63.

Aldiss, B. W. *Billion Year Spree: The True History of Science Fiction*. New York: Schocken, 1974.

Altick, Richard D. *Victorian Studies in Scarlet*. New York: W. W. Norton, 1970.

Ashton, Helen. *Letty Landon*. London: Collins, 1951.

The Athenaeum. Unsigned review of *Ethel Churchill*, by L. E. L. 518 (1837): 713.

The Athenaeum. Unsigned review of *The Notting Hill Mystery*, by Charles Felix. 1900 (1865): 520.

Bahar, Saba. "Jane Marcet and the Limits to Public Science." *The British Journal for the History of Science* 34, no. 1 (2001): 29–49.

Bankard, Jennifer Sopchockchai. "Testing Reality's Limits: 'Mad' Scientists, Realism, and the Supernatural in Late Victorian Popular Fiction." PhD diss., Northeastern University, 2013.

Barrett, R. A. F. "Mesmeric Cure of a Lady Who Had Been Twelve Years in the Horizontal Position with Extreme Suffering." *The Zoist* 47 (1854): 213–42.

Bartrip, Peter W. J. "How Green Was My Valence?: Environmental Arsenic Poisoning and the Victorian Domestic Ideal." *The English Historical Review* 109, no. 400 (1994): 891–913.

Bayne, Peter. "Studies of English Authors: Edward Bulwer, Lord Lytton." *The Literary World* 22 (1880): 328–30.

"The Belaney [sic] Poisoning Case." *Monthly Chronicle North Country Lore and Legend*. London: Walter Scott, 1887.

Beller, Anne-Marie. "Suffering Angels: Death and Femininity in Ellen Wood's Fiction." *Women's Writing* 2, no. 15 (2008): 219–31.

Blanchard, Laman. Vol. 1 of *Life and Literary Remains of L. E. L.* London: Henry Colburn, 1841.

Braddon, Mary Elizabeth. *The Black Band, Or the Mysteries at Midnight*. London: G. Vickers, 1877.

———. *The Trail of the Serpent*. New York: The Modern Library, 2003.

Brantlinger, Patrick. "Victorian Science Fiction." In *A Companion to the Victorian Novel*, edited by Patrick Brantlinger and William B. Thesing, 370–84. Malden: Blackwell Press, 2005.

"The Bravo Case." *The Spectator* 49 (1876): 651–52.

"The Bravo Inquiry." *The Medical Times and Gazette*, August 19, 1876.

Buckler, William. "Once a Week Under Samuel Lucas, 1859–65." *PMLA* 67, no. 7 (1952): 924–41.

Bulamur, Ayse Naz. *Victorian Murderesses: The Politics of Female Violence*. Cambridge: Cambridge Scholars, 2016.

Bulwer, Edward. *Greville*. In Vol. 2 of *The Life, Letters, and Literary Remains of Edward Bulwer, Lord Lytton*, edited by Victor Bulwer Lytton. 331–92. London: Kegan Paul, Trench, & Co., 1883.

———. *Lucretia; Or, the Children of Night*. 2 vols. Leipzig: Tauchnitz, 1846.

———. *Lucretia; Or, the Children of Night*. 2 vols. Philadelphia: Lippincott, 1866.

———. "Romance and Reality by L. E. L." *New Monthly Magazine* 32, no. 132 (1831): 546–75.

———. "A Word to the Public." In Vol. VI of *The Works of Edward Bulwer Lytton*. 713–34. New York: Collier, 1892.

Bulwer Lytton, Rosina. *Unpublished Letters of Lady Bulwer Lytton to A. E. Chalon, R. A.* London: Everleigh Nash, 1914.

Bulwer Lytton, Victor. *The Life of Edward Bulwer, First Lord Lytton*. London: MacMillan, 1913.

Burney, Ian. *Poison, Detection, and the Victorian Imagination*. New York: Manchester University Press, 2006.

Caleb, Williams. *Observations on the Criminal Responsibility of the Insane*. London: John Churchill, 1856.

Campbell, John W. "In Times to Come." *Astounding Science Fiction* 27 (1941): 87.

"The Case of Thomas Smethurst." *The Saturday Review*, August 27, 1859.

"Central Criminal Court, Dec. 15." *Medical Times* 17 (1847): 204–6.

Chapelle, Marie. Vol. 1 of *The Memoirs of Madame Lafarge*. London: Henry Colburn, 1841.

Chappel, J. A. V. *Science and Literature in the Nineteenth-Century*. London: Macmillan, 1986.

Ciolkowski, Laura. "The Woman (In) Question: Gender, Politics, and Edward Bulwer-Lytton's *Lucretia*." *Novel: A Forum on Fiction* 26, no. 1 (1992): 80–95.

"Circumstantial Evidence: The Smethurst Case." *Tait's Edinburgh Magazine* 24 (1859): 550.

Cobbe, Frances. "The Medical Profession and Its Morality." Vol. 2 of *The Modern Review*. London: James Clark, 1881.

Collins, Paul. "Before Hercule or Sherlock, There Was Ralph." *The New York Times Book Review*, January 7, 2011.

Collins, Wilkie. *Armadale.* Vols. 8 and 9 of *The Works of Wilkie Collins.* New York: P. F. Collier, 1895.

———. *Blind Love.* Vol. 28 of *The Works of Wilkie Collins.* New York, P. F. Collier, 1895.

———. *Heart and Science.* Vol. 25 of *The Works of Wilkie Collins.* New York, P. F. Collier, 1895.

———. *Jezebel's Daughter.* Vol. 27 of *The Works of Wilkie Collins.* New York: P. F. Collier, 1895.

———. *The Legacy of Cain.* Vol. 26 of *The Works of Wilkie Collins.* New York, P. F. Collier, 1895.

———. *The Moonstone.* Vols. 6 and 7 of *The Works of Wilkie Collins.* New York, P. F. Collier, 1895.

———. *The Woman in White.* Vols. 1 and 2 of *The Works of Wilkie Collins.* New York, P. F. Collier, 1895.

Costantini, Mariaconcetta. "A Land of Angels with 'Stilettos': Travel Experiences and Literary Representations of Italy in Wilkie Collins." *Wilkie Collins Society Journal* 10 (2007): 13–33.

Cothran, Casey A. "Mysterious Bodies: Deception and Detection in Wilkie Collins's *The Law and the Lady* and *The Moonstone.*" *Victorians Institute Journal* 34 (2006): 193–214.

"The Crime of the Age." *Illustrated Times,* February 2, 1865, 64–65.

Davies, Owen. *Murder, Magic, Madness: The Victorian Trials of Dove and the Wizard.* Harow, UK: Pearson Education, 2005.

Dawson, Janis. Introduction to *The Sorceress of the Strand and Other Stories,* by L. T. Meade. 13–40. Peterborough, Ontario: Broadview Press, 2016.

Densmore, Helen. *The Maybrick Case: English Criminal Law.* London: Swan Sonnenschein & Co., 1892.

Derrida, Jacques. *Dissemination.* Translated by Barbara Johnson. Chicago: University of Chicago Press, 1981.

———. "The Law of Genre." Translated by Avital Ronell. *Critical Inquiry* 7, no. 1 (1980): 55–81.

———. *Limited, Inc.* Translated by Samuel Weber. Evanston, IL: Northwestern University Press, 1988.

Dewitt, Anne. *Moral Authority, Men of Science, and the Victorian Novel.* Cambridge: Cambridge University Press, 2013.

Dickens, Charles. "The Demeanour of Murderers." *Household Words* 13, no. 325 (1856): 505–7.

———. "Hunted Down." Vol. 25 of *The Works of Charles Dickens.* London: Chapman and Hall, 1898.

———. *Oliver Twist.* New York: Modern Library, 2001.

Dickinson, S. "Memoranda on the Epidemic Cholera of India." *The Lancet* 2, no. 350 (1829): 139.

"Doctors and Patients." Reprinted in *The People's Medical Journal, and Family Physician,* by Thomas Harrison Yeoman. London: George Vickers, 1851.

Doyle, Arthur Conan. "The Adventure of the Speckled Band." In Vol. 1 of *The Annotated Sherlock Holmes*, edited by William S. Baring-Gould, 243–62. New York: Clarkson N. Potter, 1977.

———. "The Final Problem." In Vol. 2 of *The Annotated Sherlock Holmes*, 2nd. ed., edited by William Baring-Gould. 301–18. New York: Clarkson N. Potter, 1977.

———. *The Valley of Fear.* New York: A. L. Burt, 1914.

Dunne, Éamonn. *J. Hillis Miller and the Possibilities of Reading: Literature after Deconstruction.* New York: Continuum, 2010.

Edgeworth, Maria. Vol. 2 of *Practical Education*. New York: Self, Brown and Stansbury, 1801.

Edinburgh Evening Courant. July 21, 1865, 228.

Edinburgh Review. Unsigned review of *Mechanism of the Heavens*, by Mrs. Somerville, 55 (1832): 1.

Eigen, Joel Peter. *Unconscious Crime: Mental Absence and Criminal Responsibility in Victorian London.* Baltimore: Johns Hopkins University Press, 2003.

Fayter, Paul. "Strange New Worlds of Space and Time: Late Victorian Science and Science Fiction." In *Victorian Science in Context*, edited by Bernard Lightman, 256–82. Chicago: University of Chicago Press, 1997.

Flint, Kate. "Difference and Disability." In *The Cambridge Companion to Wilkie Collins*, edited by Jenny Bourne Taylor, 153–67. Cambridge: Cambridge University Press 2006.

A Full Report of The Evidence Taken on the Alleged Poisoning Case also, the Trial of J. C. Belany. Alnwick: G. Pike, 1844.

Furst, Lillian. *Between Doctors and Patients: The Changing Balance of Power.* Charlottesville: The University Press of Virginia, 1998.

Gilbert, Pamela K. *Disease, Desire, and the Body in Victorian Women's Popular Novels.* Cambridge: Cambridge University Press, 1997.

Griffith, George. *Olga Romanoff; Or, the Syren of the Skies.* London: Tower Publishing, 1894.

Hadley, Matthew. "Mary Shelley's Literary Laboratory: *Frankenstein* and the Emergence of the Modern Laboratory in Nineteenth-Century Europe." In *Environments in Science Fiction: Essays on Alternative Spaces*, edited by Susan M. Bernardo. 83–100. Jefferson, NC: McFarland Press, 2014.

Hallissy, Margaret. *Venomous Woman: Fear of the Female in Literature.* New York: Greenwood Press, 1987.

Halloran, Jennifer. "The Ideology behind *The Sorceress of the Strand*: Gender, Race, and Criminal Witchcraft." *English Literature in Transition, 1880–1920* 45, no. 2 (2002): 176–94.

Haynes, Roslynn. "The Alchemist in Fiction: The Master Narrative." *HYLE: International Journal for Philosophy of Chemistry* 12, no. 1 (2006): 5–29.

Hedgecock, Jennifer. *The Femme Fatale in Victorian Literature: the Danger and the Sexual Threat.* Amherst: Cambria Press, 2008.

Helfield, Randa. "The Poison Pen: Narrative and Sensation in Victorian England." PhD diss., Cornell University, 1994.

Heller, Tamar. *Dead Secrets: Wilkie Collins and the Female Gothic*. New Haven: Yale University Press, 1992.

Hogarth, George. "Poisoners of the Seventeenth Century." *Bentley's Miscellany* 2 (1837): 229–39.

———. "Poisoners of the Seventeenth Century." *Bentley's Miscellany* 3 (1838): 121–33.

Hollingsworth, Keith. *The Newgate Novel; 1830–1847: Bulwer, Ainsworth, Dickens & Thackeray*. Detroit: Wayne State University Press: 1963.

Howitt, William. Vol. 1 of *Homes and Haunts of the Most Eminent British Poets*. London: R. Bentley, 1847.

Hughes, William. "Medicine and the Gothic." In *The Encyclopedia of the Gothic*, edited by William Hughes, David Punter, and Andrew Smith, 439. Hoboken: John Wiley and Sons, 2015.

———. "Victorian Medicine and the Gothic." In *The Victorian Gothic: An Edinburgh Companion*. Edinburgh: Edinburgh University Press, 2012.

Hugo, Victor. *Lucretia Borgia: A Drama: In Three Acts*. Adapted by J. M. Weston. New York, Samuel French, 1865.

Illustrated Life and Career of William Palmer. London: Ward and Lock, 1856.

Kayman, Martin A. "The Short Story from Poe to Chesterton." In *The Cambridge Companion to Crime Fiction*, edited by Martin Priestman, 41–58. Cambridge: Cambridge University Press, 2003.

Kendra, April. "Gendering the Silver Fork: Catherine Gore and the Society Novel." *Women's Writing* 11, no. 1 (2004): 25–38.

Kennedy, Meegan. "The Ghost in the Clinic: Gothic Medicine and Curious Fiction in Samuel Warren's *Diary of a Late Physician*." *Victorian Literature and Culture* 32, no. 2 (2004): 327–51.

Kingsbury, George C. "Hypnotism, Crime, and the Doctors." *The Nineteenth-Century* 29, no. 167 (1891): 147.

Kirby, Vicki. "Deconstruction." In *The Routledge Companion to Literature and Science*, edited by Bruce Clarke and Manuela Rossini, 287–97. New York: Routledge, 2011.

Kucich, John. *The Power of Lies: Transgression in Victorian Fiction*. Ithaca: Cornell University Press, 1994.

Landon, Letitia Elizabeth. *Ethel Churchill*. 3 vols. London: Henry Colburn: 1838.

———. "Living Literary Characters No. V: Edward Bulwer Lytton." *New Monthly Magazine* 31 (1831): 443.

———. "The Venetian Bracelet." *The Venetian Bracelet, The Lost Pleiad, A History of the Lyre, and Other Poems*. London: Longman, 1829.

LeFanu, Sheridan. *Uncle Silas*. New York: Penguin, 2000.

Leighton, Angela. *Victorian Woman Poets: Writing against the Heart*. Charlottesville: University Press of Virginia, 1992.

Leighton, Mary Connor, and Robert Leighton. *Michael Dred, Detective*. London: Arno Press, 1899.

Liggins, Emma, and Andrew Maunder. "Introduction: Ellen Wood, Writer." *Women's Writing* 2, no. 15 (2008): 149–56.

Lonoff, Sue. "Multiple Narratives and Relative Truths: A Study of 'The Ring and the Book,' *The Woman in White*, and *The Moonstone*." *Browning Institute Studies* 10 (1982): 143–61.

Lynch, Martin H. "Analysis of Madame Lafarge's Trial, with Remarks on the Medical Evidence." *Provincial Medical & Surgical Journal* 1, no. 2 (1840): 17–19.

MacArthur, Sian. *Gothic Science Fiction: 1818 to the Present*. New York: Springer, 2015.

MacCulloch, Edgar. "Bluebeard: Origins of the Story." *Notes and Queries* 43 (1871): 29.

Macdougall, Alexander William. *The Maybrick Case, A Treatise*. London: Baillièrre, Tindall, and Cox, 1891.

Mangham, Andrew. "'Drink it up Dear; it will do you good': Crime, Toxicology, and the Trail of the Serpent." In *New Perspectives on Mary Elizabeth Braddon*, edited by Jessica Cox, 95–112. Amsterdam: Rodolpi, 2012.

———. "Life after Death: Apoplexy, Medical Ethics and the Female Undead." *Women's Writing* 15, no. 3 (2008): 282–93.

———. *Violent Women and Sensation Fiction: Crime, Medicine, and Victorian Popular Culture*. New York: Palgrave Macmillan, 2007.

Manning, Anne. Review of *Village Belles, a Novel*. *Athenaeum* 299 (1833): 471.

Mansel, Henry. "Sensation Novels." *The Quarterly Review*, no. 113 (1863): 482–513.

Marcet, Jane. *Conversations on Chemistry*. Hartford: Oliver D. Cook, 1822.

Marshall, John. *Five Cases of Recovery from the Effects of Arsenic*. London: McDowell, 1815.

Meade, L. T. "At the Edge of the Crater." *The Strand* 15 (1898): 86–98.

———. "The Blood-Red Cross." *The Strand* 24 (1902): 505–18.

———. "The Bloodhound." *The Strand* 16 (1898): 304–17.

———. "The Bloodstone." *The Strand* 25 (1903): 198–212.

———. "The Doom." *The Strand* 16 (1898): 416–29.

———. "The Iron Circlet." *The Strand* 16 (1898): 3–16.

———. "The Luck of Pitsey Hall." *The Strand* 15 (1898): 379–92.

———. "Madame Sara." *The Strand* 24 (1902): 387–401.

———. "The Mystery of the Strong Room." *The Strand* 16 (1898): 123–37.

———. "The Star-Shaped Marks." *The Strand* 15 (1898): 649–64.

———. "The Swing of the Pendulum." *The Strand* 15 (1898): 243–56.

———. "The Talk of the Town." *The Strand* 25 (1903): 67–80.

———. "Twenty Degrees." *The Strand* 15 (1898): 529–41.

———. "The Winged Assassin." *The Strand* 15 (1898): 137–50.

"The Medical Evidence in the Smethurst Poisoning Case." *Medical Times and Gazette* 40 (1859): 201–8.

"Medical Practitioners and Their Female Patients." *The Lancet*, December 6, 1884.

"The Medical Profession and Its Morality." *The Medical News*, September 23, 1882.

"The Medical Profession and Its Morality." *The Student's Journal and Hospital Gazette*, July 2, 1881.

Mellor, Anne K. *Romanticism and Gender.* New York: Routledge, 1993.

Miller, D. A. *The Novel and the Police.* Berkley: University of California Press, 1988.

Miller, Elizabeth Carolyn. *Framed: The New Woman Criminal in British Culture at the Fin de Siècle.* Ann Arbor: University of Michigan Press, 2008.

Morgan, Sydney Owenson. Review of *Jack Sheppard,* by W. H. Ainsworth. *Athenaeum* 626 (1839): 803.

Moscucci, Ornella. *The Science of Woman: Gynaecology and Gender in England 1800–1929.* Cambridge: Cambridge University Press, 1993.

Moss, Stephen. Review of *Wainewright the Poisoner,* by Andrew Motion. *The Guardian,* May 24, 2012. https://www.theguardian.com/books/2000/mar/01/andrewmotion

Mossman, Mark. "Representations of the Abnormal Body in *The Moonstone."* *Victorian Literature and Culture* 37, no. 2 (2009): 483–500.

Mulvey-Roberts, Mary. "Fame, Notoriety and Madness: Edward Bulwer-Lytton Paying the Price of Greatness." *Critical Survey* 13, no. 2 (2001): 115–34.

Nemesvari, Richard. "'Genres are not to be mixed. . . . I will not mix them': Discourse, Ideology, and Generic Hybridity in Hardy's Fiction." In *A Companion to Thomas Hardy,* edited by Keith Wilson, 101–16. Malden MA: Blackwell Press, 2012.

"The New Novels: *Ethel Churchill."* *Tait's Edinburgh Magazine* 4, no. 48 (1837): 745.

Nord, Deborah Epstein. *Gypsies and the British Imagination: 1807–1930.* New York: Columbia University Press, 2006.

"Novelettes." *The London Review* 11 (1865): 178.

"Offense Against the Persons Act of 1861." *SLE.* Chpt. 100 24 and 25 Vict.: Sect. 23.

Oliphant, Mrs. "Novels." *Blackwood's Edinburgh Magazine* 102 (1867): 257–80.

———. "Sensation Novels." *Blackwood's Edinburgh Magazine* 91, no. 559 (1862): 564–84.

"On the Increase of the Crime of Secret Poisoning." *London Medical Gazette* 4 (1847): 191–94.

"On the Increase of Secret Poisoning in This Country." *London Medical Gazette* 4 (1847): 105–8.

"Ought There to Be a Criminal Court of Appeals?" *The Lancet,* February 4, 1860.

Paget, John. "The Philosophy of Murder." *Tait's Edinburgh Magazine* 22, no. 8 (1851): 171–76.

Pal-Lapinski, Piya. *The Exotic Woman in Nineteenth-Century British Fiction and Culture.* Lebanon: University of New Hampshire Press, 2005.

Pamboukian, Sylvia. *Doctoring the Novel: Medicine and Quackery from Shelley to Doyle.* Athens: Ohio University Press, 2012.

Panek, Leroy. *After Sherlock Holmes: The Evolution of British and American Detective Stories, 1891–1914.* Jefferson, NC: McFarland Press, 2014.

Peterson, M. Jeanne. *The Medical Profession in Mid-Victorian London.* Berkeley: University of California Press, 1978.

"Poison." *Once a Week* 3 (1860): 277.

"Poison in the Prescription." *Leader* 6, no. 300 (1855): 1224.

"Poisoners and Slow Poisons." *Reynold's Miscellany* 17 (1856): 80.

"The Poisoning Case." *The London Review* 7 (1863): 527.

"Poisoning in England." *Saturday Review* 1, no. 8 (1855): 134–35.

"Poisoning of a Grandfather." *Annual Register* 89 (1847): 144.

"The Poisonings in Essex." *Times*, September 5, 1846.

"Poisons and Poisoners: Old and New." *Practitioner*, 65 (1900): 171–77.

Poovey, Mary. *Uneven Developments: The Ideological Work of Gender in Mid-Victorian England*. Chicago: University of Chicago Press, 1988.

Porter, Dennis. *The Pursuit of Crime: Art and Ideology in Detective Fiction*. New Haven: Yale University Press, 1981.

"The Prevention and Detection of Secret and Accidental Poisoning; Particularly with Arsenic." *Magazine of Popular Science and Journal of the Useful Arts* 2 (1836): 377.

Price, Cheryl Blake. "Probability and Capital Crime: The Rise and Fall of the Actuarial Detective in Victorian Crime Fiction." *Clues: A Journal of Detection* 34, no. 2 (2016): 7–17.

"Prospectus of a New Journal." *Punch* 44 (1863): 193.

Pyrhönen, Heta. *The Bluebeard Gothic: Jane Eyre and Its Progeny*. Toronto: University of Toronto Press, 2010.

Queen, Ellery. *Queen's Quorum*. New York: Biblo and Tannen, 1969.

Reitz, Caroline. *Detecting the Nation: Fictions of Detection and the Imperial Venture*. Columbus: The Ohio State University Press, 2004.

"Reminiscences of Bulwer-Lytton." *Appleton's Journal* 9, no. 203 (1873): 267.

"Report on Psychological Medicine." In *Half-Yearly Abstract of the Medical Sciences*, edited by W. H. Ranking and C. B. Radcliffe, 262–75. Philadelphia: Lindsay and Blackiston, 1857.

Richardson, Maurice. *Novels of Mystery from the Victorian Age*. London: Pilot Press, 1945.

"The Richmond Poisoning Case." *Annual Register*. London: Woodfall and Kinder, 1860.

Robb, George. "Circe in Crinoline: Domestic Poisonings in Victorian England. *Journal of Family History* 22, no. 2 (1997): 176–91.

———. "Out of the Doll's House: The Trial of Florence Maybrick and Anxiety over the New Woman." *Proteus* 13, no. 1 (1996): 29–32.

Rodensky, Lisa. *The Crime in Mind: Criminal Responsibility and the Victorian Novel*. New York: Oxford University Press, 2003.

Rosa, Matthew Whiting. *The Silver Fork School*. New York: Columbia University Press, 1936.

Rothfield, Lawrence. "Medical." In *A Companion to Victorian Literature and Culture*, edited by Herbert F. Tucker.170–82. Oxford: Blackwell Press, 1999.

Russell, William Oldnall, and Charles Sprengel Greaves. Vol. 1. of *A Treatise on Crimes and Misdemeanors*. 3rd ed. London: Saunders and Benning, 1843.

Rzepka, Charles. *Detective Fiction*. Cambridge: Polity Press, 2005.

Sadleir, Michael. Vol. 1 of *Bulwer: A Panorama*. New York: Little, Brown, and Co., 1931.

Sala, George Augustus. "The Cant of Modern Criticism." *Belgravia* 4 (1868): 45–55.

"The Sale of Poisons." *Pharmaceutical Journal* 16, no. 2 (1856): 117–18.

"Science in the Witness Box." *The Examiner*, January 19, 1856.

Scoffern, Dr. J. "Secret Poisoning and Medical Etiquette." *St. James Magazine* 14 (1865): 107–28.

"Secret Poisoning." *Pharmaceutical Journal* 9, no. 5 (1849): 201–2.

Shelley, Mary. *Frankenstein*. Oxford: Oxford University Press, 1993.

Sheppard, Sarah. *Characteristics of the Genius and Writing of L. E. L.* London: Longman, Brown, Green, and Longman, 1841.

Shteir, Ann B. "Elegant Recreations? Configuring Science Writing for Women." In *Victorian Science in Context*, edited by Bernard Lightman, 236–55. Chicago: University of Chicago Press, 1997.

Smajic, Srdjan. *Ghost-Seers, Detectives, and Spiritualists: Theories of Vision in Victorian Literature and Science*. Cambridge: Cambridge University Press, 2010.

Small, Helen. *Love's Madness: Medicine, the Novel, and Female Insanity 1800–1865*. Oxford: Claredon Press, 1996.

"The Smethurst Case." *The Medical Times and Gazette* 19 (1859): 214.

Smith, Andrew. *Victorian Demons: Medicine, Masculinity and the Gothic Art at the Fin de Siècle*. Manchester: Manchester University Press, 2004.

Sparks, Tabitha. *The Doctor in the Victorian Novel: Family Practices*. Burlington: Ashgate, 2009.

The Standard. Unsigned review of *The Notting Hill Mystery*, by Charles Felix. 12728 (1865): 3.

Stephen, James Fitzjames. *A General View of the Criminal Law of England*. Clark: The Lawbook Exchange, 2005.

———. *A History of the Criminal Law of England*. 3 vols. London: Macmillan and Co., 1883.

Stephenson, Glennis. *Letitia Landon: The Woman Behind L. E. L.* Manchester: Manchester University Press, 1995.

"The Suppression of the Crime of Secret Poisoning." *London Medical Gazette* 4 (1847): 284–88.

Sutherland, John. Introduction to *The Woman in White*, by Wilkie Collins, vii–xxiv. Oxford: Oxford University Press, 1996.

———. "Wilkie Collins and the Origins of the Sensation Novel." Rpt. in *Wilkie Collins to the Forefront: Some Reassessments*. New York: AMS Press, 1995: 75–90.

Suvin, Darko. *Victorian Science Fiction in the UK: The Discourses of Knowledge and of Power*. Boston: GK Hall & Co., 1983.

Symons, Julian. *Bloody Murder, from the Detective Story to the Crime Novel: A History*. New York: Viking Penguin Press, 1972.

Sypher, F. J. Introduction to *Lady Anne Granard*, by L. E. L. New York: Scholars' Facsimiles & Reprints, 2002.

Talairach-Vielmas, Laurence. *Wilkie Collins, Medicine, and the Gothic*. Cardiff: University of Wales Press, 2009.

Taylor, Alfred Swaine. *Medical Jurisprudence*. Philadelphia: Lea & Blanchard, 1845.

———. *On Poisons in Relation to Medical Jurisprudence*. 2nd ed. London: John Churchill, 1859.

Thackeray, William Makepeace. *Catherine*, edited by Sheldon Goldfarb. Ann Arbor: University of Michigan Press, 1999.

"The Theory of Suicide in the Bravo Case." *The Medical Times and Gazette*, August 19, 1876.

Thomas, Ronald. *Detective Fiction and the Rise of Forensic Science*. Cambridge: Cambridge University Press, 1999.

Thomson, Thomas. Vol. 4 of *A System of Chemistry: In Four Volumes*. 5th ed. London: Baldwin, 1817.

Times. March 8, 1851.

Times. October 8, 1853.

"Trial of Madame Lafarge." *The Edinburgh Review* 75 (1842): 359–96.

"Trial of Thomas Smethurst." *The British Medical Journal* 2, no. 139 (1859): 702–3.

Tuttle, Hudson. Vol. 2 of *Arcana of Nature; Or the Philosophy of Spiritual Existence and of the Spirit World*. Boston: William White, 1864.

"Undetected Poisonings." *The Medical Times and Register*, August 15, 1871.

Wagner, Tamara S. "The Clinical Gothic: Sensationalizing Substance Abuse in the Victorian Home." *Gothic Studies* 11, no. 2 (2009): 30–40.

Watson, Katherine. *Poisoned Lives: English Poisoners and Their Victims*. New York: Hambleton and London, 2004.

Weiner, Martin. *Men of Blood: Violence, Manliness, and Criminal Justice in Victorian England*. Cambridge: Cambridge University Press, 2004.

Westminster and Quarterly Review. Unsigned review of *Lucretia*, 46, no. 2 (1847): 618.

"What Is Mesmerism?" *Blackwood's Edinburgh Magazine* 70 (1851): 70–85.

White, Hayden. "The Good of Their Kind." *New Literary History* 34, no. 2 (2003): 367–76.

Wilde, Oscar. "Pen, Pencil and Poison: A Study in Green." *Fortnightly Review* 45, no. 265 (1889): 41–54.

Williams, Anne. *The Art of Darkness: A Poetics of Gothic*. Chicago: University of Chicago Press, 1995.

Williams, Lucy. *Wayward Women: Female Offending in Victorian England*. Barnsley, South Yorkshire: Pen and Sword Press, 2016.

Willis, Chris. "The Female Moriarty: The Arch-Villainess in Victorian Popular Fiction." In *The Devil Himself: Villainy in Detective Fiction and Film*, edited by Stacy Gillis and Philippa Gates, 57–68. London: Greenwood Press, 2002.

Willis, Martin. *Mesmerists, Monsters, and Machines: Science Fiction and the Culture of Science in the Nineteenth-Century*. Kent: Kent State University Press, 2006.

Winter, Allison. *Mesmerized: Powers of Mind in Victorian Britain*. Chicago: University of Chicago Press, 1998.

"The Woman in White." *Saturday Review*, August 25, 1860.

Wood, Ellen. "Another Passage in a Dark Story." *Bentley's Miscellany* 38 (October 1855): 388–401.

———. "Beech Lodge." *Bentley's Miscellany* 42 (September 1857): 306–19.

———. "A Draught of Poison." *Bentley's Miscellany*, 38 (September 1855): 266–80.

———. "Ellen Leicester." *Bentley's Miscellany* 42 (June 1857): 626–38.

———. *Gervase Castonel; Or, the Six Gray Powders*. New York: Dick and Fitzgerald, 1863.

———. *The House of Halliwell*. New York: National Book Co., 1890.

———. *Lord Oakburn's Daughters*. 3 vols. London: Bradbury & Evans, 1864.

———. "A Midnight Dream." *Bentley's Miscellany* 42 (August 1857): 181–93.

———. "Mr. Castonel." 295–424. Reprinted in *Ashley and Other Stories*. London: MacMillian & Co, 1901.

———. "The Passing Bell." *Bentley's Miscellany* 42 (May 1857): 514–28.

———. "The Six Grey Powders." *Bentley's Miscellany* 42 (July 1857): 84–98.

"'A Word to the Public'—The Art of Secret Poisoning." *London Medical Gazette*. 4 (1847): 242–48.

Worthington, Heather. "Against the Law: Bulwer's Fictions of Crime." In *The Subverting Vision of Bulwer Lytton: Bicentenary Reflections*, edited by Allan Conrad Christensen, 54–67. Cranbury: Rosemont Press, 2004.

———. *The Rise of the Detective in Early Nineteenth-Century Popular Fiction*. New York: Palgrave Macmillan, 2005.

Youngston, A. J. *The Scientific Revolution in Victorian Medicine*. London: Billing & Sons, 1979.

INDEX

abortion, 81, 84–85, 95, 156n63
Adams, Charles Warren, 103. See *Notting Hill Mystery, The*
alcohol, 124–25, 127
Aldiss, Brian, 168
Allnut, William Newton, 110, 121
antimony, 94, 104, 108, 116–20
Armadale (Collins), 13, 73; Lydia Gwilt in, 47, 145–46, 148, 152–53
arsenic, 7, 45–46, 51–52, 64–65, 83, 94, 110, 119, 147; Arsenic Act, 107–8; household uses of, 169
"Arsenical literature," 21
Ashton, Helen, 29
Asimov, Isaac, 141

Bahar, Saba, 41
Bankard, Jennifer Sopchockchai, 142n8
Barrett, R. A. F., 113–14
Barton, Robert Eustace, 157
Bate, Jonathan, 176
Battle's Vermin Killer, 110
Belany, James Cockburn, 68, 79–82, 89, 95
Beller, Anne-Marie, 71n13
Black Band, The (Braddon), 26–27
Blanchard, Laman, 30
Blind Love (Collins), 74
"Bluebeard" (fairy tale), 72–73, 79, 81–82, 89–91, 97
Bohn (chemist), 44

Borgia, Lucrezia, 22, 50, 151
Bowers, J. Milton, 69n2
Braddon, Mary Elizabeth, 26, 37
Bravo, Charles, 108, 123, 128
Brodie, Benjamin Collins, 95
Brotherhood of the Seven Kings, The (Meade), 25, 140–44, 148, 152–68, 172–75
Buckler, William, 103n1
Bulamer, Ayse Naz, 64
Bulwer-Lytton, Edward, 24, 32, 36; Landon and, 48–49. See also *Lucretia*
Burdock, Mary Ann, 46
Burney, Ian, 8–9, 14, 23, 118

Campbell, John W., 140–41
Carey, John, 176
Carpenter, William Benjamin, 134
Chapman, George, 69
Chappel J. A. V., 143
"chemical criminal" character: attributes of, 3, 5, 16, 18; contemporary uses of, 175–76; Fosco (*The Woman in White*) as exemplary, 4–13, 16; paradoxical nature of, 10, 76; progression of scientific criminals to criminal scientists, 143–44; women as, 9, 24–26, 30, 32, 36–37, 43–46, 51–52, 57, 75n22, 140, 142, 144–46, 151, 158
chemical products, eventual ubiquity of, 169–70

INDEX

Chesham, Sarah, 64–66
Ciolkowski, Laura, 53, 55
Cobbe, Frances, 86–87
Collins, Paul, 103n1
Collins, Wilkie, 4–5, 8n30, 12, 37, 102; doctors in, 73–75; later writings of, 13, 74. *See also book titles*
Constantini, Maria, 10
Cook, John, 5
cosmetics, 144–45, 147, 166–67
Cothran, Casey, 131
Cream, Thomas Neill, 9n34, 69
Cross, Philip, 68–69

dandy fiction, 34–35
Danesbury House (Wood), 72
Dawson, Janis, 145, 149
deconstructionism, 20, 23
Densmore, Helen, 148
Derrida, Jacques, 17–21; on genre, 23
detective fiction, 3, 13–14, 16, 103–8, 112–38, 123, 141–42, 177; bodies in, 105–28; gothic irrationality in, 105; locked-door subgenre, 24; prevalence of poison in, 25; three phases of, 14; typical endings of, 167
Dewitt, Anne, 149
Dickens, Charles, 4, 35; "The Demeanour of Murderers," 4n12; "Hunted Down" 176
discipline and crime fiction, 18–21, 177
doctor poisoners, 24, 68–102
domestic realism, 35, 75
Dove, William, 110–11, 121, 123
Doyle, Arthur Conan, Sherlock Holmes stories of 14, 26, 68, 139–40, 142n8, 154
Dunne, Éamonn, 20n69

Edgeworth, Maria, 40, 42–43
Eigen, Joel Peter, 110, 112
Elements of Materia Medica (Pereira), 111
Elliotson, John, 134
Essex Poisoning Club, 64–66
Ethel Churchill (Landon), 24, 29–33, 35–47, 52–54, 56, 66, 151–52, 175; influence of, 32–33, 49–50, 144–45

Fayter, Paul, 141
female education. *See* scientific education for women
feminism and chemical crime, 46–47, 58, 64, 66, 142, 145, 148, 157–59
Fenning, Eliza, 45–46
Flint, Kate, 130
forensic science, 7, 15, 58, 64, 82, 95–96, 108, 139; in detective fiction, 14, 16, 25. See also *Moonstone, The*; *Notting Hill Mystery, The*; toxicology
Forster, John, 29, 49, 53
Foucault, Michel, 14, 17
Frankenstein (Shelley), 70, 141–42, 144, 149–50, 155, 159

Gaboriau, Émile, 104
gender: crime and, 9, 174–75; hybridity and, 32, 39, 42, 54–56, 59; science and, 21, 25–26
Genette, Gérard, 23
genre experimentation and innovation, 3, 19–20, 23–24, 175–77
Gilbert, Pamela, 41
gothic fiction, 13, 70, 82, 95–96, 105, 151; medical gothic subgenre, 24–25, 70–71, 75, 78, 85, 89, 92, 97, 102
gypsies, 104, 115, 122, 124, 135

Hadley, Matthew, 155
Haggard, H. Rider, 168
Hallisy, Margaret, 8
Halloran, Jennifer, 164
Hardy, Thomas, 176
Haynes, Roslynn, 144
Heart and Science (Collins), 13, 73
Hedgecock, Jennifer, 146
Helfield, Randa, 19
Heller, Tamar, 133
Herapath, 118
"hocussing," 127–30
Hogarth, George, 9
Holl, Edward, 128–29
Hollingsworth, Keith, 33
Howitt, William, 31
Hughes, William, 71, 78, 85

"inheritance powder," 9
Invisible Man, The (Wells), 149–50
Island of Dr. Moreau, The (Wells), 25, 70, 141

Jack Sheppard (Ainsworth), 34
Jerdan, William, 49
Jezebel's Daughter (Collins), 8n30, 13

Kendra, April, 34–35, 37
Kennedy, Meegan, 70, 102
Kucich, John, 76

Lafargue, Marie, 51–52, 57–58, 60–61
Lamson, George, 68
Landon, Letitia Elizabeth, 24; Bulwer relationship, 48–49; death of, 28–31, 49, 51–52, 63, 66, 172; poetry of (as L. E. L.), 28–29, 42, 48; rumors about, 48–49. See also *Ethel Churchill*
Lefanu, Sheridan, 24
Lifted Veil, The (Eliot), 145
Liggins, Emma, and Andrew Maunder, 101
Lonoff, Sue, 138
Lord Oakburn's Daughters (Wood), 24–25, 72, 75, 81, 89–93, 96–102
Lucretia (Bulwer), 19, 24, 49–67, 145, 176; Bulwer on, 52–53, 62; Clavering surname in, 51, 64; Landon's influence on, 32–33, 36, 47–50; as Newgate novel, 47, 50, 52, 60–64, 66–67; revised ending to, 53n81, 63
Lynch, Martin H., 51

Maclean, George, 28–29, 49
"mad scientist" character, 25, 140, 142, 145, 149–52, 154–55, 158–61, 173
Maginn, William, 49
Mangham, Andrew, 8, 71n13, 76, 102
Mansel, Henry, 22
Marcet, Jane, 41
May, Mary, 64
Maybrick, Florence and James, 147–48
Meade, L. T., 19, 25–26, 140, 144, 148–49, 168–69. See also *Brotherhood of the Seven Kings, The*; *Sorceress of the Strand, The*

medical case studies, 14
medical profession, power and authority of, 75, 84–85, 93, 96–97. See also science and medicine
Mellor, Anne, 42
mesmerism, 25, 104, 106, 113–16, 125, 134
Michael Dred, Detective (Leighton and Leighton), 24
midwifery, 84
Miller, D. A., 14, 16, 19
Miller, Elizabeth Carolyn, 145, 156n63, 157–59, 161
Montagu, Mary Wortley, 36
Moonstone, The (Collins), 19, 24–25, 103, 112, 126–38; forensic science in, 104–5, 106–8, 126–27, 130, 134–39
Mossman, Mark, 131
Motion, Andrew, 175–76
"Mr. Castonel" (Wood), 19, 24, 72, 75, 79, 81–89, 96–97, 100, 102; novella version of (*Gervase Castonel*), 79
Mulvey-Roberts, Mary, 64n129

Nemesvari, Richard, 176
Newgate fiction, 3, 13, 22, 24, 33n13, 35, 37; Bulwer and, 47, 50, 52, 60–64, 66–67; definitions of, 32; Landon and, 32–33, 47; silver fork fiction and, 33–35
New Historicism, 17, 20; Derrida and, 21n70
New Women, 140, 144, 148–49, 154, 158
Nord, Deborah Epstein, 124
Notting Hill Mystery, The (Adams), 19, 24–25, 103–8, 112–27, 130, 138; forensic science in, 104–6, 112–13, 116–17, 120–23, 126–27, 139; narrative structure of, 104n3, 123, 125–26

Offenses Against Persons Act, 127
Olga Romanoff (Griffith), 150–52, 158
Oliphant, Margaret, 5–6
Oliver Twist (Dickens), 35–36
opiates, 8, 17, 145; opium and laudanum in *The Moonstone*, 103, 126–27, 129–30, 133–34, 136–37; suicide by, 83
Oswald Cray (Wood), 72

Paget, John, 1–2, 7
Pal-Lapinski, Piya, 18, 107
Palmer, William, 4–5, 12–13, 22, 68, 79, 86, 96n93, 107, 111, 117–18
Pamboukian, Sylvia, 18, 20, 130
Panek, LeRoy, 157
Paul Clifford (Bulwer), 34
Pelham (Bulwer), 36
penny dreadfuls, 26–27
Peterson, M. Jeanne, 96
pharmakon concept, 17–20, 23
poisoning: ambiguity of, 17–18, 20, 107, 112; "circumambient presence" of, 1–2, 25, 107; civilized qualities of, 6; domestic nature of, 8–9, 12, 24; foreignness and, 9–10, 12, 19, 26; intent and premeditation in, 108–12; mind-body relation and, 10–11; poisoner profile, 2; romance and, 8; scientific methodology and, 3, 7, 14–16; transformative power of, 10–12, 18, 44–45, 106; violence vs., 6–7, 83, 109; as woman's crime, 9, 24, 37; writing as poison, 21–23, 62, 177. *See also* doctor poisoners; women: as poisoners
Pommerais, Edmond-Désiré Couty de la, 87
Poor Miss Finch (Collins), 171
Poovey, Mary, 84
Pope, Alexander, 36
Porter, Dennis, 16
pregnancy and childbirth, 75, 81, 83–84, 89
Pritchard, Edward William, 68, 87
prussic acid (cyanide), 7, 28, 30–31, 44, 80–81

Queen, Ellery, 142

Reitz, Caroline, 141–42
Richardson, Maurice, 104n3, 123
Robb, George, 37, 148
Rodensky, Lisa, 108–9
Romance and Reality (Landon), 48
Rzepka, Charles, 14

Sala, George Augustus, 22–23
scapegoating, 18–19
science and medicine: anxieties about, 4, 9, 25, 38–39, 85, 92; domestic threat of, 3, 9, 12–13, 71, 73–76, 96–97; female practice of, 158–59; increasing specialization and inaccessibility of, 143–44, 168; knowledge and methodology of, 2–3, 14, 135; professionalization of, 2–3, 12, 41, 70, 73–74, 86, 143, 165. *See also* forensic science; medical profession; scientific education for women
science fiction (scientific romance), 3, 140–42, 157–58, 162, 168; definitions of, 141
scientific education for women, 24, 27, 40–42, 65, 172–73; in *Ethel Churchill*, 30–33, 36–40, 42, 45–46, 60; in *Lucretia*, 33, 36, 53–54, 56–57, 59–60, 63; in Meade's stories, 140, 142–43, 172–73
scientific progress narrative, 13, 16
Scoffern, John, 6, 9
Scudéry, Madeleine de, 42
sensation fiction, 3, 6, 19, 22–23, 66; Collins's contribution to 4, 13; defining features of, 4, 13; Landon's contribution to, 32, 47, 66; medical sensation subgenre, 25, 71, 102; as poisonous, 22–23; social impact of, 23; Wood and, 72–74, 77, 79, 102
Shakespeare, William, 10–11, 165
Shteir, Ann B., 41
silver fork fiction, 24, 32; as crime fiction, 33–36, 66; *Ethel Churchill* and, 36
Smajic, Srdjan, 105
Small, Helen, 56, 60
smelling salts, 8, 11
Smethurst, Thomas, 68, 93–96, 100, 117, 118–19
Smith, Andrew, 69
Smith, Madeleine, 107
society fiction, 35, 36, 37, 47
Somerville, Mary, 40
Sorceress of the Strand, The (Meade), 25, 140, 142–43, 144, 148, 152–61, 163–71, 173, 175
Southgate, Hannah, 64
Sparks, Tabitha, 70, 73–74, 102
Stephen, James Fitzjames, 5, 147–48
Stephenson, Glennis, 42–43
Strange Case of Dr. Jekyll and Mr. Hyde, The (Stevenson), 25, 70, 142, 149, 159

strychnine, 7, 111, 118
supernaturalism and the occult, 26, 39, 44–45, 70, 105, 136–37, 164–66
Sutherland, John, 22
Suvin, Darko, 141
Symons, Julian, 103–4
Sypher, F. J., 49n70

Talairach-Vielmas, Laurence, 70, 74, 83, 102
tartar emetic. *See* antimony
Taylor, Alfred Swaine, 17, 64, 94–95, 108, 117–20, 133
Thackeray, William M., 32n12, 34
Thomas, Ronald R., 14, 104–6, 122, 134
toxicology, 15–16, 63, 105, 116–19
Trail of the Serpent, The (Braddon), 26–27, 145

Uncle Silas (LeFanu), 24

Victorian womanhood ideals, 11, 57, 152, 159
Vyse, Ann, 110

Wagner, Tamara, 71

Wainewright, Thomas Griffiths, 45, 50–51; Motion's biography of, 175–76
Warder, Alfred, 68
Watson, Katherine, 83
Weiner, Martin, 6
Wells, H. G., 25, 70, 141, 149
White, Hayden, 23
Wilde, Oscar, on Wainewright, 50, 175–76
Williams, Anne, 73
Williams, Lucy, 128
Willis, Chris, 158, 160
Wollstonecraft, Mary, 40, 42–43
Woman in White, The (Collins), 4–13, 16, 22, 73–74; influence on *The Notting Hill Mystery*, 104n3, 123, 125
women: essentialist views of, 24, 42–43; as poisoners, 9, 24, 26–27, 32, 37, 45–47, 50–52, 64–66, 142; scientific knowledge and, 24, 25–26, 27, 32. *See also* "chemical criminal" character: women as; scientific education for women
Wood, Ellen, 24–25, 71–102; early stories by, 76–82
Worthington, Heather, 13–14, 34–35

Youngston, A. J., 86

www.ingramcontent.com/pod-product-compliance
Lightning Source LLC
Chambersburg PA
CBHW020947230426
43666CB00005B/211